FIELDWORK IS NOT WHAT IT USED TO BE

FIELDWORK IS NOT WHAT IT USED TO BE

Learning Anthropology's Method
in a Time of Transition

**Edited by
James D. Faubion
and George E. Marcus**

**Foreword by
Michael M. J. Fischer**

CORNELL UNIVERSITY PRESS ITHACA AND LONDON

First published 2009 by Cornell University Press
First printing, Cornell Paperbacks, 2009
Printed in the United States of America

Library of Congress Cataloging-in-Publication Data
Fieldwork is not what it used to be : learning anthropology's method in a time of transition / edited by James D. Faubion and George E. Marcus ; foreword by Michael M. J. Fischer.
    p. cm.
  Includes bibliographical references and index.
  ISBN 978-0-8014-4776-1 (cloth : alk. paper) — ISBN 978-0-8014-7511-5 (pbk. : alk. paper)
  1. Anthropology—Fieldwork. 2. Ethnology—Fieldwork. 3. Anthropology—Methodology.   I. Faubion, James D., 1957–   II. Marcus, George E.   III. Title.
  GN34.3.F53F52 2009
  301.07'23—dc22
2008049124

Cloth printing   10 9 8 7 6 5 4 3 2 1
Paperback printing   10 9 8 7 6 5 4 3 2

Contents

Foreword: Renewable Ethnography

Michael M. J. Fischer

In Part I of this volume, six authors offer their projects, done as dissertations under the mentorship of James Faubion and George Marcus, as texts for pedagogical reflection. In the book's Introduction Marcus provides a framing in terms of pedagogy of first projects and an opening to treat such projects as inevitably exploratory. He thus expresses his hope that "unfinished" as well as more polished dissertations have lessons to teach in worlds where it is either not possible or not desirable to reproduce older forms of ethnographic projects. In Part II Faubion presents a meta-meditation for framing the doing of ethnographic projects in terms of shifting forms of connectivity and concomitant forms of ethics.

What I can offer, having only been an interlocutor on two of these projects, and a contributor to the Rice Department of Anthropology for eleven years (1981–1992) in an earlier incarnation, is a reading of these six projects from a different space, that of attempting to help midwife and defend the possibility of an anthropology of science and technology in my subsequent and current position in the History, Anthropology and Science, Technology and Society (HASTS) graduate program at MIT (see Fischer 2003, 2007a, 2007b). There are two aspects to this perspective: First, I cannot help but be impressed by the degree to which all six projects have science and technology interfaces, interfaces which not incidentally have complex topologies having to do with what Kim Fortun in Chapter 8 of this volume calls complex issues of scale and context, sometimes involving spatio-temporal recursions and looping effects not unlike Möbius strips and Klein bottles. Second, and related, are my understandings of the legacy of earlier manifestations of Rice anthropology's insistence on reinventing forms of cultural critique within and for globally distributed and differentiated processes in our contemporary world.

Let me call the first of these themes "Reading for the Ethnography in a Technoscientific World" and the second "Reading for the Rice Mark."

Reading for the Ethnography in a Technoscientific World

I read these six projects as substantively rich arenas in today's world to be read for their ethnography, importantly including the mediations of guarded, packaged, and traded elusive information. It is often as important to understand the structures of the circuits as to challenge or guesstimate the veracity in the information packets. Assemblages (Marcus and Saka 2006) are another passing metaphor hinting at modernist ancestors (montage, collage, constructivism).

The six projects are about (1) the made-up statistics and corruption stories that not only inhabit but structure the transnational humanitarian and development industries in places like Nigeria, Switzerland, and Washington; (2) venture capital industries and their claims to innovation based on a kind of "social capital" that itself proved to be a finance bubble; (3) indigenous justice forums that mediate First Nation autonomies and nation-state devolutions of court, bureaucracy, and jail burdens; (4) an Ethical, Legal, and Social Issues (ELSI) project associated with the HapMap genomics program that characterizes worries about commodification of, and regulatory capture of, bioethics; (5) the classificatory technologies and interpellations of human and civil rights NGOs in Washington, D.C., drawing on the (illusions of) proximity to power, and deployed like fishermen's nets to catch and adjudicate the past and prepare the future; and (6) archaeologists and the local communities whose labor they hire, whose land they excavate, and whose precursors they prepare for tourists.

Reading them in this way, I think, is more productive than seeing them as somehow messy or unpolished examples of the inability to live up to what is satirically referred to in many of the essays as the Traditional or Malinowskian model of ethnography. They are ethnographies constructed within—to borrow an intellectual property metaphor—"new compositions of matter." The six authors might be read as applying to each of their cases three doubled or split dimensions: audits (listening, accounting), projects (promissory logics, transitional objects), and the active value-added work of interpretations—cultural encounters that are "between different modes of perception and representations of reality (what one could call culture, I suppose)," as Nahal Naficy puts it.

Reading for the Rice Mark

I think it productive to read these six offerings in ways that do not satirize older anthropologies and instead build upon, and extend into a new era, a recursive series of intellectual conversations and experiments that were notable features of a distinctive Rice anthropology from the 1980s through the early 2000s. These include the Rice Circle discussion group; the inaugural editing of the journal *Cultural Anthropology;* the writing and debate surrounding *Anthropology as Cultural Critique* (Marcus and Fischer 1986) and *Writing Culture* (Clifford and Marcus 1986); the Rice Center for Cultural Studies and its six-year-long hosting of a Rockefeller Residential Fellowship program; the decade-long Late Editions Project; the follow-on volume *Critical Anthropology Now* (Marcus, ed. 1999a) a decade after *Anthropology as Cultural Critique* and *Writing Culture;* the engagement with Foucauldian thematics, with the arrival in the 1990s of James Faubion (both in the idiom of classical Greek philosophemes, Faubion bringing his expertise as a scholar of Greece, and in the translation and codification of the Foucauldian corpus, Faubion being one of the editors of an important recent multi-volume collection of Foucault's essays in English [Faubion 1993, 2001a; Faubion, ed. 1998, 2000]); the forging of conversations regarding both transnational (China and East Asian) cultural studies and the influential "public culture" initiative of Arjun Appadurai and others (through the presence of Ben Lee, who succeeded Appadurai as the provost of the New School University); and the early (from the late 1980s) and persistent presence of science studies in the department through the hiring, first, of Sharon Traweek and then of Chris Kelty and Hannah Landecker (Traweek 1988; Kelty 2005a, 2005b, 2008b; Landecker 2007).

This is not an occasion to write out this history, only to try to distill a few indexical features.

(1) *Cross-discipline experiments:* The Rice Circle was a faculty discussion group composed of a core of two philosophers, two historians, at times religion scholars, and literature scholars, as well as the anthropology faculty (which included the comparative literature scholar Kathryn Milun, who was hired in the anthropology department and whose brief was to help graduate students assimilate the critical philosophies that arose with interests in third world and postcolonial literatures and poststructuralist and deconstructionist reading strategies. Her own work was on modernist projects of settlement via terra nullius claims and empty centers in reconstructed cities inducing agoraphobia). The group staged cross-disciplinary engagements on annual themes. One of the more coherent themes, for instance, was the comparison and even stronger contrasts between the practices and theories deployed by psychotherapy and ethnography,

precisely because psychodynamics and psychoanalytic hermeneutics (in its various and derivative forms) had so infused the humanities generally. One year, this included a collaboration with family systems practitioners at the Texas Medical Center, observing and discussing together tapes of family consultations and interventions. One of the organizing thematics was an exploration of different forms of "dialogic encounter" led by Tullio Maranhão's interest in psychotherapy and Stephen Tyler's interest in pushing to the limit the implications of writing as an alienated form of encounter and thus recognizing only face-to-face encounters as ethical forms of engagement (Maranhão 1990; Tyler 1987).

(2) *Re-reading, recontextualizing, and reformatting for the contemporary world the modalities of anthropology as cultural critique* developed at various historical conjunctures (World War I, the Great Depression, World War II) and engagements with adjacent practices: (a) social anthropology in a generational shift between nineteenth-century grand comparative work and twentieth-century detailed fieldwork; (b) 1930s–1940s documentary and photographic realism, surrealism and the Collège de Sociologie, and the Frankfurt School's retooling of Freud and Marx for mass politics, mass propaganda, and mass consumer society; (c) a generational shift again in the 1960s involving the integration of political economy and cultural analyses as well as the reopening of questions of how understandings of subjectivation and subjectivities rework older notions of affect, emotion, and personhood; (d) an agenda of continued experimentation for the 1980s. The subtitle of *Anthropology as Cultural Critique,* "an experimental moment in the human sciences," signified both meanings of experiment: modernist experimental art forms, and the increasingly de-idealized and nonuniform understandings of the methods of the experimental sciences as analogues of, and subjects for, validity in the communicative and human sciences. If *Anthropology as Cultural Critique* focused on fieldwork reports as the crucibles for social theory formation and epistemological testing grounds for cultural and social critique, *Writing Culture* renewed discussions about composition of and rhetorical forms in ethnographic writing, again using a cross-disciplinary conversation, in this case, with historians and literature scholars (cf. Fischer 1992; Taylor 1998).

My own experiments, with Mehdi Abedi, in *Debating Muslims: Cultural Dialogues in Postmodernity and Tradition,* paying attention to the weave of oral, literate, and visual media in pre- and post-revolution, domestic and diasporic Iranian social-cultural contestations and transformations, was a concomitant multi-sited ethnographic exploration with contemporary stakes (Fischer and Abedi 1990), but the fullest expression of such an exploration was in Kim Fortun's *Advocacy After Bhopal.* In her dissertation version, she literally wrote different chapters in the various rhetorical genres required by the communicative situations of Bhopal activists among whom she did her initial fieldwork. The intent was performatively to display and explore modalities of making form fit and interrogate content and to explore how form made content. In the vastly reworked and now comparative and cross-national version of the project (Fortun 2001), these genres were integrated with a matrix of analytic questions into one of the most powerful and well-tuned critical ethnographies of the contemporary "new world order," anticipating many of the questions raised by, and duly acknowledged and built upon by, Kris Peterson and others in the current volume. I don't think either of these ethnographies has been dismissed as merely being about writing and not about fieldwork or the materiality of political and economic issues as the critics of *Writing Culture* have often insisted.

(3) *Reinventing the ethnographic interview form.* The Late Editions Project, a series of topical volumes under George Marcus's editorship, over the decade of the 1990s experimented with paired collective editorial workshops (including all authors) to plan each year's thematic topic and then to workshop draft papers. Form was meant to be determined by the richness of ethnographic content, and could vary from lightly edited transcripts, to *New Yorker*–style profiles, to French-style "entretiens" in which questions and answers were reworked by their respective enunciators until they were satisfied with the polished product, to even, in one case, collages of documents. The topics moved from directly topical concerns formatted in standard categories—new *Perilous States* (Marcus, ed. 1993) in the aftermath of the collapse of the Soviet Union; *Technoscientific Imaginaries* (Marcus, ed. 1995), media, corporations—to topics responsive to, intensified by, and reformatted by the dramatic revolution in media of communication (the World Wide Web came in 1994): *Paranoia within Reason* (Marcus, ed. 1999b); *Para-Sites: A Casebook against Cynical Reason* (Marcus, ed. 2000a); *Zeroing in on the Year 2000* (Marcus, ed. 2000b). For a review of how the shifts in writing style over the decade tracked the shift in media consciousness, see "Before Going Digital/Double Digit/Y2000" (Fischer 2000). Many of these again are precursors to the ethnographies of the early 2000s represented in the present volume.

(4) *The shift from anthropology's primary interlocutors being in the humanities (1980s) to science studies (1990s–2000s).* Marcus makes this point in his introductory essay in this volume, and my "reading for the ethnography" notes the explicit reference points in the six dissertation projects even though none are explicitly framed or disciplined as science studies. That Kim Fortun and Chris Kelty provide two of the key pedagogical touchstones in the volume reaffirms the point.

(5) *Interventions in academia and the world outside academia.* The Rice Center for Cultural Studies, founded in 1986, and which I directed until 1993, was a Humanities Division response to a reorganization on the Rice campus instituted by the then new president of Rice, George Rupp, to create interdisciplinary centers

of excellence in each school of the university. That a member of the School of Social Sciences should head a center housed in the School of Humanities was a recognition of the strength and national reputation of the graduate program of the Department of Anthropology, as well as a recognition that the humanities at Rice had not kept up with the interest in interdisciplinarity in the 1980s. The Rice Center for Cultural Studies was a pioneer in the move to foster conversation among social science and humanities approaches, especially in a global context. The Rockefeller Residency Fellowships obtained by the Center were a mechanism to bring to campus representatives of topics and approaches not well represented on the faculty, with the hope that their presence would encourage the hiring of people with such skills. In this way, and in creating and welcoming Rice Circle–style faculty reading groups, the Center helped foster the creation on campus of expertises in feminism (Jane Gallop), film studies (Tshombe Gabriel, Hamid Naficy), African studies (Atieno Odhiambo, D. S. Masolo), comparative religion (Masolo, Anne Klein) and the like. The journal *Cultural Anthropology,* under Marcus's inaugural editorship, also attempted to reach out to contributors in fields other than anthropology in order to enrich the discussions in both directions. It signaled its ambitions physically in the "little journal" format of uncut edges and rag-textured covers. This ambition and signing have been reinvigorated and updated by the current editors, Rice graduate Kim Fortun and Mike Fortun, with a series of innovations—physically in returning to the little journal format now in color; in content configurations and topical foci sections; by a complementary website; and through the effort to build a public board of adviser-interlocutors outside of academic anthropology.

Outside academia, there is an underappreciated pioneering of anthropologists in the corporate and design world. Marcus alludes in the Introduction to his long interest in the arts, his periodic participation in design studios at the Rice School of Architecture, and his writings on museum worlds. Jamer Hunt, a graduate of the Rice department, has built a career in design worlds at the Philadelphia University of the Arts and now the Parsons School of Design at the New School. His graduate research on Sylvia Bataille (actress, wife of Georges Bataille and Jacques Lacan) was one of the dissertations around which our experimental writing discussions revolved, along with dissertations by Jeff Petrie (a highly evocative collage of meditations and ethnographic accounts of the Christian minority rebel groups in northern Burma), Ryan Bishop (a novel about the cultural horizon at the time of Beethoven's death in Vienna), David Syring (short stories about the culture of the hill country in Texas [Syring 2000]), and Bruce Grant (reconstructing the layerings of erased and thinned cultural accounts on Sakhalin island [Grant 1995]). Hunt's dissertation, he joked at the time, was a dissertation with a missing center and a recursive spiraling structure: Sylvia Bataille was still alive in Paris, but elusive, not willing to be a subject, yet her moving locus in a network of celebrities and productions made the topic still eminently explorable and configurable.

Given new developments, such as the formation of the annual meetings of EPIC (Ethnographic Praxis in Industry Conference) and the visibility of anthropologists working in major corporations such as IBM and Intel, the story of Rice graduate Melissa Cefkin's remarkable career is also worth attention. The modalities of reflecting upon the practice of anthropology within corporate worlds is the subject of a parallel book to this one, edited by Cefkin: Ethnography@Work.com (Cefkin, ed. 2009). Recent Rice graduate Michael G. Powell has followed her into this world, and Beth Tudor, a Rice graduate in the 1980s, preceded her. Petrie, too, ended up not in the American corporate world, but in Thailand in cultural broker roles in the tourist industry and in the planning offices of the Thai government. Bishop, remaining within the academy, has helped build an American Studies center at the National University of Singapore, and has defined an important Southeast Asia node for the *Theory, Culture & Society* and *Cultural Politics* journal networks. Stella Grigorian's dissertation on conflicts among three generations of migrants to Armenia was conducted in the aftermath of a major earthquake while serving first as a translator and cultural broker for international relief teams and then as the on-site manager for building a health clinic.

The science studies thematic had its early manifestations in the dissertations of Priscilla Weeks (on aquaculture and labor disputes between fishermen and marine biologists), Maziyar Lotfalian (on scientists in Iran, Pakistan, Malaysia, and Iranian scientists and engineers in the United States [Lotfalian 2004]), and Myanna Lahsen (on climate modelers).

Ethnographic Pedagogies and Reinventions

The complexities of our times require ethnographic skills. This is a matter of opening up simplified accounts, making accountability possible at different granularities, signposting the labyrinths of possible inquiries for their relevance, their points of no return, their conceptual reruns, acknowledging in a politics of recognition pebbles of resistance that destabilize easy theories.

The essays here explore training for the ethnographic skills required by the complexities of our times. George Marcus has been toying with the term "para-site" since the volume *Para-Sites*. The term, revivified in his articles with Douglas Holmes, picked up on the *Anthropology as Cultural Critique* arguments that the ethnographic style of cultural critique depends upon the locating of critiques in the play or dialogue of discourses in the world, rather than in the inventive genius of the writer, after fieldwork, alone in his or her study (Holmes and Marcus 2006). This was also the argument of locating "immanent critique," that is, looking to the internal cultural resources and their deployments in critique, as well as cross-cultural critiques, in a global world, that motivated the experimental essays in *Debating Muslims*. The Late Editions Project also was premised on trying to reposition interview subjects as collaborators who together with the ethnographer were jointly interested in puzzling out the ways in which the changing world has outrun the pedagogies in which practitioners as well as analysts have been trained. At the University of California, Irvine, Marcus has turned these reflections into a studio-design technique (see http://www.socsci.uci.edu/~ethnog/), and the term "para-site" has taken on the literal meaning of a space alongside, and different from, an actual fieldsite. Dissertation writers bring in colleagues and ethnographic subjects from the discursive spaces in which their research occurs and design the discussion in such a way that other academic colleagues can get a taste of the problematics and contribute their perspectives, disciplinary practices, and insights. This is a more dimensional modality of pedagogy than the usual workshopping where the sources of insight come from essentially one discipline or from academia alone.

In Part III of this book both Kim Fortun and Chris Kelty in their chapters on teaching ethnographic research stress the "fateful consequence of technical design." Fortun's combinatorial exercises for a course in Advanced Cultural Analysis recognize the transitional object mobility of ethnographic work (scanning across virtual matrices, filtering varying epistemic objects through different screens), as well as multi-player coordination of "obsessive-compulsive" and "paranoid" disorder tendencies in all interpretive circuits (cf. Fortun 2003). Kelty compares fieldwork's commitments to those of robust, recursive, and never finished open source Linux software, "over against a commitment to research design that sets questions in advance and for which fieldwork is mere data-gathering." This needs to be understood by institutional review boards (IRBs) if they are to work with, rather than against, ethnographic creativity and utility. "Ethics," Kelty observes, all too often designates a residual or supplementary space for professionals "not part of everyday practice," something to which professionals must "also" attend but which is not inherent. Ethical, legal, and social issues are often treated as parasites rather than para-sites, to be quarantined, marginalized, and pre-empted. In fact, however, the "ethical" (or "socially responsible," "political economy," or "social justice and access" issues) marks out troubling terrain as meriting ethnographic help. Even if initially conceived as something to be managed, the ethical is a space of anxiety, where epistemological encounters can be recursively staged under controlled, productive, therapeutic, or pedagogical facilitations.

In such ways, ethnography can contribute to robust civil society and what Kelty has called its "recursive public spheres."

FIELDWORK IS NOT WHAT IT USED TO BE

NOTES TOWARD AN ETHNOGRAPHIC MEMOIR OF SUPERVISING GRADUATE RESEARCH THROUGH ANTHROPOLOGY'S DECADES OF TRANSFORMATION

George E. Marcus

Fieldwork projects in anthropology are not what they used to be—at least as they have been imagined in an aesthetics of practice and evaluation that define anthropology's highly distinctive disciplinary culture of both method and career-making. In recent years, there have been a number of stimulating volumes that have reflected on the changing nature of fieldwork practices challenged by contemporary conditions, informing the concepts and ambitions of anthropological research (see, e.g., Amit 2000; Gupta and Ferguson 1997a; Marcus 1999; Rabinow 2005; Strathern 2004). After the so-called reflexive turn of the 1980s, virtually all ethnographies themselves are interesting sources of such reflection, since they include, almost as a requirement, meditations on their conditions of production. Indeed, accounts of fieldwork within ethnographies constitute a primary form of evidence for arguments, and often *are* the primary form of argument.[1] But these sources are mostly written from within this professional, disciplinary culture of anthropology, rather than making this culture and its shaping effects on

---

1. Anna Tsing's *In the Realm of the Diamond Queen* (1993) comes to mind as one of the most influential and intricate ethnographic texts that builds a strategy of theoretical argument around a narrative account of fieldwork. This narrative character remains an important dimension of how she develops argument in her more recent work, *Friction* (2005), which is exemplary of how ethnographic accounts might develop arguments about globalization. More generally, the volume *Women Writing Culture* (Behar and Gordon 1995), a response to, but quite independent of, *Writing Culture* (Clifford and Marcus 1986), constitutes a kind of primer on how fieldwork narratives within ethnographies have become integral to their core strategies of description and interpretation—at least in one of the most influential contemporary styles of ethnography.

research visible; they think of the broadening horizons of research projects and deliver critical assessments of fieldwork while still holding the aesthetics and the regulative ideals of the Malinowskian paradigm of research—more crucial than ever to the signature identity of anthropology—centrally in place.[2]

What we believe is distinctive about this volume is that it begins to relativize the role of fieldwork, as classically and normatively conceived, within a broader view of the production of anthropological research today. So emblematic of disciplinary identity, fieldwork remains the focus of the accounts offered here. Yet they unfold from varying situations and retrospective degrees of distance from career-defining initiatory projects of ethnographic research. They are studies of the variable role of the classic practices, images, and expectations of fieldwork, with which anthropologists are so familiar and of which they are so proud, in the playing out of complex, often ad hoc and opportunistic designs of research for which the classic aesthetic of distinctive method alone is no longer an adequate imaginary. Indeed, two of the essays (by Fortun and by Kelty) are accounts of personal efforts in teaching fieldwork to conserve the traditional imaginary of fieldwork even while reconceiving and remapping it onto altogether different topologies or scales of research design.

The essays of this volume represent two perspectives: that of the graduate supervisor and that of the former student. They offer the longer view of how initiatory fieldwork that earns degrees turns into finished first projects of research, and then into later projects. In doing so, they open a new discussion of fieldwork

---

2. "Malinowskian" is repeatedly used as a shorthand in my introductory essay to stand for a complex history of variation in fieldwork practices in the modern history of anthropology (including in the pre-Malinowski, British tradition, something as vogue-ish in the contemporary fashion for collaborations as the Torres Strait expedition of 1898 [see Herle and Rouse 1998]). Still, despite interesting efforts today to revive alternative styles to the mythos of Malinowski (see Bunzl 2004, in his plea for a Neo-Boasian practice of anthropological research), the basic training model of first fieldwork in anthropology graduate programs preserves the substance and outline of Malinowski's fieldwork in the Trobriands, reported effectively in the introductory chapter of *The Argonauts of the Western Pacific* (entitled "The Subject, Method, and Scope of This Ethnography" [Malinowski 1961 (1922), 1–26]). This text, along with a few influential later essays by Clifford Geertz, instantiates in many programs the ethos of fieldwork practice and especially the metamethodological practices that define it as central to the professional craft culture of anthropology. The central tendency in the craft culture of fieldwork is deserving of this particular shorthand, not just because Malinowski wrote effectively about fieldwork, but because he established legendary pedagogical practices that were effectively passed on generationally (see Firth 1957).

While many different theoretical brands of anthropology have been incorporated within the basic model (e.g., during the 1960s, fieldwork in cognitive anthropology had a distinctively different feel from fieldwork, say, in economic anthropology), the critiques of the 1980s (signaled in *Writing Culture* and *Anthropology as Cultural Critique* among other texts) had the effect, in my view, of reinstantiating the basic Malinowskian processual model of fieldwork in training, in new guises and with new licenses like "the reflexive turn," even though the works of Malinowski and those of Clifford Geertz are more and more consigned to courses on the history of the discipline.

and its changing functions in the complex courses of anthropological research careers. In short, the variable ways that the defining practices of fieldwork (participant observation and sustained encounters in stable sites of occupation by the anthropologist) function in the under-conceptualized diversity of the research processes that engulf them are the concerns of these essays. In effect, we argue that the transformation of classic research practices is already well under way within the full array of apprentice to mature projects of research today, but that the deeply committed disciplinary culture of method and symbolic capital of disciplinary identity does not provide an articulate understanding of that transformation on which any collective rethinking of and innovations in how ethnographic research is imagined, taught, and undertaken would depend.[3]

So, we proceed from four basic, connected propositions:

(1) The conduct and outcome of fieldwork are less a matter of training in method, or specific techniques of inquiry and reporting, than of participating in a culture of craftsmanship that anthropologists embrace.

Mentorship (the importance of the supervisor), expectations and strong shared images of ideal practice (young "Malinowskis" engaged with key informants and telling incidents), exemplary performance (the published ethnography that attracts attention beyond specialization), and an aesthetics of evaluation of results (what is "good" ethnography, effective material, rich translation) define collective standards of fieldwork in this culture of craftsmanship. For us, then, fieldwork is already well understood as a method through the many formal and informal accounts of it that exist (see fns. 1 and 2). There are always more stories

---

3. For a very recent account that exposes the workings of the basic training model that I term Malinowskian, see Allaine Cerwonka and Liisa H. Malkki's *Improvising Theory: Process and Temporality in Ethnographic Fieldwork* (2007). This work, which documents the exchanges between adviser/mentor and student while the latter is doing fieldwork, is of special value here not only because it exposes the pedagogical context of first fieldwork in progress, as no other work does, but also because it involves a student from another discipline (political science) and thus the anthropologist mentor (Malkki) displays, perhaps more didactically, her own personal assimilation of the craft of Malinowskian anthropology which she is passing on in her advising of Cerwonka's fieldwork.

Suggesting a reform (rather than a replacement) of the basic model of research long at the core and self-identity of anthropology as a discipline, as this volume does, is a tricky exercise, precisely because of the flexibility of this model and its realization in the experience of each and every person's becoming an anthropologist, and then in his or her experience of passing on this method to students and others. "How is this different from what I do?" "How is this different from what was always done (in fact)?" or "This may be what you do, but it is not what I do" are expected reactions to generally intended discussions of shifts in the way that conditions of research refigure key ideological aspects of research practice (see my debate with Judith Okley [Marcus and Okley 2008]). It is both the glory and the weakness of anthropology's professional culture of method, in whatever shorthand it is characterized, that it depends on this profoundly individualistic form of training, flourishing, and reproduction. We intend in this volume the difficult task of working both with and against this tendency of anthropology's craft culture.

to be told, new reflections on familiar norms and forms, but these are a reinforcement of the same, which I suppose is important for the solidarity of a profession that understands itself as a craft and prides itself on a certain mystique of practice.

What is not well understood are the metamethodological aspects of the anthropological research process, that is, fieldwork's production as a valued object of a professional culture. These aspects both exert a highly restrictive influence on the range of discourses that anthropologists can have about their distinctive research process, and encourage a flexible covering over of the variety of activities, of what is done as research "out there" in fieldwork's name, whether or not they resemble the classic mise-en-scène of fieldwork.

So one sense of "metamethod" in which we are interested concerns the norms of professional culture that shape the actual form of research. Other metamethodological issues define the conditions for research today that exceed the discourse of fieldwork that exists. These define unrecognized predicaments or possibilities of research about which anthropologists are either frustrated or are finding ready-made solutions, revealed perhaps in the changing character of the stories of fieldwork that they tell each other informally, but are otherwise unregistered in the regulative training model of fieldwork (Marcus 2006).[4] We believe these issues of professional culture and research practice, once articulated, would define the bases for certain reforms in the way that anthropologists think about and teach their classic research practice as a craft. Most of the essays in this volume are not explicitly reformist in this way, but a number are just this side, so to speak, of suggesting alternative practices that accommodate the critiques or ready-made adjustments of fieldwork that they have undertaken. This brings

---

4. In my impressionistic hearing, corridor chat and stories among graduate students whom I have known are about routes, connections, mapping, knowledge distributions—in short, about networking with keen ethnographic sensibilities—rather than about sites, what goes on in a situated community, or location of observation. I am sure that all fieldwork now and in the past has included movement in networks and within sites, and there have always been stories about both milieus, but it is my impression at least that the milieu of the network outweighs the milieu of the site in many current conversational fieldwork stories. This could be a shift in style of self-presentation, but I think it has to do more with changing objects of study, the influence of "theory" (critical cultural and social theories and their ideologies), and real changes in the tempo of research, in access to sites, and in investments in sticking with particular specialized sites of classic participant observation (see Marcus, ed. 1999a). As one raised on "peoples-and-places" research (a year and a half in Tongan villages), I hear too little in fieldwork stories today of conversations with informants, anecdotes of observations and situations, but instead more about findings, juxtapositions, and events familiar through media reportage. These students could produce interesting and in-depth stories of the more traditional kind if asked, but it seems as if their preference and concern in informally reporting their fieldwork are of a different quality. If there is in fact a tendency that could be documented here, I am not prepared to judge whether it is good or bad, but in any case, it would be significant.

us to the need to shape a discourse that escapes the restrictive constructions of fieldwork while preserving its valued characteristics.

(2) The exercise of the decoupling of fieldwork in its enduring classic construction as an essential and defining characteristic of doing anthropology is crucial in being able to think differently about fieldwork in broader contexts of inquiry today, to which the essays of this volume are committed.

In his essay, James Faubion both performs and argues for this exercise of freeing fieldwork as we have known it from the heavy symbolic, identity-defining load that it has carried. For Faubion, what is distinctively anthropological are ways of problematizing inquiry and conceptually defining its objects, rather than the practices of a particular conduct of inquiry and the professional ideological functions that have historically come to bear. To quote him:

> If anthropological (field)work today thus looms as the specter of a Sisyphean labor, endless and never redeemed, it does at least permit of functionally distinct divisions that give it a rather different look from fieldwork of the past. Neither the extended sojourn nor the serial return to the same or closely related physical sites yields a correct model of its physiognomy. Good anthropology will always take time. Yet I can see no reason for concluding that the time it takes must in every case be spent in its bulk in a physical fieldsite.... The ethical profile of the good anthropologist, in short, yields no methodological a priori concerning the appropriate duration of a project. Everything hinges on the terms and requirement of the question of research itself.

Just so.... The turning of an anthropologically conceived question into research requires different ways of thinking about the actual design or practices of research that are free to roam from the deeply inculcated aesthetics of fieldwork by a professional culture of craft. Faubion continues:

> Given the marked inertia of granting agencies, the anthropological (field) project of the future...may well end up looking in fact much as it has looked for several decades: one roughly year-long, more or less continuous encampment at a primary physical site, a few satellite trips here and there, and probably a two- or three-month mop-up before the dissertation or monograph is complete. Yet, in a less conventional understanding of what constitutes an anthropological project, an understanding more in accord with the practices of our contributors, a seriality comes to light that is not merely that of the repeated return to the same physical site (classically, in order to develop an ever richer and deeper comprehension of the people inhabiting that site), but more

frequently that of a concatenation of legs—some passed in what we still customarily expect a site to be, but others, no less integral a part of the project itself, passed at the library or in conversation with students and colleagues, legs in which the primary but still altogether integral activity is not that of encounter but instead that of the evaluation, articulation, thinking, and rethinking of what one has already encountered and what one is likely to encounter on the next go.

Faubion makes it possible to see classic fieldwork as a variable component of a broader process of research, and thus to see the need for distinctively anthropological understandings of this broader process. In his essay, he ventures a fascinating scheme of his own to conceive of this broader process, which develops seriality (rather than reflexivity or recursivity), connectivity, and a topology of conceptual innovations as its key ideas. He understands anthropological research as playing out on different scales required by its contemporary ambitions to pursue questions that fieldwork itself in its conventional aesthetics cannot answer. We need many more such schemes, proposals, and inventions to think about at this juncture.[5] The essays of this volume suggest where in the professional culture of research careers the rethinking of fieldwork as we have conceived it might most cogently emerge—which brings us to our third proposition.

(3) Thinking about how anthropology's culture of research and professionalization shapes what is usually thought as method, the process of dissertation research, of apprentice research, and, by extension, how first research gets "finished," and then how one moves on to other projects that should share something of the same character as first fieldwork is a strategic focus of attention for us.

The aesthetics of craft in a culture of knowledge production that takes mandatory courses on method insouciantly, while highly valuing tales of fieldwork that recount surprise, discovery, and unanticipated findings,[6] are much more

---

5. At present, such schemes sometimes emerge as novel experiments or projects, especially in the orchestration and management of collaborations (see Lassiter 2005a). In the context of training and pedagogy, Burawoy's *Global Ethnography* (2000), representing a collaborative project among him and his students, is an example of one such effort to revise the standard practices of ethnographic research to produce coordinated fieldwork on processes that take place on a global scale. Such examples of multi-sited ethnography, as I have defined it (Marcus 1998), would seem to be the natural terrain on which to conduct self-conscious experiments with the Malinowskian parameters of fieldwork, but as the essays of this volume demonstrate, there are as many conceptual varieties of recentering the classic fieldwork process in broader domains of research activity as there are dissertation projects revised by later reflection.

6. The rhetorical frame that corresponds to this special contribution of ethnography is the common indication at the beginning of texts that the research fortuitously took different turns from the way it had been conceived before fieldwork. This is one key way of establishing authority for an ethnography through the venerable aesthetic in anthropology of knowing by discovering. Thus, fieldwork habitually is reported as having taken often quite abrupt shifts or turns in direction.

defining of fieldwork than training in particular skills or techniques of inquiry in the conventional sense of method. But still, we argue in this volume that this arena of metamethod, as we have termed it, needs conceptualizations and experiments with alternative practices just as much, and even regimes of training in terms of them, that would substitute for what is now imagined by regulative ideals about the doing of research as fieldwork. These latter assimilate at their limit what anthropologists—both apprentice and mature ones—are actually doing in their research these days, without explicitly undergoing redefinition themselves.

This rethinking of the craft, and its regulative ideals or aesthetics, can best be done by looking closely—as autoethnographic objects themselves—at the experience and process of first fieldwork in a broader context that most anthropologists define initially as students, then as mature researchers looking back, and continually as mentors/supervisors. First fieldwork is thus a common object of reflection by which the entire culture of research craft in anthropology can be rethought. That is the spirit in which the contributors to this volume think about fieldwork today—not to celebrate its virtues, despise its flaws, or to admire its adaptability—but to look squarely at how it plays variable roles in larger designs of research that the present training model can only vaguely accommodate.

There are at least two reasons why this focus on first fieldwork is strategic for us rather than being merely convenient or interesting. As training model, first fieldwork is where what is most authoritative and regulative in the Malinowskian tradition of fieldwork most visibly meets the complex array of research questions and concepts that challenges the parameters of this tradition. These questions are imported into anthropology through its interdisciplinary engagements and are what have primarily drawn many students to the discipline.[7] The emphasis in some graduate programs may well be to limit quickly the ambition in apprentice inquiry that some of these questions encourage so that the training function of that first project can be successfully, effectively, and efficiently achieved. There are also ready-made narratives of research conception available on various current

---

7. This is an appropriate point to indicate that we make no effort in this volume to explain why, in recent disciplinary history, ethnographic practice plays such a large role not only in the symbolic identity of anthropology and anthropologists, to judge whether this should be so (that indeed anthropology, social and cultural, should be more than ethnography), or to suggest the major sources, internal or external, which have altered the forms and norms of the practice of fieldwork and the writing of ethnography in recent times. One of the press readers for this volume posed the issues in this way: "Was it new modes of fieldwork that produced recent changes in anthropology, or did new theoretical questions in anthropology bring about and necessitate new forms of fieldwork?" or, "Are we discussing 'new reflections on fieldwork' or 'reflections on new fieldwork?" These are indeed big questions that deserve their own treatment, but we sidestep them for the sake of a more strategic (but we believe just as important) critique and intervention that focus on a neglected side of the many discussions concerning fieldwork and ethnography in recent years. For my own preliminary and fragmented attempts to address the big questions, see Marcus 1998, 1999, 2005, 2007, 2008b; Rabinow, Marcus, et al. 2008.

problem arenas within which the Malinowskian ideal can be easily followed.[8] But, more frequently in my experience and observation, first fieldwork projects in many departments today are more like experiments managed by students and their supervisors in negotiating the limits of the norms and forms of the traditional paradigm to take on dimensions of problems that "fieldwork as usual" has not been designed to address.[9] It would certainly be preferable not to have to conduct such training as de facto experiments under the burden of conserving the valued norms of a culture of craft. We believe there are others means by which this very same culture can be preserved, but it requires thinking differently about first fieldwork, more in line with what the ongoing mentor-student negotiations tell us than what the long-standing regulative ideals in play impose.

So, the value of innovation, originality, discovering something conceptually new through fieldwork trumps the countervailing pressure to work within the available anthropological "takes" on the problem arenas that it has recently entered. In particular, exemplary ethnographies by younger scholars, which are of key pedagogical use, are carriers of this value, provide models of what to strive for, and also indicate where the self-esteem of anthropology lies today. What is interesting to us, then, in first projects are their edges, the negotiations by which they satisfy the traditional norms and gesture beyond them. It is in these negotiations and what is settled for in the production of dissertations—and thus, perhaps most crucially, in what remains to be done afterwards to finish or complete

---

8. These are discussed in a volume of conversations mainly between Paul Rabinow and me (Rabinow, Marcus, et al. 2008). These are the scripts that situate locales, communities, or groups, usually of subaltern subjects, at the vortex of contemporary complex changes involving global-scale processes, events, and multiple agents and forces (for influential recent examples see Petryna 2002; Tsing 2005). Ethnography preserves its Malinowskian aesthetics by staying with human-scale lives of accessible subjects. Some would say this is what ethnography does best and is also its limit. The spirit of this volume is to renegotiate this limit by rethinking the formal dimensions of the research process, held in place by powerful craft aesthetics, so that the role of fieldwork in specific projects can be conceived beyond the conventionally situating current scripts for it.

9. Simply incorporating experts as ethnographic subjects, or the production of a particular kind of rational, bureaucratic knowledge as an ethnographic object, into a field of research that traditionally focuses on sites of everyday and ordinary life stimulates such negotiations in graduate training (see Boyer, in press). This negotiation is not about simply adding sites of elites to sites of subaltern subjects; rather, it is about encompassing in fieldwork something of the complexity of contemporary processes, which the habit of setting up ethnography by distinguishing between the global and the local belies. The ethnography of policy processes provides exemplars for defining this more complex terrain in the conception of fieldwork projects. Greenhalgh's magisterial account of China's One-Child policy (2008) derives from a complex path of research, rooted in fieldwork, over twenty years. The challenge of negotiating dissertation projects today is how to incorporate such scale—or not—into the design of career-defining ethnographies of apprentice anthropologists. Such a design involves not just doing fieldwork in the Malinowskian pattern, but a different compass in which fieldwork itself can have variable functions and forms.

research—that the glimmer of an alternative and coherent conception of the present research process can be perceived.

Second, while I have written about the way in which later projects of research operate on very different principles than first projects, even though they share the same ideology of craft (Marcus 1998, 233–45), it is first projects more than later ones that are responsible for guaranteeing the reproduction of the entire research enterprise of anthropology in its traditional form, even though it appears sometimes that second projects are "running away" from the training model. This frequent discomfort or at least ambivalence with how first projects end, at least at the dissertation stage, is a major and ironically valuable encouragement in the production of finished first work, and later projects as well; it is indeed a symptom to note in the imagining of the alternative, remodeled practices to which I will return.

Indeed, whether first fieldwork was done in the classic era of sustained discipline-developed problematics for it (e.g., problems of kinship, ritual, classification, language, the essential character of cultures) or now, when problems of inquiry often exceed the imagined and literal places in which first fieldwork in the classic mode can take place, first fieldwork nonetheless provides in almost every case a personal, even intimate constitution, carrying in an embodied way the culture of craft that anthropology so much values into highly diverse careers of research. Many of these are in the pursuit of projects very far from the training model, while still hanging on to the influence of its imaginary.

Thus, through first fieldwork the authority of the discipline as craft comes to live on within careers of diverse research activity. It is the anchor of lore in practice, through the affect of memory—positive or negative. It tells one what the "classic" model is in one's own experience and later trajectory; it is a compass, however much one's research and circumstances vary later. In this volume, we depend on the power of that "looking back" on first fieldwork in a sampling of today's projects of research, as represented in the essays of former recent students at different degrees of distance and in various subsequent professional situations. Their accounts think of first fieldwork not as a professional legitimation, bittersweet in some cases perhaps, for what one does later, but as a key means to begin to imagine alternative visions of craft that respond to the "symptoms" encouraging them in such distanced reflection on experiences of first fieldwork. This leads us more explicitly to the state of the pedagogy of first projects of anthropological research and to our fourth guiding proposition.

(4) Finally, and more briefly, the object of the exercise undertaken collectively by the essays of this volume and the critiques of anthropology's professional culture of method, centered on fieldwork, is to encourage experimentation with alternative pedagogical strategies that might enhance graduate training

consistent with a long view of how fieldwork fits practically, ideologically, and variantly into anthropological research careers today.

What is called for are more debates arising from better ethnographic understandings of the contemporary research process itself. This is a very large task that we can only hope to evoke and provoke in this volume. But the common concerns of these essays with first fieldwork, across the perspectives of the supervisors of the dissertation projects in question in the various essays, of former recent students, and of two teachers of fieldwork with a decidedly experimental orientation to pedagogy, are an effective way to begin.

The Essays

The essays by Faubion and me are reflections by long-time dissertation supervisors, who worked together over the years in this capacity. Indeed, we were co-supervisors of the first fieldwork projects of the six former recent students who contribute essays to this volume. Appropriately, our essays bracket and frame their accounts, mine by overview, Faubion by theoretical implication. Taken together, our reflections are not about specific projects, but of the changing nature and function of fieldwork of the classic sort over the past two decades in the kinds of contemporary research careers that are exemplary and emerging among younger anthropologists.

Faubion goes much further than I do in venturing a theoretical framework for an alternative understanding of what fieldwork might be about these days. We both, however, see the need, from the shared supervisions that we have done, to evolve apprentice projects differently. Both of us work with an ethnographer's eye for the metamethodological habits that currently shape the production of ethnography—the subtle affective and attitudinal factors that characterize anthropology's explicit and core culture of method as it is challenged today: its sense of tempo, of patience, slowness, in the presence of rapidly changing events; its anxieties about scale, about being pulled away from the Malinowskian scene of encounter; and its multiple accountabilities, with the professional community being only one. I have tried to capture some of these characteristics below in a set of notes and observations about predicaments of the training process. Faubion uses ethics as a conceptual frame to evoke some of the same issues.

About the six core essays by former recent students variously situated now and at various degrees of distance from the first fieldwork process in graduate degree programs: the temptation, given the dominant genre in existence for such accounts, would be to treat these as simply more "tales of the field" that, however bittersweet and even critical, wind up validating the professional ideology of fieldwork as worthy "trial and tribulation." I would encourage readers not to do so, but to see them as fieldwork accounts that begin to challenge, from different angles of distance and current situation, the adequacy of the classic paradigm of fieldwork to account for their research experiences, which overflow it. Each case of near or more distant "looking back" and the intellectual value and function of first fieldwork performed, within the canonical environment of training as I described, is quite different from every other. If there is a single overweening issue that enters, more or less prominently, into each account, it is about scale and scaling: how to make the phenomenological intimacies of fieldwork, made even more canonical by the so-called reflexive turn of the 1980s, speak to larger theoretical, more abstract, but nonetheless empirical engagements with systems, institutions, networks, and global processes. How research in each case after the dissertation develops in this larger arena of both conceptual and literal spaces determines what kind of value first fieldwork has in a relative sense.

First fieldwork barely allowed Kristin Peterson and Jae Chung to grasp, or even operate in, the problem arenas in which they are now dealing. Their essays most directly address issues of the scale of ethnographic work versus the scale of the anthropological object in question. They continue to do anthropological research, but whether it has any significant resemblance to the Malinowskian scheme is a question on which the working out of new metamethodological practices, in which this volume is interested, depends. In each case, first fieldwork was valuable for doing a certain kind of messy conceptual labor of extraordinary importance to what has come later.

The essays by Jennifer Hamilton, Deepa Reddy, Nahal Naficy, and Lisa Breglia are portraits of the situational constraints of fieldwork, the juggling of independence against several different sources of blockage, and imposition of research norms and terms of conduct not their own. In both first and later projects, they wrestle under contemporary conditions with the absence of the space that Malinowski and later fieldworkers (even if primarily in a psychological sense) had. Many fieldworkers today are simply not free in a practical sense to impose the classic conditions of fieldwork, or the difficulties of so doing are quite different from those related in classic accounts. Thus, in such accounts as these four essays especially present, there can be read the glimmer of alternative understandings of fieldwork that are being formed within essays that in a hybrid sense are still within the conventions of genre-writing ("tales of fieldwork").

Hamilton's and Reddy's essays overlap substantively: after different first fieldwork experiences they have until recently been working within the same environment of medical research that has made places for ethnography. While also explicitly addressing problems of scale, Hamilton's is a discussion of the "recovery" from the apparent failure of the first project (but see the book that was later derived from that experience [Hamilton 2008a]) to the establishment of a certain elbow room in the course of taking on the second project with Reddy (see also the book that Reddy generated around her first fieldwork [Reddy 2006]).

The essays by Reddy, Naficy, and Breglia are less about the problems of scale than the problems of association with one's subjects and the ecology of the contemporary ethnographic encounter, which redefine the "site" or mise-en-scène in which fieldwork is classically imagined to take place. Of course, this "site" has always been instead a "field" in which the ethnographer moves for a period. These movements accumulate an inventive recursivity, composed of the de facto mix of design, serendipity, and choices that creates in turn a distinctive coherence and imaginary to fieldwork these days, as Faubion discusses. The problem is that this recursivity spins research out of the traditionally imagined confines of fieldwork (where "good ethnography" can be done) and suggests the need for practices that redefine these "confines" of fieldwork to keep up with the expanding and moving ground of research.

Breglia makes perhaps the strongest argument for the marginalization of the Malinowskian standard in favor of found concepts and circuits of inquiry in a very complex ecology of movement. Indeed, fieldwork for Breglia is at once an identity, a foil, and, as she says, a phantasm of heightened "common sense," against which to think creatively. All of these essays suggest the need for different training models, worked out, rather than the revised Malinowksian model of craft that is proudly open to what the student might find.

So, as a dissertation supervisor, I ask myself how many of the retrospective insights in these six essays about what fieldwork in its classic modality means in larger frames and longer views of particular research problems could have been thought through proactively before "going into the field"? And if many could have been (as I believe), what would the capacity to think through ethnographically or imagine the field more thoroughly before "going there" suggest about different preparations and conceptual boundaries of research projects, even in the performance of first fieldwork with its symbolic load as "rite of passage"? More on this later.

This volume ends appropriately with two experiments in teaching research that are alive to the issues that we are raising. They provocatively conduct these experiments on first fieldwork at the very beginning of careers, where, as argued, metamethod is the symbolic heart of the discipline's identity. Kim Fortun was trained in anthropology at Rice and is author of *Advocacy After Bhopal* (2001). She teaches now in a science studies program at Rensselaer Polytechnic Institute. Christopher Kelty was trained in science studies at MIT and is author of *Two Bits: Free Software and the Social Imagination After the Internet* (2008b). Until recently, he taught anthropology at Rice. There is a sense of license in both papers in experimenting with anthropology's method that would not be found commonly in anthropology programs. And this is significant. They emerge from the borderlands of the crossover between the anthropological project of ethnographic research and the interdisciplinary field of science and technology studies (sometimes known as STS) in which the focus is on the conception of objects of study and how to articulate research problems that will stimulate collective work on particular topics (in this, STS tends to mimic the concern of research in the sciences themselves for operating within limited, vetted, and collective research programs) rather than on methods, about which STS is eclectic.[10]

From the perspective of anthropology programs, science studies is clearly a vibrant arena in the current orientation of anthropological inquiry toward problems and objects of study novel to it, which inevitably challenges very settled ideas of what research as fieldwork should be like. This arena is a veritable laboratory of new ideas about alternative conceptions of fieldwork. But of course, not all anthropologists do science studies, and science studies programs in their eclecticism care little about staying true to the classic norms and forms of anthropology. The trick is how the experimental spirit and license of these two papers in rethinking first fieldwork might migrate suggestively and more generically into the diverse range of problem areas in which anthropologists conduct research today. This is indeed already happening on a large scale in contemporary anthropology and as represented here in the crossovers that structure the essays by Fortun and Kelty. Both provide useful ways for teaching fieldwork relevant to any contemporary subject of interest and for addressing issues, which run through this volume, of scale, research environments of collaboration, and how fieldwork can be conceived flexibly to participate in research on questions for which anthropological fieldwork has little past experience in providing answers.

Finally, it will not be lost on the reader familiar with the recent history of anthropology that the contributors to this volume are connected by more than common interests—they have all been associated with the Rice department of anthropology in various ways: Faubion a current member of the faculty and Kelty (who was also a student of Michael Fischer's at MIT, a former longtime faculty member at Rice who reflects on the history of the Rice department in his foreword to this volume) nearly current; a former faculty member now at the University of the California, Irvine (myself); six former recent graduate students; and Fortun, a former graduate student at Rice in the late 1980s and early 1990s.

The Rice department collectively was a leader, among others, and a mildly controversial one at that, in the seminal critiques of the 1980s that contributed

---

10. For exemplary recent works that reflect the vibrant crossover between anthropology and sciences studies, see Fischer 2003; Downey and Dumit 1997; and Franklin and Lock 2003.

to the broader trends that have reshaped the research agendas of contemporary anthropology and its styles of ethnography over the past two decades. But I would ask readers not to move quickly to the conclusion that the concerns of this volume thus represent the concerns of a smallish faction within anthropology, either in the guise of a survival of past fashion or of an avant-garde. While the spirit and intellectual capital of the critiques of the 1980s perhaps endured somewhat more strongly in the Rice department than in others, on the whole, the legacies of those critiques have become quite mainstream. At least a large number of anthropologists, and many students who are entering the discipline, think of research today in terms that would be quite familiar to and compatible with ideas and arguments circulating especially through the 1980s and early 1990s.

In any case, we would claim that much of what we are arguing for now encourages anthropology to move on from the influences of that period and the points where the discipline has become stuck, so to speak. The way to do this, we think, is to concentrate on remaking what is least up for debate, but which is deeply shaped by once critical ideas becoming a kind of orthodoxy, or at least an authority for preserving very old and ideologically highly valued practices of a culture of craft. Accordingly, we believe that we are addressing significant current tendencies of change at the heart of the discipline—its culture of method. Further, we think the Rice connections are a distinct advantage in so doing. They provide a context of working within an important, if not decisive, recent history of the discipline, and they provide a coherence and rationale in purpose at a level that few edited volumes achieve.

My own recent move to the department at the University of California, Irvine, one that has been prominent in contributing to, even in defining, current research trends, confirms for me the importance of rethinking our culture of method, especially in graduate pedagogy. The student predicaments at UCI and the culture of method here impress me as not markedly different from their counterparts at Rice in recent times, or from the situation of graduate training in many programs that I have visited in recent years, both in the United States and abroad.

I would make a broad and relative distinction about the level of current awareness among anthropology graduate programs, or even projects case by case, regarding the state of the discipline's culture of method and their motivation to remodel the pedagogy of training. On the one hand, there are those programs or projects that are undertaken within strong facilities and traditions of area studies (e.g., universities where anthropology develops alongside substantial institutional resources for the study of particular regions)—even though area studies as a concept and program has itself undergone searching critiques since the 1990s. On the other hand, there are those programs and projects that are driven by "problems of the contemporary" (phrased often in terms of modernity, alternative modernities, globalization, or identified with various formulations of public anthropology or activism), wherever they may be situated geographically. This distinction is of course relative, and projects so distinguished are pursued side-by-side in the same departments. But it seems to me that fieldwork projects backed by strong area studies traditions are not as troubled, or as stimulated, by problems of metamethod that we have been discussing here. The motivation to remodel pedagogy is likely to be strongest among those teachers and students who are most vexed by problems of scale in what they do, for which the apparatus of culture/geographical areas is not an adequate or available framework.

So today we often deal with first fieldwork projects in which students situate the complex things that they do (made complex by transcultural, transareal structures that fieldworkers have the ambition to get "inside" as they once desired to get inside structures of kinship, for example) in specific cultural zones nonetheless (which the Malinowksian model, especially in training, requires— "go far away and work on ordinary people"). With the aid of mentorship and advising, they are left to figure out a research path that will satisfy these parameters: what culture is in the vortex of changes at different scales; what the relation of micro to macro is; how power is constituted in systems of many agencies. Without the supporting context of organized area studies, which often has specific, usually historicist narratives for the ethnographer to write within and the fieldworker to structure her experience in terms of, many projects today, though still deeply invested in understanding other places, require a different kind of working through of a problem that matches the complexity of its recognition and encounter in a pathway of fieldwork that neither begins nor ends with the gathering of material for a dissertation.[11]

---

11. Xiang Biao's *Global "Body Shopping"* (2007) provides, for me, an ideal example of how a dissertation project evolved into a transnational, multi-sited and manageable ethnography of a truly global object of study: an Indian labor system on which the computer industry has depended. Granted, Xiang is dealing with subjects quite congenial to a tradition of fieldwork research: the study of workers and working conditions. Yet I am impressed by the preservation of "the cultural" within the ethnography without it being the dominant frame of the study (he is not primarily asking about the "Indian-ness" of this system, although he captures it), and I am equally impressed by how appropriate the depth of fieldwork is in the different sites explored. Malinowskian detail is there; but the account of the operation of a system is foregrounded. It is as if Malinowski actually made the kula voyages.

Xiang's project accomplishes conventional fieldwork on a scale and in terms of a complex object about which supervisors are often hesitant, if not skeptical, when they negotiate dissertation projects with students.

Revisions of the Culture of Training and Observations from Graduate Supervision: A Brief Exercise in Ethnographic Memoir

I want to use the remainder of this essay to present in note form a collection of observations and suggestions about graduate training in the metamethod of anthropology's craft that addresses the concerns of this volume. Perhaps this should be thought of as a contribution to pedagogy rather than methodology. These notes are developed from the perspective of my role as a graduate supervisor in a single program over more than two decades during which the actual nature and content of initiatory fieldwork across the discipline have changed markedly, though the pedagogical routine with its considerable virtues has not. I do not argue for a revolution in or reformation of pedagogy, but rather a morphing of it to catch up with what research, and fieldwork within it, have become in many apprentice situations. The ethnographer's eye for the subtlety, detail, and contradictions or ironies of process is what I hope to have turned, however briefly, upon our culture of craft, in which I have participated and which I have observed during a time of its transition, the nature of which, I would underscore again, has not yet been effectively articulated.

I preface this exercise with two personal observations, impressions really, about shifts in the graduate training process that have affected my experience and thinking about supervision. First, for many years after the 1980s critiques and the interdisciplinary ferment around the study of culture of which they were a part, at least until the late 1990s, the best candidates for graduate training in social-cultural anthropology were motivated primarily by the excitement and complexity of those largely academic debates. Critique, critical theories, and changing conceptions of culture, society, and identity drove students from a variety of academic trainings in these interdisciplinary movements into anthropology which, for its legendary method of engagement in the world, its self-critical acuity, its long-standing identification with conceptions of culture, and the objects that its broad historic ambitions had evoked for inquiry had considerable cachet in these interdisciplinary movements. So, I had come to presume at least at Rice that the students with whom I would be working came with this theoretical, essentially academic interest and image of 1980s anthropology, and that fieldwork, while desired as a trope of practice, would be the major challenge—how to operationalize the theory of that period and its habits for the shocks, cultural and otherwise, messiness, and ad hoc qualities of fieldwork's distinctive intellectual labor. After the turn of the century, I came to realize that the priorities of the best candidates had shifted (even at Rice). The excitement of theory and academic debate about changing social and cultural orders had receded among students in favor of activism, driven by a healthy combination of pragmatics and idealism. The "typical" highly motivated candidate today comes with experience from work in the world of NGOs and activist organizations. One can no longer count on a background in the knowledge of, or at least the desire for, the theories and debates that brought students into anthropology previously and about which they were better informed, even though academic training in anthropology still heavily depends on working within the debates and theories of the earlier period. It is just that students are unfamiliar with—and thus have to be taught in a more elementary way (which, by the way, is a very great problem for the economy of effort in graduate teaching in many programs)—this still active apparatus.[12]

So, if my impression is at all correct, students enter anthropology today for what fieldwork can do in sites of the world with which they already have considerable experience or affinity. In a sense, today's students are ahead of the discipline in thinking about the terrains of the "real world" in which fieldwork-based projects of research must be forged. We could simply adapt the pedagogy we have to these NGO-experienced students, which is the state of play in many departments, but in my opinion it is much better for anthropology and its own debates and ideas to rethink and recast its pedagogy to where younger generations are pulling it in the present era. One might say that the 1980s were a congenial intellectual preparation in less engaged times for the shape and inclinations of research careers being formed now. Rethinking graduate pedagogy is a crucial middle term and disciplinary task in this transition.

Second, in participating in the pedagogy of first fieldwork over the years, I have long felt that the period of the defining of the dissertation, through fieldwork, to the dissertation writing-up process encompasses the most obvious and interesting activities in which to intervene with new thinking and experiments in the remodeling of practices. Certainly, they remain the most critical activities by which to observe the negotiation of anthropology's aesthetics of craft and in

---

12. In my own current department, there is a brilliantly conceived and effective three-term procourse designed in part to instill this "apparatus"—this tradition and influence of theory from the 1980s and 1990s—in new students. In my former department at Rice, we at one point hired Kathryn Milun, a scholar in comparative literature, to teach students preparing to do fieldwork this synergy, so to speak, of the mastery of contemporary theory (Michel Foucault, Gilles Deleuze, Jacques Derrida, Jürgen Habermas, Hans-Georg Gadamer, Gayatri Spivak, Julia Kristeva, etc.) and its innovative applications in text-based cultural analyses, for it was then in comparative literature that such synergy was most effectively realized. Milun had to work yearly with students who arrived (for better or worse!) with considerable conversancy with the range of theoretical works. Now, in both departments, there is the need to begin at the beginning in teaching these sources (or those whose currency has survived, such as Foucault), even though the role that such theory plays in constructing ethnography is still decisive (for a critique of the kind of ethnography that the era of theory produced, see Marcus 2007).

relation to which to suggest changes in practice. But under current constraints, I have come to see the little-reflected-upon postdoctoral process as the part of first research that most accurately and explicitly manifests the real predicaments of contemporary anthropological research. Of course, this process is often beyond formal supervision and pedagogy, but probably most supervisors, and I myself, remain involved with this key part of the research projects of former students. For me, it has become more fun and personally satisfying than trying to forge alternative pedagogy in the current process of dissertation research. And for my interest in the remodeling of pedagogy, it has become a very instructive and inevitable phase in the present training model. I find the kind of "second-wind" rethinking and renewed initiatives in inquiry that sometimes go on in this phase fascinating and a source of inspiration for my rethinking of the pedagogy that precedes it.

In many cases, former students substantially revise their dissertations or put them aside altogether in the postdoc period. Certainly they functionally relativize the dominant role of first fieldwork in the dissertation process, which shares much with the enterprise of this volume. Increasingly, almost as a standard practice nowadays, jobs are awarded to candidates who have remade their research in postdoc periods of one to two years, however well supported by fellowships or temporary jobs they are—or are not—and have completed ethnographic volumes to show for it. So the following notes take the present process as it is, but they are inspired by the reinvention of research that often goes on in the postdoc period today.

Observations

In the spirit of the previous discussion about what of consequence for rethinking the paradigm of training these days occurs off the radar, so to speak, in the postdoc period, the following observations are mere gestures, of varying degrees of elaboration, from a contemplated memoir of a career of supervising first research projects. They are about where to look—where there are "seams" between present practices and alternative possibilities legible within them. This legibility itself depends on the ethnographer's art, and each one deserves an article or a chapter in an ethnographic memoir of a career of supervision that savors the subtleties and subversions of the informalities of a culture of method central to a discipline that itself savors the subtle and critical edges of its research productions.

Tales of Fieldwork Now

Fieldwork stories—not so much those written into ethnographies almost habitually since the 1980s as a consequence of the so-called reflexive turn of that period, but the kinds of narratives that are the currency of courses, conferences, and informal occasions of all kinds in anthropology departments—have been a key modality in the instilling of method and its culture in anthropological training and beyond. They are the medium by which anthropologists reveal to one another what really goes on in fieldwork. While some older anthropologists may have tired of listening to such stories, even given the sense of professional solidarity that they provide, I observe that the shape and frequency of occasionally told fieldwork stories today, coming especially from research in arenas where Malinowskian conditions of fieldwork are most challenged, are key loci of access to the seams, revealing expected and alternative practices that I mentioned. In my hearing, I find that such informal accounts of research by younger fieldworkers—apprentice and later—are less indulgent of the canonical "trial-and-tribulation" form of reporting on an initiate's testing and less naturally about Malinowskian, situated encounters than about the kind of recursivity that Faubion discusses—the moving around various kinds of sites and sources and the problems of the coherence of informing concept and research problem to which this movement—defining a cumulative density—gives rise.

Several of the essays begin to tell, or suggest the telling of, different such stories. For example, Jae Chung does this by beginning with "a feint," luring us into a comfortable tale of fieldwork (hanging out with subjects in relaxed company after hours), only then to tell us that such settings do not inform the kinds of questions with which she was centrally concerned. Her research was very much like canonical first fieldwork, but stories of this sort were not central to what her research was about. Further, the teaching experiments of Fortun and Kelty each suggest the telling of different sorts of modified traditional stories of the field. In Kelty's case, fieldwork stories would be organized around the problem of "composition" that he discusses and would not be reducible to the Malinowskian mise-en-scène.

Fieldwork stories today are thus less about a fieldwork experience bounded by the Malinowskian scene of encounter (these can always be elicited on demand, but they are not so naturally offered in corridor talk) and more about what I will describe below as the design of anthropological research for which anthropology does not yet have an adequate articulation. So increasingly, this de facto design gets articulated along the way of research and careers in changing genres of talk derived from fieldwork stories that serve professional solidarity. These are worth listening to in a different register.

The Pedagogical Role of Reading Exemplary Ethnographies

Reading ethnographies as another way of learning what the signature method of anthropology is and what it should produce as a discursive result has long been of pedagogical importance. In a sense, students are to learn both the aesthetic standards and the procedures of fieldwork from reading their published results; in many departments, obligatory fieldwork courses have for their textbooks exemplary ethnographies. Ethnographies have served classically as the basis of thought experiments, providing materials to be "worked through," augmenting conceptual debates over description, and crucially showing what fieldwork is to be about, what is expected of it in a discipline that has been remarkably silent in a formal way about research design. After all, who else would read ethnographies with any care—no matter how appealing their romantic origins in travel?

Before the 1980s, there were classics and models of ethnography that circulated in such an exemplary, pedagogical way. After the 1980s, it has no longer been so much the classics that have circulated for their pedagogical influence, except perhaps symbolically, as texts of self-consciously experimental ethnography, calling attention to their critical, innovative aspects. In student culture, for example, one reads Michael Taussig rather than, or at least more carefully than, Malinowski. And contra the older more stable system of pedagogy based on classics, for a time these experimental ethnographies circulate in an inflationary manner, turning over every year or so, emphasizing the first or second works of younger scholars, and very much defining the marketplace of reputation on which secure careers are established (see Marcus 2007). Indeed, the considerable demand for innovation and revival of ethnography determines the primary readership for such ethnographies. Significantly, this pattern of circulation and influence continues to the present. It still creates the pedagogical models, fashions, markets, and perhaps most crucially the form of knowledge for ethnography, especially for students, who learn in a back-loaded way what fieldwork is to accomplish through strong images of how it is to do so as portrayed in exemplary ethnographies since the reflexive turn.

While I appreciate that exemplary ethnographies are powerful purveyors of what we have called in this volume the metamethods of the discipline, and that their use in teaching as vehicles for thought experiments about the conduct of fieldwork is invaluable, I also believe that they bear too much of the burden of conceptualizing research in pre-fieldwork training, since as a genre they are still written as if the fieldwork experiences that they canonically evoke are the core and limit of the process of inquiry—a presumption that we are calling into question in this volume. Also, given a broader imaginary for the research process that we are advocating, the ethnographic form itself in its current exemplars is no longer necessarily the ideal textual outcome of such a reimagined research process. In some current exemplary ethnographic works, the limits of the classic form are clearly pushed, but in my observation, this is not the lesson that is clearly drawn from them by their use in teaching within the culture of method.

In any case, how certain exemplary ethnographies become reread during the course of a project before and after fieldwork would make for an interesting topic for elaboration within a fully realized ethnographic memoir of supervision.

The Private Data Sets of Fieldwork

The "stuff" of fieldwork, its raw materials, has always been primarily between the fieldworker and her notebooks, but formerly the traditional topics of anthropology (kinship, ritual, religion, and so on) offered more exposure to this material and to its "working through" in the scholarly community in its near-to-primary form than they do now at almost any stage of processing (see Sanjek 1990): supervisor-student interactions, seminar presentations, write-up, and the production of published texts. It is much more uncertain what the data sets of various fieldwork projects are now, and there is very little discussion of them in these various contexts of training. In fact, the acuteness of the challenges to what the objects of ethnography are today makes the raw form of fieldwork material a crucial subject for direct attention and analysis in common. For example, in my experience, supervisor-student discussions are mostly about positioning moves, conceptual fixes, and how to make and support an argument; there is rarely the working from an inventory of material, but rather the negotiation of selectivity from a corpus of material, largely off-stage to these discussions. Given that training keeps the finished ethnography in view, and the fact that the ethnography is supposed to do more theoretical work of an abstract, or at least more interdisciplinary, sort than the classic ethnography as analytic-descriptive report was ever expected to perform, it is not surprising that primary materials get very little direct attention in training or in processing for publication or, for that matter, in professional reception.

Still, what are ethnography and the labors of fieldwork all about if not basic materials that have specific forms and processes of presentation in which they can be collectively discussed and reviewed at some phase of research? It is perhaps ironic that outside the culture of method of anthropology, those intimate materials of the field are probably more public in character than they have ever been. In their raw form, they exist as documents among overlapping documents and discourses of a parallel nature being produced by others—subjects, media, parallel inquiries—in the field of research (this is especially the case with the emergence of blogs as a "form" of anthropological writing; see Saka 2008 and the e-seminar based on it). As such they are subject to constant change and engagement with their counterparts even as they reside in fieldwork notebooks (or whatever other media of recording are in play today). As such, research, including fieldwork, conceived of as a design process or design studio—to be suggested below—might allow for the capturing of this dynamic character of data through the staged presentation of basic materials at different points of development, along with continual revision. Such an opportunity is lacking now.

Greater exposure of the stuff of fieldwork by design would mean at this juncture a challenge to present practices that tend to encourage the production of the dissertation as the first draft of a book. It might be better to think instead of ways to deal more directly and processually with the personal archives from which the dissertation is produced. Perhaps the dissertation is the one phase in the current production of research where the working through of material is most exposed for review by a specific (departmental) community. How to compose materials for the purposes of scholarly communication is at the core of Kelty's innovations in teaching. The challenge is to develop forms and ways of processing, conceptualizing, and paying attention to raw material in common as pedagogy, without being overwhelmed by it. If the raw material, the data sets of fieldwork, are increasingly composed with public dimensions, amid various active collaborations and receptions in play, then again, a design process incorporating staged occasions of broad review might best serve this present absence of what otherwise gives anthropological research with fieldwork at its core, more than ever, its distinction.

Surprise and Discovery: The Expected Derailment of Original Research Plans

There is not only a tolerance for, but even an expectation of, a shift in plans in fieldwork. This has the standing of a trope in ethnographic writing, a story of "correction" as I call it: the anthropologist starts out with the idea of researching one thing, but good, promising fieldwork often leads to something completely different, unexpected, and more interesting. This is as much a part of the rhetoric of ethnographic authority as the well-known tropes establishing "being there." It is most eloquently articulated by Faubion in his essay:

> The worthiest of questions are not at all guaranteed to remain stable through the empirical course of their resolution, and what instability and mutation they exhibit make unstable and liable to mutation every one of their epistemological and ontological fortifications.

Certainly, these accounts of how what one intended to study becomes something else during fieldwork are one common currency of discussion between supervisors and students. Finding something new, a sense of discovery and surprise, and a surrogate for the traditional affinity for the exotic, no longer respectable but still traceable within the romantic side of anthropology—these are all aspects of the regulative aesthetics of ethnography that are performed in the "turning course" stories of fieldwork. Such stories are also at the core of the sense of double agent-cy in the production of first research, discussed below.

In one sense, what these stories communicate is the essential unpredictability of fieldwork, its virtuous unruliness, and its resistance to standard ideas about research design and methodology in the social sciences. But is this deep orientation of anthropological metamethod a reason for indulging it entirely? It is worth considering how this valorization of changing the question in midcourse can be further thought through and better understood with the aim of changing, if not method, then the metamethod of training to accommodate it.

For example, I have begun to make a collection of these stories and expressions and to think in reverse about them: Could the projects in question have been conceived differently to have accommodated earlier on, before fieldwork, the turns that they cast in the rhetoric of surprise, discovery, and of what was unanticipated? In what kind of process of organized research preparation could such turns at least be conceived as satisfying and worth approving while also explicitly or implicitly not calling that process into question? In this, I suppose I contest Marilyn Strathern's recent celebration of the surplus capacity of the uncertain turns of traditional anthropological research, especially in new environments. As she says:

> Social anthropology has one trick up its sleeve: the deliberate attempt to generate more data than the investigator is aware of at the time of collection...a participatory exercise which yields materials for which analytical protocols are often devised after the fact... [Ethnography allows] one to recover the antecedents of future crises from material not collected for the purpose...to anticipate a future need to know something that cannot be defined in the present. (Strathern 2004, 5–7)

Well, yes, but there is method (or metamethod) to this restatement of the traditional aesthetic of the distinction of anthropological inquiry in new research environments. It is worth exploring rather than valorizing the virtues of established practices.

So, are there ways to reorganize the current metamethod of anthropological training around this aesthetic and enhance it? This question presages my discussion below about imagining a broader process of design for anthropological research.

Double Agent-cy

Anthropology's thriving, distinctive culture of research, composed of a cluster of informal practices and standards such as those just described, has an uncertain, often ill-fitting relationship to the demands of the larger institutional structure and ecology of research in terms of which it must define and shape itself, for the sake both of such quite tangible "goods" as research funding and disciplinary recognition and of public and academic conversations in which anthropology would like to count as participating. The deeply regulative norms of metamethod often conflict with the larger contexts in which anthropology must be successful—and, I observe, this tension is felt and most consequentially plays out in the current pedagogical process itself. At least part of the solidarity and identity of anthropologists today is based on a premise of their own disciplinary "cultural intimacy" (see Herzfeld 1997), a shared understanding that they are playing a game of double-ness, or fancifully, double agent-cy, on the level of individual project development. There is the sense in training projects of producing research for both "us" and "them" at the same time, in different registers.

Though widely shared among anthropologists, the playing of this game is learned in training, and primarily in the crucial funding application process, which has a critical shaping or enhancing effect on some of the characteristics of the current informal training norms (e.g., it enhances the previously discussed expectation, and pridefully so, that proposed research will change course after the formal proposal has ceded center stage, as it usually does; it also tends conceptually to reify fieldwork as coterminous with "research" more than we think should be the case, because fieldwork is what methodologically stands for anthropology in its reception as a social science). The labor and importance of producing funding proposals thus often exclude a distinct marking of this double-ness in pedagogical process in favor of collusion. Such a marking would be more desirable, I believe, under present conditions.

The formulation of research within the culture of method, as described above, differs from its formulation for a funding proposal that responds to the authoritative norms, forms, and categories of the social sciences, with which the former fits badly. Under current conditions, the former deserves its own expression before or aside from translation into the latter. Such translation is possible, and anthropology has in fact been very successful in fitting into funding structures, but there is neither the time nor the resources in the training process to give to the parallel development of a proposal that more fully reflects anthropology's culture of metamethods and to perform this double-ness in a satisfactory, balanced way.

As it now stands, the formal proposal requirements push the expression of the alternative discussion of research—how it really works—to the realm of the informal and the marginal and tend to make it a bit of the outlaw as well. This has consequences for all of the issues that I have been raising about how anthropology's metamethods affect its research projects. These issues exist in the shadows of more formal procedures that are in tension with them. Better would be a transcending of this awkward situation of double-ness by a developed expression, a remodeling, of its metamethods, drawn from an auto-ethnographic appreciation of how they work at present, and the eventual offering of this formulation or model to the institutional ecology of support for anthropology as the appropriate standard by, and form in which, its proposals should be assessed. (Actually, there is a commission under way to advise organizations like the NSF about how to evaluate "qualitative research" in the social sciences on its own terms; my suggestion here is in line with this promising development.) It would mean substituting for fieldwork, as the emblem that indeed stands for anthropological method in its present institutional environment of support, a broader conception, such as a design process, as discussed below. In so doing, the awkward aspects of the double agent-cy game, especially visible in training, might be reduced.

Suggestions

Finally, here are some specific ideas for reshaping the crucial training process at the beginning of careers through which anthropologists learn practices as well as an aesthetics or embodied ideology of method to think about them. They are about strategy (metamethod, directed toward the pedagogical process), rather than tactics of inquiry (research techniques—e.g., how to do interviews, how to count things). They are presented in broad strokes and emerge from memoirist observations such as the preceding as well as from my engagement with the essays in this volume.

The first suggestion is a large one, about an alternative concept of form or framework as distinctive of the anthropological research process. The other three suggestions can be viewed either as aspects of this alternative form or as potentialities, as under-realized features, within current pedagogy. Though advocating more than mere "tweaking," these suggestions follow what I have called the seams of alternatives already present in current practices under the challenge of changing conditions of research.

A Design Process

We come to the conviction that some broader, elaborated view and model of the anthropological research process is needed today, rather than just "fieldwork," to serve especially the task of training ethnographers-in-the-making. While acknowledging that anthropological research is mostly composed of projects of individual conception and execution and is about defined cases—this much is guaranteed by the discipline's mythic construction of fieldwork—virtually everything else about research these days pulls a project into collaborations, collectivities, institutional arrangements, and networks of various kinds that are not simply its objects, but are integral to the process of making knowledge out of the traditional individual, case-bounded project of fieldwork.

Once again, to quote Faubion:

> [Anthropologists] offer us anthropology as a topology that refuses to abandon the particularity of its various cases even as it manages to pursue and indeed to grant pride of place to a topologically modulated enterprise of comparison. [Research today is] executing a practice in and beyond the literal site of the field that has no need of an ethnographic totality or of any contribution to some generalist's gamut of human types in order to assert its anthropological credentials.

My candidate for a concept that conceives of research practice in a way that provides the long view, encompassing the phases of research today in a coherent way, retaining the focus on individual research while incorporating and making visible and accessible to the professional community the complex relations that compose it, is that of the design process. I am not thinking of the idea of formal research design, which is a standard category in the implementation of social science methods, but of design as it is defined in studio fields like art, graphic and industrial/product design, and architecture (the latter of which I have experienced as a process, and think of as a model in making this suggestion).[13] In design processes with which I am familiar, the individual and collective as agents of knowledge

---

13. There is much diverse writing on the design process and its pedagogy in these fields that can generate models with which one can experiment in deriving analogous design frames for developing an alternative research process in anthropology that both encompasses Malinowksian fieldwork and allows for systematic treatment of the ways that it is getting stretched, redefined, and contextualized in current projects. One work on the pedagogy of teaching graphic design that I recently discovered through a (graphic) presentation of it at a conference in Oslo is by Theodor Barth and Maziar Raein (Barth and Raein 2007). Barth is an anthropologist who works closely with Raein in developing the pedagogy of design development in Oslo. With appropriate translation, I found aspects of it particularly suggestive for how the teaching of ethnographic research might be thought through in terms of design process. There is constant feedback in the development of a design; research is built into the conceptual work at the core of this development (the idea of "a holding pattern," a theme of their cited article, conveys how the conceptual work from beginning to end in ethnography "hovers" in the operations of fieldwork); and key ethical issues have cogency, not so much in the process of data collection itself as in the transaction that makes the materials of ethnography public, comparable to the stage when a design is turned over to a client with whom one has had a relationship during the entire process. In my view, some of what they have written fits, some not, but I am finding that the frame of design pedagogy is "good to think" in reconceiving the research process in anthropology. Earlier, I had found inspiration in the work process of conceptual, site-specific artists (Marcus 2008a), whose conduct of fieldwork-like research within the production of installations or

production are constantly in play. There is conceptual and practical rigor in applying ideas. There is reporting and constant feedback by diversely composed audiences from beginning to end. The final result has multiple accountabilities which are thought about through the entire project, and so the final result is not final, at least conceptually—there is an ideology of open-ended design and of a work being a solution that is subject to revision by later and other work.

It seems to me that anthropological research today rethought as a design process would encompass and preserve classic fieldwork perhaps still as a core modality. It would, however, both relativize its functions and blur its beginning and end in conceiving it within the broader contexts and operations that so much research now entails, as the essays of this volume illustrate. This would lead immediately to the three other issues that I take up briefly below: incompleteness as a norm, at least of the dissertation phase of a project; the more complex role of collaborations in producing individual projects; and the more formal or conceptualized incorporation of the receptions of the project into its design and doing.

Further, a model of a design process would map easily onto the research process that we have today and would give it an articulation for which we have been calling. At least such a model would serve as the framework for a practical discussion of many of the issues that we have raised here about the workings of the present informal culture of metamethod in anthropology, most visible in the pedagogy of first research leading to the production of dissertations, but not ending there. Moving to understand this venerable disciplinary process according to one or another model of a design studio would bring into the open—for anthropologists, students, anthropology's publics, and for institutional supporters demanding accounts of its methods in return for funding—the longstanding distinctiveness of the experimental ways that anthropologists have produced ethnographic knowledge. It would usefully displace the mythos of fieldwork and the informal professional culture that supports it, which no longer offers sufficient clarity about the research process and its dimensions, either to anthropologists themselves or to their subjects and publics. It would finally give this experimental dimension of anthropological research full expression as a framework of practices rather than remaining just a professional ethos and set of regulating aesthetics.

I cannot actually lay out a blueprint for this idea here; there are many possibilities. Such a proposal deserves its own full account (in my case it probably would depart from the procedures of the architectural studio to model similar

---

works of conceptual art, resembles that of ethnography, but their practices lacked both the coherence of process and the concern with pedagogy that I have found in the literatures on design.

practices for anthropology) and certainly lots of discussion in response. Because a design process would map readily onto what we already do traditionally as anthropologists, discussion of its feasibility alone would provide the framework to systematically question the process that we have now, as registered in my above observations. A design process should be open-ended. It should incorporate scenarios of anticipation and changing course. It requires the presentation for review of an ethnographically sensitive research imaginary before the undertaking of fieldwork that overreaches it and is revisable in terms of it. Research conceived as a design process keeps attention focused on material—data sets—all along the way and insists on results that are closely accountable to it. Thus, it encourages theoretical work at the level of material—the "stuff" of fieldwork as I called it—and privileges found concepts that emerge from it. It also looks beyond the confines of its own production to response and revision. While still preserving the responsibility of individual work, it recognizes collaboration as a normative principle, incorporates broad receptions, and finds a place for the anthropological community in this. What could be better, given how anthropological research is moving today anyhow?

A Norm of Incompleteness

Any traditional fieldwork project defines a massive task compared to what a researcher can practically hope to do with the time and resources available. Thus, a rhetoric of incompleteness is very common in finished ethnography. It is sometimes a hedge for inadequate evidence or analysis; it is sometimes a pro forma apology. It sometimes reflects a certain edge of anxiety or tension about the way an individual researcher handles both the limitations and the possibilities of the discipline's regulative culture of metamethod. We are most interested in the latter aspect motivating this rhetoric. Both under present conditions and in research imagined as a design process as just discussed, incompleteness would be a positive norm of practice, even a theorem of practice, expected of kinds of inquiry that remain open-ended even when they are "finished." Incompleteness is a dimension of thinking about what can be said about one has done. It is not about incompleteness in relation to the general and future unknown, but in relation to a design or research imaginary that has been thought through ethnographically but investigated only in part (e.g., the dissertation phase of research that produces first projects). That partial knowledge, so to speak, which is the product of first fieldwork, is partial in relation not to some unknown or vaguely conceived larger whole (in my view, this leads all too often to the justifying, dominating moral discourses of so many ethnographies today), but to a known and carefully conceived incompleteness, a ground or terrain of possible ethnography that is deeply imagined as such and in terms of which the partial results of fieldwork are specifically argued. Incompleteness thus defines a norm for contextualizing conditions of fieldwork research today at a thoroughly imagined ethnographic level for which the researcher should be responsible.

For example, the state or economy is not the context for a bounded site of fieldwork; certain ethnographically imagined processes and their connections to the foci of fieldwork are. The anthropologist may not do fieldwork in these contextualizing realms, but she projects an ethnographic imagination upon them as if she had. I would say most if not all objects of interest today can be known in this speculative way. And some degree of so doing could be part of a norm of incompleteness and the pursuit of research projects as they are today. The processes of a design studio would simply make this operation of incompleteness as a practice visible, indeed normative, and metamethodological in a formal way.

Design processes thus call attention to such edges of a project and develop contexts of discussion for them in the same terms and styles that characterize the work of the focused individual effort of fieldwork and its defined objects of inquiry. But even without the imaginary of research today as a design process, a norm of incompleteness under current practices could provide context, ground theory, and calm anxieties in researchers who move recursively around a field of inquiry and are uneasy or hedging about the partiality of what they are doing. They might otherwise embrace incompleteness as defining knowledge of something also in a speculative way. Scenarios are the instruments for dealing with the specificities of incompleteness by the informed imagination, and they can be implemented to good effect now or within some future regime of anthropological research as design studios.

Collaborations

Collaborations have always been integral to the pursuit of individual fieldwork projects, and their importance has been widely acknowledged at least since the *Writing Culture* critiques of the 1980s (see Lassiter 2005a). They never have been, however, an explicit aspect or norm of anthropology's culture of metamethod. The fieldworker, for example, is not held accountable or judged by the quality of his collaborations and his ability to manage them. Yet, today, collaborations of various kinds are increasingly both the medium and objects of fieldwork, quite aside from the long-established collaborative character of the relationships between fieldworkers and their once labeled "key informants" in the Malinowskian scene of encounter.[14] Virtually every observation made in this

---

14. In a recent paper (Marcus, in press), I attempt to describe some of the distinctive current predicaments and imperatives that move anthropologists to experiment with forms of collaboration in their research projects. One major ongoing concern of the Center for Ethnography that I founded

volume about relativized fieldwork in broader contexts of research practices suggests the incorporation of explicit norms and forms of collaborations into the culture of metamethod. If this were to happen, then anthropology would have to develop far more varied ideas about the ethics and the nature of fieldwork collaborations and the significance of what gets transacted in them.

For example, nowadays relationships with experts or counterparts (and not just colleagues or consultants) very often provide the intellectual capital for conceptually defining the bounds of fieldwork. Such relationships are neither outside fieldwork, nor are they one-dimensional in purpose. They define contexts of mutual appropriation when the anthropological project itself sometimes undergoes the "turning of course" that I have described as one of the common expectations for it. So, collaborations with what I call epistemic partners, those who come to inform the very conceptual frame of the research, push at the boundaries that keep the "scholastic" space (Bourdieu 1990) distinct and distant from the situated intellectual work of subjects. I suppose this might be seen to constitute a latter-day threat of "going native," made more threatening perhaps when the practices studied overlap with the intellectual apparatus and terms of the observing analyst. This movement of a project's intellectual center of gravity into the bounds of fieldwork probably can't be helped, nor can it be contained by keeping this operation normatively invisible in the culture of metamethod.

Under the present conditions of this culture, I see no way for collaborations to gain explicit identity as a form with normative status in terms of the practice of metamethod, since the latter so resolutely focuses on individual research and its achievements. The promise of remodeling the culture of metamethod as a design process is a different story, since such a process constantly incorporates collaborations of different sorts as part of its fabric—within the studio, out there in the field—as very visible and explicit parts of producing work, transacted in the constant feedback and revision by which a design process is characterized. Within the framework of design, such collaborations would be bound to become a much more explicit concern for anthropology's remodeled culture of metamethod, as

---

when I moved to UCI is "Ethnography In/Of Collaboration" (http://www.socsci.uci.edu/~ethnog/). Pedagogical experiments are part of this project as well, the most notable example of which so far has been the sponsorship of "para-site" exercises within the frame and process of dissertation projects that otherwise are conceived and conducted in the individual voice of the lone, responsible ethnographer. The para-site is a surrogate for collaborative design in that at appropriate phases of a project it injects carefully staged (and designed) events like seminars in which ethnographers, research subjects, and select others do conceptual work critical to the development of the research (this is similar to the reviews that punctuate design projects in all phases). This operation introduces a collaborative dimension into fieldwork as conventionally conceived and in so doing suggests alternative models for the fieldwork research paradigm itself that can be explored through design thinking that I am suggesting here.

eventually something that the assessment of "good" ethnography depends on by the aesthetic judgment of craft.

Receptions

The widespread call today for a public anthropology (Marcus 2005) already signals the intense interest of anthropologists in the responses to their work by the publics of varying composition and scale that it is able to touch. These responses matter more to many anthropologists, at least affectively, than professional responses to their work within the discipline, which I believe are weaker in intensity, and often less substantive, than sources of broader reception—both academic and nonacademic. The question for us here, again, is how this interest in receptions can be built into the fabric of research projects themselves, that is, how it can become part of the culture of metamethod. The question especially, given this volume's focus on pedagogy, is how such an interest can become a dimension of the process of first research. This is not just a question of what the subjects think of what the anthropologist has written about them—this sort of exercise began to be developed after the critiques of the 1980s (Brettell 1996)— but how diverse responses to a project as it develops become part of its integral data-sets, so to speak, the raw materials that need exposure somewhere in the process of research, certainly in dissertation research. Folding receptions into the metamethods of anthropological research at this stage would surely influence the habits and aesthetics of more mature research no longer subject to the specific constraints of training, but still shaped by its regulative ideologies.

As with collaborations, building norms and forms for reception into current research practices is difficult to accomplish, except piecemeal, where there are such tendencies anyhow as legible seams of particular current projects. The systematic integration of these tendencies depends on the implementation of a larger frame for research that, again, I have argued for here as a design process. In the manner of design studios, through the constant phased critiques and discussions of research by diverse audiences, including subjects, receptions would find an integral place in the production of anthropological research.[15]

---

15. This final suggestion on incorporating "reception" as an integral dimension (and site) of contemporary fieldwork prompts a final source of experiment where alternative forms of the classic research process of anthropology are emerging. This concerns blogging as a medium of ethnographic research and opens for consideration the whole arena of new forms of digital communication with the introduction and expansion of the Internet. I avoided this domain in my essay (though it is taken up in the essay by Kelty, who is a scholar of emerging forms of communication) because I am not sufficiently familiar with it and because the state of development of this medium in research is too inchoate at present, although I am sure that it is likely to be the eventual basis for the reconfiguration

Envoi

At its very best, in the supervising of ethnography-in-the-making, students gradually become one's teachers. In my passion for crafting new practices of training out of anthropology's old ones, this has especially been the case with the essays collected here, in their distanced insights of what their authors have made of fieldwork as they have developed contexts of work beyond it. In this, they have provided me with new ideas for inhabiting this venerable set of practices that stand for as well as perform the discipline, and thus, they have renewed my career-long romance with anthropology in a different and optimistic register.

Appendix: A Note on the Literature Relating to Fieldwork and Ethnography

Of the voluminous, long-standing, recent and accumulating literature on fieldwork in anthropology and related disciplines, the influential volumes by Vered Amit (1999) and Akhil Gupta and James Ferguson (1997a) are the two sources with which this volume is perhaps most closely engaged. We share with these volumes the sense of the altered circumstances in which fieldwork is undertaken today as well as the necessity of rethinking it conceptually. Both of these volumes are indeed concerned with what we term metamethodological aspects of fieldwork (that is, fieldwork as shaped by certain expectations of form and practice encountering changing objects of study and conditions of implementation), but neither develops a framework or a set of questions that delve into the professional culture of research and, within that, the pedagogy of first research, to focus on these aspects. We believe that this is the original contribution and advance of this volume.

Still, there are hints, clues, and discussions embedded here and there in the huge literature on fieldwork, primarily as method, that touch on the meta-

---

of conventional research practices, about which I am currently thinking in terms of design. Still, I want to draw the reader's attention to an "e-seminar" (May 20–June 2, 2008) occurring as I write these notes, administered by the EASA Media Anthropology Network (http://www.media-anthropology. net/workingpapers.htm), that in my view is the most stimulating ongoing source from which to learn of ethnographic research conducted on and through alternative and emerging media. This seminar concerns a paper on blogging as a research tool by Erkan Saka (Saka 2008). Saka is a Turkish graduate student at Rice, about to complete his dissertation on journalism, Turkey, and the European Union. He has produced a highly successful website and blog since he returned to Turkey three years ago that serves multiple functions in his fieldwork. The interesting exchanges produced by the e-seminar suggest that Saka's work is a kind of design studio itself for the revision of the conventional forms of ethnographic research practice. The e-seminar on Saka's blogging provides stimulating discussions that cover each of the topics that I have been describing in the final section of this essay as central to making over the conventional terms by which fieldwork is produced in training.

methodological concerns of this volume. This literature is located primarily in the disciplines of anthropology and sociology, but has developed markedly in recent years, as the popularity of and demand for ethnography has grown, into an industry of manuals and topically specialized treatments of more generically conceived "qualitative methods." Publishers, most prominently Sage, AltaMira, and Routledge, have developed extensive lists in this area. As a bibliographic link to my introductory essay and this volume, I cite a range of "methods" books in which discussion of issues regarding the craft of fieldwork as a distinctive professional culture of inquiry is more or less legible: the comprehensive seven volumes of *The Ethnographer's Toolkit* (LeCompte, Schensul, and Schensul 1999) and the three editions of the massive *Sage Handbook of Qualitative Research* (Denzin and Lincoln 2005) can aptly stand for the large manual-style literature on fieldwork and its various topics (interviewing, participant observation, and so forth). In anthropology, many of the best known and most effective texts on fieldwork address undergraduates or graduate school novices (see especially Agar 1995; Crane and Angrosino 1984; Spradley 1979, 1980; Watson 1999). Recent overviews of and readers on anthropological fieldwork show clearly the impact the analysis and critique of ethnography as texts and a genre of writing from the 1980s have had on treatments of fieldwork practice as method (see Lucas 2000; Robben and Sluka 2006). Also useful for getting at a kind of implied culture of method in terms of what is expected from fieldwork as written result are two important works on fieldnotes (Sanjek 1990; Emerson, Fretz, and Shaw 1995).

Two works that parallel my conceptual but not methodological apprehension of the details of the ethnographic (or qualitative) research process are Howard Becker's *Tricks of the Trade* (Becker 1998) and John Law's *After Method* (Law 2004), although neither is explicitly concerned critically with a professional or pedagogical culture (sociological or anthropological), as I am. In particular, Law, known for developing Bruno Latour's actor-network theory as a sociological method, shares my sense of how methodological traditions (he is not specifically concerned with the ethnographic tradition) do not serve well the experience of trying to do research in the present, but he tends to emphasize coping with factors like fluidity, multiplicity, and messiness more than I do. Perhaps, this is because he critiques established methodological practices in sociology that abhor these factors, while I am dealing with a disciplinary tradition that has long embraced them—to a fault perhaps.

Finally, while this volume addresses contemporary developments in the distinctively anthropological tradition of method, it is also concerned more with the comprehensive process that produces ethnography rather than with what ethnography produces—that is, more with the fieldwork process in the broader research contexts of specific projects than with ethnography itself as a distinctive kind of writing or style of analysis. But, in terms of separate literatures, this is not a hard and fast distinction, since I have often found more attention to and insight regarding the metamethodological issues of interest here in the literature on ethnography as genre and research product than in the usually more didactic and less critically acute literature on fieldwork. This is particularly the case with sociological studies of ethnography (e.g., see Denzin 1997) and works of socio-logical ethnography that include interesting metamethodological reflections on the process of inquiry and its requisite conceptual artifice (from the myriad examples, the following have been among the most important for me: Burawoy 2000; Glaeser 2000; Waquant 2003; Willis 1981). These reflections, in my view, are different from typical examples of the "reflexive turn" in anthropological ethnographies from the 1980s forward (see fn. 1). Yet, in anthropology, there are also many examples of recent ethnographies that have within them specific suggestions about rethinking the traditional compass of fieldwork practice in a metamethodological frame (Holmes 2000; Maurer 2005; Riles 2000).

Part 1

REFLECTIONS ON FIRST FIELDWORK AND AFTER

1

PHANTOM EPISTEMOLOGIES

Kristin Peterson

In 2001, I attended the annual African Studies Association meetings a few
months after returning from dissertation field research in Nigeria. I went to a
panel where a scholar gave a talk about Nigerian capital flight and transnational
corruption. I wanted a copy of the paper for a couple of reasons. One is that
even though I had just completed research on AIDS, development aid, and the
intellectual property law that governs HIV treatment access, the paper and certainly my own fieldwork experience stimulated my thinking about a troubling
Orientalist notion that distinguishes between legitimate (transnational business
and aid practices) and illegitimate (internal state corruption) capital flight. A second reason I wanted the paper was because the author had quantified the level of
capital flight—upwards of several trillion dollars over the last ten years. She presented numbers that sounded firm and confident when all I had heard while in
and out of Nigeria was only speculative, though it indeed involved incredible and
varying sums of money. How much was stolen out of Nigeria was anyone's guess.
I wanted to see what this certainty was all about.

The oral presentation critiqued the usual calculation of capital flight—
calculations that ignore off-the-books or shadow economic dynamics. To put a
value on capital flight, to explicitly calculate it, means to do so with information
that can be accessed and abstracted. Such approaches cannot account for secret
deals, hidden Geneva-based bank accounts, or the way fleeing capital comes back
into the country to fund government privatization schemes or other lucrative
deals. As such, the literature tends to fetishize calculable material objects and
spaces such as the state treasury, which is described by Nigerians and outsiders

(and I don't dispute this) as being looted by state officials. The implication is that the "native" state alone possesses agency or that the state is a monolithic entity without internal contests over the fiscal management of any given political geography (Emeagwali 2001; Krugman 1998). The discourse here is about indigenous greed and not the many different national and international monetary and legal policies or European and North American banks and actors at work. The sole focus on indigenous activities contributes to a phenomenon that easily misses a form of state and transnational consumption held over from the days of indirect rule. What sort of analysis would be possible if the murky realms of capital movement were just as significant as the visible ones?

One of the objectives of the conference that launched this volume was to understand how apprentice ethnography largely encounters the "already known" while developing and crafting ethnographic training. Yet my feeling is that the "already known" has been overstated—data, results, and surprises are buttressed by pre-existing expectations, which empty the prospect of something not yet in view. To get at something else lying within our own methodological frameworks, I propose the idea of "phantom epistemologies." Specifically, I refer to empirical elusiveness, unspoken common sense, a politics of (in)commensurability, and how the presence of any "ghost" becomes viewable to those who believe—these are the ethnographic entryways into what is knowable. Yet what is knowable will often lie in the realm of uncertainty; that is, the very thing of empiricism cannot be absolutely defined in the presence of phantoms and unknowable possibility. My thinking is partly informed by "shadows" theorized by Carolyn Nordstrom and James Ferguson. Both refer to "shadow" political economies that are liminal, hidden, or simply unaccounted for. James Ferguson writes:

> A shadow is not only a dim or empty likeness. It also implies a bond and a relationship. A shadow, after all, is not a copy by an attached twin—a shadow is what sticks with you. Likeness here implies not only resemblance but also a connection, a proximity, an equivalent, even an identity. A shadow, in this sense, is not simply a negative space, a space of absence; it is a likeness, an inseparable other-who-is-also-oneself to whom one is bound. (2006, 17)

The desire here is directed toward recognition, not one marked by an empiricism that provides a finiteness or certainty of something, but a recognition of some hidden essence, implication, connection—one that sits, for a moment, underneath or beside our apprehension. While the shadow waits to become known in some concrete form, a phantom epistemology does not count on revelation. Rather than dismissing our quandaries of "not having all the data" that may not be gotten, a phantom can inhabit the data in ways that do not always desire the fullest of answers—one that allows the unknowable to remain as powerful an analytical figure as the known. That is, the phantom—the stuff of familiarity, yet also the stuff of the unknowable—is the ethnographic object of inquiry, rather than being some shadow whose materializing requires further patience and digging. Finding one's way through (or even detecting at all) the presence of such ghosts is difficult, as the latter occur at different levels of scale, not only in fieldwork but at the level of interpretive circulation. Indeed, both capital flight and the conference paper I was seeking were "phantom indexes" of an AIDS epidemic in which capital and drugs were made scarce via political-economic processes that generated a common sense about political leadership, development aid, and elusive practices of governance.

After we both returned home from the meetings, I e-mailed the presenter asking for her paper. She responded by stating that I should get the original unpublished paper from which she derived her own talk—but she needed to get permission. Once that was done, I was told that I could not use the author's real name or institutional affiliation. The author of the original paper claimed that due to the sensitive nature of the material many powerful people would be exposed, which would cause trouble for him and his place of work. I understood, agreed to these terms completely, and anxiously read the paper.

The truly remarkable aspect of this unpublished piece was that it recounted the same stories I had heard on the street from people selling fruit, from taxi and bus drivers, from the home of one of Nigeria's wealthiest men, from Nigeria's most senior UN officials and, indeed, in articles about post–military dictatorship Nigeria. These are stories such as: a governor of one of the oil producing delta states fears he could lose his bid for reelection and calls in a trusted ally, one of the transnational oil companies, for help. As soon as the polls close, the governor's men are in place and clear the way for the oil company's helicopter to land. The ballots are stolen, the helicopter flies them off to the governor's mansion, and later that evening he is reelected. Or this one: a newly installed military general travels to Geneva, meets with a top bank official, and inside his office pulls out a gun and demands, "Give me the names of all of those from the previous regime with secret bank accounts!" The bank official drops to his knees and declares that he would rather die right there than trade away the identity of his clients. The gun-toting man then pulls out a suitcase filled with money in large denominations, puts his gun away, chuckles to himself, and says, "You can have my account and look after my money!"

The point of the paper was to argue that the sociopolitical truths about corruption are often anecdotal data; and, too often, the very definitions of corruption do not take into account its reciprocal role, one that begins to widen the predominant understandings of capital flight. That is, "what happens" in Geneva or London manages to circulate back to the Nigerian city and village street in a way that indicates something far more than the stereotypical idea that Nigeria is the most corrupt place on earth. Rather, Nigeria is an open society in terms of public political debates combined with long-term windfall oil profits where the state remains the primary form of accumulation. Such a scenario allows a view inside a more secretive and perhaps predominant form of capital mobility and accumulation that represents a huge proportion of the world's wealth; this mobility is rarely accounted for, even though authors such as Graham Hancock (1994), Carolyn Nordstrom (2004), and William Reno (1999) have pointed us in these directions.

The empirical is difficult to tag here because realities and elusiveness exist in the same space. The reality is that capital flees Nigeria and international banks provide secretive and safe harbor, that state officials are investigated for corruption, that wealthy elites perform grandiose displays of their own material worlds in public places—in the view and earshot of those who have not eaten for days. Indeed, Daniel Smith (2006) has eloquently pointed out that the prevailing ideas and discourses of corruption are launched via inequalities on national, community, and individual levels. Hunger and the thin line between public/private performance together facilitate the circulation and scale of the stories themselves, and so do development workers and academics. Their elusiveness consists in their being stories resonating at the level of common sense, circulating in the most powerful ways, that have literally defined a sense of national public discourse and what it means to be Nigerian. Historian Luise White argues that the stories of rumor need to be taken at "face value, as everyday descriptions or ordinary occurrences" (2000, 5). In referring to accounts of bloodsucking during the colonial period in Africa she writes, "the inaccuracies of these stories make them exceptionally reliable historical sources as well: they offer historians a way to see the world the way the storytellers did, as a world of vulnerability and unreasonable relationships" (5). Stories of capital flight are equally instructive because they provide a space for ordinary people to narrate inequality and how they engage the state (see Gupta 1995), and, indeed, provide profound insight into the dynamics of both militarism and, more recently, civilian rule, often referred to as "democracy." These "knowables" emerge in secondhand stories that reflect a reality that truly cannot be unreal. Yet, the contours of "reality" are also not always traceable.

These phenomena are distinct from partial or situated knowledge, which recognizes that the possibilities of knowing never lie within an imagined totality, that knowing can be achieved only in parts—and apprehending such parts is shaped by positionality and subjectivity. Douglas Holmes and George Marcus (2005) employ the term "para-ethnography," with which they identify the ethnographic knowledge of central bankers such as Alan Greenspan—a knowledge that, more often than not, emerges in the form of anecdote. Anecdote, as a crucial form of data, is gathered by such experts in order to produce reports on the status of the national American economy, but it disappears as acknowledged data in the reports themselves. Para-ethnography functions at the level of both method and knowledge and, like phantom epistemologies, must determine and enter into the shadows of knowledge and systems. Phantom epistemologies do not seek out parts in order to fit into a whole that is imagined to exist out there somewhere. Rumor, anecdote, stories, evasiveness, and not being able to ever know are their own sets of data and knowledge. They point us not in the direction of desired concreteness, as in "facts," but rather offer an analytical opening to something just as fascinating and analytically provocative as a traditional sense of the empirical. That is, the phantom asks us to rethink the very essence and contours of the "empirical" itself.

When the rumor on the street in Lagos, for example, is that forty percent of all Nigerian crude oil "goes missing" every year, it is not a matter of believing or not believing the numbers. Many of these numbers simply do not exist as something that has already been calculated; or if they do, the numbers are completely different among official and unofficial quarters for any given community, institution, or individual who has something at stake in them. For example, Benue state, located in the central part of the country, reported the highest percentage of HIV infection in 1999 at eighteen percent. The numbers did not garner any additional funding or declarations for special emergency relief. Rather, they created the stigmatization of an entire state. Two years later, Benue reported that its infection rates were below ten percent without providing an explanation of, or hypothesis for, the supposed decline.

Another example: Alhaji Umaru Dikko was a Nigerian minister and had the sole power to grant import permits. Wealthy expatriates took suitcases of money to his back door in order to keep their businesses going. Some say he collected over US$5 billion. Once Dikko's Nigerian colleagues heard about the amount they were not getting, they set out forcibly to take their share (the trickle down of payments inside any business/government agency is expected and a standard procedure). After escaping across the Nigerian border (the anecdote: by tossing wads of cash out both windows as he approached armed border guards, distracting them and zipping on past into the Republic of Benin), he was eventually found and kidnapped in London (the anecdote: while an Israeli anaesthetist kept him unconscious—suspicious customs officials detected and found them inside a crate; it was suspected the Nigerian High Commission ordered the kidnapping). Nigeria requested his extradition on the grounds that he had stolen over US$5 billion. Publicly the United Kingdom invited Nigeria to submit the necessary paperwork to initiate extradition proceedings. But anecdotal knowledge and rumor claimed that if extradition procedures were commenced on the grounds that he stole money, the U.K. threatened to release the names of all those Nigerians holding more than US$5 billion in British banks. Dikko was never extradited and remains in London.[1]

While drawing on Foucault's concept of epistemes and Thomas Kuhn's notions of limits and paradigms, Nancy Scheper-Hughes has provocatively argued that the structure and norms of research are situated within naturalized paradigms of positivist research practices (Foucault 1973; Kuhn 1962; Scheper-Hughes 1997). She has called for a "demography without numbers" that would render both the social and the biological powerful analytical indicators and constraints to demonstrate what gets missed or passed over in conventional quantitative research. Yet not even numbers can always constitute the "factual." Numbers can work the same way that stories and anecdotes do—capital flight and HIV infection rates calculated with only cursory sets of numbers do not take into account the shifting alliances that produce numerical data in the first place; and here it is productive to think about the relationship between secrets and official numbers or official numbers as secrets. Secrets are crucial data points because they must operate at public and private levels. As the Dikko story above shows, the implications inside the anecdotal knowledge are that capital flight, generated by corruption, is not condemned but highly encouraged. The secret is juxtaposed against an idea publicly articulated by banks and government that corruption is a no-no. Here, the anecdote reveals a productive tension between the allowable and the condemned. The tension functions as yet another shadow that masks a rarely accounted-for capital mobility. Therefore, numbers can often only remain inside the common sense of a national consciousness that seeks to explain the conditions of its own existence. This was the crux of the ethnographic challenge for me: not discerning what was newly knowable inside the givens, but figuring out how possible it was to discern the givens themselves.

Revisiting Multi-sited Ethnography for a Moment

Following elusive "facts" and the traveling fantasia of stories is one of the modes of operation that multi-sited ethnography proposed as its initial experiment.

---

1. While several scholars (such as White 2000; Geschiere 1997; Ashforth 2000) have demonstrated the power of rumor intersecting with postcolonial realities in Africa, others have analyzed such phenomena as deeply ambivalent relationships to capitalism and inequality (Smith 2001; Comaroff and Comaroff 1993; West 1997; Sanders 1999). Most of the literature analyzes such phenomena via witchcraft, the occult, and vampires. But the public secret and the audacities of capital flight have their own sensibilities of rumor and anecdote, even if the accumulation of wealth via capital flight is generated by occult activities.

One of the great misunderstandings that I have encountered about multi-sited ethnography is that it is often viewed as a methodological approach that is purely spatial or simply a matter of scaling. That is, multiple physical sites of research tend automatically to count as a thorough rendering of any given object of analysis, which ultimately collapses the "comparative" with the "multi-sited." This collapse misses the point of the *Writing Culture* debates in the 1980s and 1990s, which in large measure were responding to both 1970s critiques that linked anthropology to imperialism and the poststructuralist literature that posed questions about the production of knowledge—what George Marcus and Michael Fischer referred to as the "crisis of representation" (Marcus and Fischer 1986). The response to these critiques (see also Clifford and Marcus 1986; Gupta and Ferguson 1997b) and, subsequently, the schematization of the methodology of multi-sitedness (Marcus 1995) remained inside these questions of epistemology. The bare-bones Malinowskian paradigm of ethnographic research did not go away here. But new changes included how the question of scale, the production of knowledge, and textual strategies especially determined how we understand "culture" (and see Faubion in this volume). While questions of new objects of study have emerged in this context, I am more interested in how the "experimental moment" actually shifted established ideas over what counts as data, method, and knowledge. That is, I am interested in the shift from the spatial as a limiting factor of research design and procedure to spheres of knowledge in which new analytical and epistemological domains have arisen as primary questions of the anthropological project. Given that phantom epistemologies operate at different levels of the real and the fantastical, the question then becomes: What constitutes any given consonance between objects of study and sites of study? How do stories of meetings between Geneva bankers and Nigerian generals suddenly become a point of data even though they remain "empirically" in the shadows?

In the opening of *Friction*, Anna Tsing describes how her project on environmental social movements became possible when she "stumbled on a curious misunderstanding" (2005, x). She recounts that because she arrived in the aftermath of an original campaign against logging, she had to rely upon tellings of the story of the campaign itself. To her informants' and her own surprise, they all seemed to describe incongruent events, finding each other's descriptions and experiences unreal and completely incommensurable. In thinking about how to handle such an experience methodologically, she states:

> How does one do an ethnography of global connections? Because ethnography was originally designed for small communities, this question has puzzled social scientists for some time. My answer has been to focus on zones of awkward engagement, where words mean something different across a divide even as people agree to speak. These zones of

cultural friction are transient; they arise out of encounters and interactions. They reappear in new places with changing events. The only ways I can think of to study them are patchwork and haphazard. The result of such research may not be a classical ethnography, but it can be deeply ethnographic in the sense of drawing from the learning experiences of the ethnographer. (Tsing 2005, xi)

The interconnection here is one that may be a matter of scale where the process of scaling is methodologically always presenting itself—the haphazard and zones of awkward engagement. Like most research, mine poses questions that are already situated within distinct frames of analysis, even when my examples may stand in stark contrast to the norm of theorization. Yet I am interested in locating those people, movements, objects, and the things germane to understanding the system itself that are constructed as the most deeply at stake, as being the most generative—yet quite invisible—dynamics of political economies. But narrowing down who and what are in play—that is, accounting for a range of actors and institutions whose actions are consequential for the larger system of things at multiple scales—makes the question of consonance between objects and sites of study perhaps one of the most important in ethnographic fieldwork. Marcus has addressed the crisis of representation by suggesting that multi-sited ethnography treat methods as firmly embedded in the research conceptualization and design itself (1995). Similarly, the notion of consonance becomes a matter of both critique and method where neither can be pulled into separate parts.

Tsing suggests that consonance is haphazard, that zones of awkward engagement rise up out of fractured ethnographic forms, where consonance puts questions of method itself at stake. I would suggest that consonance and scaling are still carefully articulated methods even if one trips over them in a moment of surprise, leading data collection down an altogether unexpected path. In *Advocacy After Bhopal,* Kim Fortun first confronts the problem of how to demarcate the site of research that tracks and understands a disaster such as the Union Carbide gas leak in Bhopal, India (Fortun 2001). She points out that the Bhopal disaster lingers nonspatially as the dire health effects of the gas leak continue in time. One of the keys in determining the conceptual and physical scaling of such a project lies in Fortun's shifting of discursive contexts and frameworks inside her research questions—a strategy that begins to open up an entire range of new questions and insights that are "givens" already firmly embedded in her existing frames of analysis. For example, in making sense of advocacy, Fortun decides to use the term "enunciatory communities" instead of the development and policy term "stakeholder." For Fortun "stakeholder" is static; it assumes consensus, agreement, and an existence prior to the disaster itself, whereas enunciatory communities show shifting articulations, contradictions within "groups"; they cannot exist prior to the double binds in which they live (see her essay in this volume). While she holds to the stakeholder model—there is something at stake for different communities—the shift to enunciatory communities allows her to see new subject formations take place while existing ones undergo their own shifts and changes. At the same time, it allows for an accounting of different and contradictory epistemologies, discourses, and forms of advocacy. The very physical and linguistic encounter with Bhopal brings legal issues and legal language into everyday living; notions of "health, fairness, and progress" are radically redrawn, giving rise to new and shifting social formations. It is these articulations across time and borders, which move in and out of Bhopal and in and out of India, that demand understanding of how a "shifting world order" emerges out of a single disastrous moment. As such, through ethnographic, conceptual, and textual strategies, Fortun shows how the Bhopal disaster articulates India's own globalization policies and the various contradictions (of citizenship and national identity in particular) that arise as a result.

I use these examples of (in)congruence and scale to make particular claims about phantom epistemologies and the ethnographic practices used to apprehend them. The key moments in both Tsing's and Fortun's work hang on a particular explosive event: a spatially bound logged forest intersected by competing epistemologies and disparate apprehensions; a single disastrous gaseous moment that spirals out across time and space, hailing new subjects and subjectivities into both necessary and unpleasant consonance. My own research shows a different problem of scale that does not emanate out of an experience that demands the immediate attention of everyone and everything in its path. Both Fortun and Tsing mark the trace of past and current presences. But what kind of attention is needed when such dramas do not exist or mark the very thing we wish to understand?

Revitalizing Failure: Tracing "Not Knowing"

I first went to Nigeria and Cameroon in January 2000 to conduct preliminary dissertation research, which ultimately led to my first career-defining failure. I set out to understand new transnational institutional assemblages between several U.S. and West African universities, militaries, NGOs, and government institutions, all of which were bioprospecting forests across the Nigeria/Cameroonian border—endeavors that aimed to find new therapies for infectious diseases. I was particularly fascinated by the problem of how trade-related intellectual property law would play out across nation-state and institutional "partnerships" in the wake of a recently formed World Trade Organization. I was working with one of the NGOs, which was directing these activities, and my research project fell apart after about six months. Part of the failure had to do with internal politics, but a greater part was due to implicit expectations that I would be writing a journalistic account of the various bioprospecting programs. In fact, toward the end, one of the project leaders requested that my dissertation be a narrative and not an analysis of the program. Complying with this request of course was not possible. So, after three years of graduate school, two grants, and no project, I had to rethink what I was doing.

My time as a graduate student in the anthropology department at Rice University was instrumental in the action I took. Much of our training as students in and out of the classroom stressed a rigorous thinking of the "conceptual writ large" framed squarely inside a unique pedagogy—one that did not micromanage our thinking or doing, but one that constantly opened up space to reassess and rethink our objects of inquiry. In the classroom and before the field experience, this meant, for example, writing and rewriting many times a "research imaginary" as first-year graduate students. I remember after I gave George Marcus the fifth draft of such a piece in the pro-seminar, he handed it back to me and said, "Good, now do it again, and this time don't use the word 'globalization'"—an exercise that produced new realms of thinking over the question at hand. Moreover, my long and extensive e-mails to Jim Faubion and George Marcus from the field documenting the slow and painful demise of the first project were circulated to the first-year students in the pro-seminar as an example of the generativity of failure. At first, I was mortified at the thought. But when students told me what they got out of the mailings, I realized that they treated them as objects of analysis—that the collapse of a project was not something to be feared, but rather that any outcome of our initial research efforts has meaning. Moreover, it helped me rethink the politics, social dynamics, and materialization of the very assemblages I was studying.

The graduate students also had their own offices on the same floor; late nights included trips into one another's offices where chalkboards were rigorously used to get feedback on one another's thinking. It also meant weekly reading and writing groups conducted in cafés that gladly gave us the remnants of chocolate cake at closing time. Students plugged in and out of such activities as they pleased, but I do not think that these endeavors we initiated on our own would even have been imaginable without the pedagogical style that framed and inculcated us as researchers.

There were a number of issues at play at the heart of this practice. The primary one was decentering power relations within the department itself, certainly not at the level of administration but rather at the level of pedagogy. This had its ups and downs. On the one hand, students looking to get training in a particular area or subfield were often on their own, meaning that the training was not about instructing students on what to read in order to prepare for the field and, indeed, it never included this sort of management at all. On the other hand, a space was created in order always to engage in dialogue about the research at hand. This did not often come in the form of committee meetings (I actually only had one such meeting, and it was my dissertation defense), but rather in the spirit of generous open-door policies, meetings in cafés, hallway chit-chat, and dinners. Even after a few cocktails, one always came away with something new to think about, to tweak, to open up, to explore. Another issue included the fact that all students were funded equally upon entering the program. While I have no evidence for this sociological observation, my feeling (via conversations with colleagues at other universities) indicates that when there is less competition for funding, more cooperative and theoretically engaged interactions take place among students.

With this training as a backdrop, I was torn between two interesting problems I wanted to explore: one was the legal and policy conundrums brought forth by bioprospecting and the other was the question of Nigeria itself. The former took me on a detour to Quito, Ecuador, in the hopes of scouting out a project to be conducted within legal organizations that had begun to construct newly conceptual and theoretical frameworks over the intersection of intellectual property and bioprospecting in fascinating ways. But I was pulled quickly back to Nigeria, not only because I had covered a great deal of ground on my initial two-month visit, but perhaps because I was trained to be curious about things not traditionally located in area (African) studies as well as anthropology. Before I first arrived in 2000, my attention was drawn more to conceptualizing assemblages with less of an emphasis on theorizing the place that made such linkages possible. That soon changed.

Although I was following Nigerian politics closely, not least because the country had recently transitioned from military to civilian rule, I was not prepared for what I would encounter on the streets of Lagos. I was fascinated by the hope and hype of "democracy," which in everyday discourse was interchangeable with "civilian rule." But democracy was the freedom to articulate suffering; how "nothing works," the inability to eat and procure medical care; "how things are getting worse." Democracy was also about social redemption. In fact, both the public and the government have used the term "democracy dividends"—the hopeful means to alleviate suffering and to retroactively cash in on an imagined social contract—from the mid-1960s to this moment.

Unlike suffering, democracy in Nigeria was elusive, intangible, idealized; yet both suffering and democracy immediately depended upon and referred back to each other in every space where they were discussed. These discourses piqued my curiosity and although I did not know what any of this would mean in the larger scheme of things, it felt right to follow; I decided to stay.

I switched my project topic to HIV drugs and AIDS activism and policy-making. As the new civilian government took power, development and other international organizations (which left the country after the Abacha government executed Ken Saro Wiwa and the Ogoni 8) returned. Along with the government, these actors rediscovered AIDS and began to redirect their programming in this direction. Social movement activism against dictatorship quickly gave way to the formation of NGOs, which established business relationships with their donors and "partnerships" with the state and multinational corporations. In this snippet of time, the discourse of democracy was not simply something that was fascinating or to be witnessed at a moment of vast political transition. It turned out to be the glue, the thing that harnessed these new assemblages and structures to one another. What did democracy dividends mean in the context of an AIDS activism that was demanding access to treatment based upon one's HIV status? What did it mean in the context of a restructuring state, one that was privatizing, signing numerous trade agreements, while promising more security to its citizenry?

To trace the contradictions rising out of these scenarios, I decided to return to my questions on intellectual property and trade by doing an ethnographic analysis of Nigeria coming into compliance with the World Trade Organization. In my fondness for scale and complexity, I encountered my first slough of phantoms. I specifically focused on the Trade Related Intellectual Property (TRIPs) Agreement, which governs the global circulation of pharmaceuticals. The country signed the agreement under Abacha, during one of the worst military dictatorships; now it had to negotiate the implications of its implementation as a civilian actor.

For Nigeria, as with many other TRIPs signatories, compliance requires an overhaul of the country's intellectual property (IP) law. The struggle over the actual anatomy of a new IP law was a largely subdued and unnoticed affair, especially in 1999–2004, when actual debates and conferences on the issue began to take shape. The task at hand was to use the space of TRIPs debates, housed in conferences and workshops, taking place among selected, invited policymakers (and others) located within specific networks. Among these actors, some of the most invested interests and views of what I assumed to be at stake were rarely articulated in public, but rather were whispered in corridors and behind closed office doors—a more secretive para-ethnography and one that did not inform the outcome of legal proceedings and documents in the way Greenspan's methods and practices did.

It was clear that an ethnography of compliance had to happen at several levels. Getting at the real and unreal would turn out to be a daunting task, as even those working in the highest or any other level of government did not know how events were transpiring beyond their immediate environments. Moreover, with few exceptions (many of whom I interviewed), neither government elites, invested in particular avenues of compliance, nor the public, including AIDS advocates, had much awareness of the global debates on trade-related intellectual property. There are several reasons for this. A chief one concerns the direction of activism itself. International development organizations constructed the contours of activism (via funding mechanisms) that fit into the immediate needs of newly configured AIDS activists. These included addressing traumatic stigma and discrimination, initial encounters of which were in hospitals; creating support groups for HIV-positive people; and finding ways to access treatment—at the time, there was virtually no antiretroviral medication in the country. Even with the burgeoning hundreds of workshops conducted on these topics, however, no major donor ever set out to provide education on the implications of treatment access in the context of various TRIPs compliance scenarios (with the exception of United Nations Development Program, which worked with government policymakers in several African countries, but not Nigeria).

In terms of business, the dialogue on intellectual property enforcement mechanisms was largely restricted to the in-country circulation of goods. Only Nigerian lawyers representing the interests of multinational companies articulated interest in developing intellectual-property protection mechanisms for such actors. Moreover, all government and private actors I interviewed claimed that there was virtually no communication between Nigerian negotiators at the WTO and the relevant ministries. No dialogue ever took place among private business actors on the shape or context of TRIPs compliance.

Thus, the Nigerian public and private sectors did not have an analysis of their own national context. So the objectives of my project began elsewhere, with the need to ask how to conduct an ethnography of "not knowing," that is, to understand how phantom epistemologies existed in layers at multiple levels. "Not knowing" about a fundamental shift in the future trajectory of HIV treatment and its landscapes exists in a field of affects within which outcomes are partially known and maneuvered in a narrow field of vision. This observation, of course, was informed by my own sense of what was important, derived from what I knew from international debates. When I began to listen more to what was important to Nigerians, which was highly contested, questions of property and compliance began to make more sense to me, as did my larger questions of "not knowing."

Another aspect of my own "not knowing" developed into a curious paraethnographic intersubjectivity: tracking down the latest IP draft or bill proved to be a difficult endeavor. There was always more than one draft floating around different ministries or the U.S. government (which was highly involved in the rewriting of Nigerian law) in divided parts—no one could ever confirm which was valid or authentic, and I was constantly chasing phantom drafts.

The global battles over TRIPs have made international headlines over the years and have incorporated what were once little-known concepts in patent law into social movement slogans; it is not my intention to elaborate on these events. I do, however, want to draw attention to the fact that a great majority of the literature on the subject constructs a dichotomy between two main players caught in a struggle of power—wealthy pharmaceutical corporations versus poor people worldwide who face few treatment options. This picture is not entirely accurate, which became more than clear once an ethnographic approach to compliance was well under way. There are numerous national and international actors and institutions enmeshed in cooperation and competition over far more complicated discourses and practices that lie outside of this dichotomy, something that global AIDS and anti-globalization activism often misses. Moreover, the TRIPs Agreement in the past has been constructed as one of the fundamental obstacles in generating and distributing generic drugs. This is not accurate either, because the Agreement does make clear provisions for the generic drug market at least to exist, if not flourish. TRIPs patenting rules actually create a blueprint for technologies of negotiation and subjectivation. The rules themselves are not necessarily at stake, but the anatomies of negotiation feed into already existing histories of inequalities. Inequality here should not be thought of as strictly a divide between have and have-not nation-states. Rather, inequality can be detected in commonplace statements such as that made by a lawyer I interviewed, who commented on TRIPs compliance: "If we don't comply, there could be trade sanctions. To that extent, we will benefit, if we comply." The lens of a subjectification that focuses the conferral of benefits is precisely the lens through which the production of knowledge can shape decisions about TRIPs compliance and ultimately the future trajectories of the drug market. It may even shed light on the more complex characteristics of power and sovereignty.

By the time TRIPs arrived—after dictatorship and severe economic decline—all that was known, and articulated to me, was this: telephones do not work in the ministries; computers and Internet access are nonexistent in government and policymaking offices, making it impossible to access the politics of trade and intellectual property or even IP databases; the patent office has no compiled databases—if you have filled out the two-page form properly, you get your patent, a practice hardly competitive with forces in Europe and the United States; Nigeria is on the "wrong side" of digital technology; billions of dollars can be made in the commercialization of folklore, music, and genetic resources, all of which slips out of Nigeria and Africa's grasp; globalization, for some, compressed space and time, something needed to compete in the global patent race, but in Nigeria, time and space are painfully elaborated, making the "benefits of globalization"—a common phrase among policymakers—difficult to reap; and TRIPs compliance was the answer to bringing Nigeria into its "rightful place in the world." Like privatization, multilateral trade-related intellectual property—for those who organized conferences and agendas—was the magic bullet, and it was this imaginary of the bullet that left no time or space for "not knowing." By analyzing Nigeria's ongoing steps toward TRIPs/WTO compliance, my purpose here has been to think about a post-practice where recent political economic artifacts inform and motivate strategies toward manifesting what "appears" to be known.

My experience of not being able to count on the "factual" as an avenue of entry into ethnographic fieldwork as well as a site of analysis has provided a methodological exploration of what is possible within ethnography. The phantom epistemologies that my research inhabits have led me to understand how policy, capital, and development function at different levels of scale, but more important, how they show up and reveal other nonintuitive linkages. Pulling together aggregate knowledge such as that of economy, dictatorship, intellectual-property policies, and drug politics in the context of macro-politics and economics is not a process that is always or necessarily shaped by a factual archive—which should make us question in turn the very reasoning and ontology of empiricism. Elusiveness, common sense, and phantom epistemologies are the things that provide a different kind of gateway into and outside of the givens in our analytical frames.

2

ETHNOGRAPHIC REMNANTS

Range and Limits of the Social Method

Jae A. Chung

Not Drinking up the Scene: The Social as Remnant

After a long day's work in a media technology venture firm, my co-workers and I ended up at Go To, one of the many bars and drinking spots typical of young Seoul.[1] There were about six of us from the start-up firm, in the third and last phase of investment negotiations with a venture capital company. The bar was a loud but nondescript place that served beer and the latest synthesized pop underneath a spinning Day-Glo mirror ball. Within the world of South Korea's (henceforth Korea's) corporate culture, such a get-together is a given, and we fell to it with as much enthusiasm as any. These drinking occasions, called *suljari* (lit. alcohol place), are a counterpoint to the social order of the day, holding the rules that govern the latter in abeyance, and anticipated (and dreaded) for their compulsory alcoholic merriment.[2]

---

1. Some definitions: The "venture capital industry" in Korea includes both venture firms (the recipients of venture capital money) and the investing venture capital firms. Venture firms are the companies selected by the Small to Medium Business Administration, a governmental agency established in 1996 to oversee the sector, to receive investment, while venture capital companies are the ones investing. Here I follow the usage common in Korea, where "venture" often refers not to the venture capital companies but to the venture firms. This differs slightly from the usage popularized in the United States in the late 1990s.

2. The Revised Romanization of Korean, the official transliteration system since 2000, is followed whenever possible.

The wit of our party was the firm's managing director, a man in his early thirties and a former stock trader for a *chaebol* (large family-controlled firm in Korea). That night, he picked up a strain of a larger story he had been telling me throughout my time there—a Chekhovian drama about the brutalities of all-male high schools and the gangster-corrupted docks in the southern seaport city of Busan. Midway through this story, the usually composed director shifted in his chair and choked back tears; soon the others, all men perhaps five years younger, followed, patting him on the back and muttering about the corruptions of power. One of them said: *Those assholes should really be all killed.* The assholes to whom he referred were, of course, the victors of Korea's recent past, the presidents and the men whose machinations had brought them to power. It was only in 1998 that the first unequivocally democratically elected president, Kim Dae-jung, came to power. And even he was not spared harsh criticism.[3] For the manager and those present, the narrative leap from the corruption in the high schools and the unregulated docks to the dark days of the struggle for democracy was short and laid bare the sense of loss that lurked beneath the normality of life in 2002.[4]

The tears and the immediacy of the charged historical memory here are complex. Some parts of this complexity have to do with the Faustian Korean bargain between economic progress and political freedom.[5] Others involve the rapid erosion of the past as new developments rise to take its place. Still others invoke a bond of nationalism among males who have spent their entire organizational lives among other males, in schools, in the military, and now at the workplace (Jager 2003). This, I thought with only the slightest guilt at the voyeurism of ethnographic work, was good stuff. After all, this mise-en-scène of historical remembrance represented my moment of transformation from an outsider to, if not exactly an insider, a quasi-member, in momentarily sharing the subjective space of the aggrieved Korean.

Back at the office, I had been assisting on multiple projects—doing paperwork for the upcoming investment rounds, and helping in negotiations with

---

3. Although Kim Dae-jung (known as DJ in Korea) spent decades in prison for his democratic activities, he was criticized because he was seen to be partly responsible for the delayed realization of robust democracy in Korea. In 1986, after he had promised to stay out of the presidential race so as to avoid a split in the vote for democracy between himself and a rival, Kim Young Sam, DJ nonetheless entered the fray (Kim 1989). The resulting split-vote scenario allowed the former general Roh Tae-woo to become president, delaying the onset of full civilian government by more than a decade.

4. For a review of the role of dictators in Korean history since 1954, see Lee 2005.

5. For an examination of Korea's politico-economic development in the 1950s—1980s, see Lie 2000 and Woo 1991. For analyses of class and gender politics, see Koo 2001 on the labor movement and Chun 2003 on female workers' fight for equality within it. For a discussion on corporate life in Korea during the early 1990s, see Janelli and Yim 1993.

their European and Japanese partners—but I remained, on the whole, a curiosity to the others. There I was, an ambiguous figure evoking anxiety and a touch of envy, an English- and Korean-speaking Korean American female, working at the firm without clearly defined responsibilities, and thus set apart from the others. After months of working side by side with these men, enduring the strange discomfort of being a nuisance that is often the lot of an ethnographer, I had finally entered into a privileged, textured subjective space through this moment of affective sharing. Indeed, after this exchange, I was accepted as part of the company, in the robust narrative sense of that word, as both witness to and participant in the suljari, a place where the carnivalesque rules of inverse social orders obtain, and where the playful, private aspect of personhood, as a manifestation of social critique, can be exercised without fear of reprisal. The beginning, if you will, of a "beautiful friendship" (Graeber 1996).

Work at the office the next day continued undisturbed: papers were filed; e-mails were sent; the overnight interest rates issued by major national banks— the European Central Bank and Bank of Korea, for example—were tracked for lending environment; data for the Korean over-the-counter market for technology companies, KOSDAQ, were collected; lunches were eaten; the work on calculating the multiple proceeded;[6] a report on the personal media technology trend was left languishing; and so on and so forth. These essential activities of the firm—conceptual and bureaucratic—remained unchanged, even as the social relations within it shifted, at least for me, inward. However, this hard-won sociality left me no closer to answering the question I was addressing in my dissertation: How does the venture capital market work in South Korea? Instead of providing insight, the social nature of the office remained apart from the logic of the market that gave meaning to its activities.

Throughout this project, the issue of the "social" as the source of diacritical data for ethnography as a whole became a question in itself. (Here, I do not use "social" as a gloss for society or even structure, as in Emile Durkheim's or Talcott Parsons's analyses, but the social in its colloquial meaning as face-to-face interaction [Durkheim 2006; Parsons 1991].[7]) The sociality of my experience was not

---

6. "Multiple" is the shorthand for what is commonly known as the price earnings multiple. When a company is asking for investment, its earnings are multiplied by a projected factor to give a sense of its market value. This is very important since accounting methods such as PE or DCF analysis do not adequately represent the worth of the company and so the multiple determines the company's attractiveness as public investment. The technology venture firm where I worked was in the process of being thus evaluated.

7. When Mary Poovey writes, "Whether one uses the social to invoke an objective infrastructure that underwrites cultures, as members of the *Annales* school did, or to suggest a gradual, continuously changing process that establishes threshold conditions for cultural and political events, as Marx or Tocqueville did, or to identify one in the series of relatively autonomous domains that compose

the Rosetta Stone or structural grounding in constructing the object of my study. Though, at the time, I considered as a drawback my failure to materialize the invisible ties that bound the apparently disconnected pieces—the social life of the office, for example—into a coherent cultural phenomenon, unexpectedly what became clear through the fieldwork is the ambiguous and sometimes bracketed nature of the social in analyzing, even defining, the ethnographic object. In other words, I had entered the field through the social only to find in the end (in fact much after the completion of my dissertation) that the ethnographic object so conceived created a framework that externalized the social domain, which is often imagined as the concretely authentic, traditional site of ethnographic authority.

From the perspective of my research, being "inside," occasioned by this and other incidents of affective solidarities and witnessing, had little impact on clarifying the then inchoate questions about the rise of new financial technologies, the broad subject of my dissertation. Such technologies are fashioning the old cultural accretions into new objects, no longer located simply in the projected understandings or doings of their participants but grasped only in their emergent effect. For this reason, I use the term "remnant" to describe the social, in order to foreground its fragmented nature as one material in these larger sociotechnical objects. The word "remnant" connotes the holistic role that the social has played in the anthropological past, perhaps overly schematized (on my part), while pointing to the more recent practices that fracture and reassemble diverse domains into an object of indeterminate duration and efficacy, a subject I discuss in the next section. Indeed, for all the richness of the classic Geertzian moment in the bar, the participation in and observation of the social as a method remained liminal in my analytic framework (Geertz 1973b). Grappling with the whys and hows of the social as a fugue-state is the object of this essay.

Using this framework, I posed the question of the social precisely because of its classic status as a source for ethnographic authority (Geertz 1983; Gluckman 1955, 235–52; Stocking 2001) and its evolving role as one knowledge site among many others (Fischer and Downey 2006; Gudeman 1986; Holmes and Marcus 2006; Luhmann 1996; Marcus 1998; Maurer 2002, 2005; Miyazaki 2003; Strathern 1991). I am interested in exploring the tension between these two—the social as the foundational ground for integrating the dispersed parts and its newer, more limited analytical role.

---

modern life, as Niklas Luhmann tended to do, deploying the social as a noun automatically mobilizes certain theoretical claims implicit in the term's grammatical status" (2002, 125), she points to the continuing opaqueness of what seems most readily graspable, social behavior. For the purpose of this essay, I rest with the more colloquial usage of "social" as face-to-face interaction as the central means to apprehend the cultural.

The first step in this argument is an account of how an ethnographic project, my own, was conceived as a response to two forces: from without and from within. Following the project from its conception to the field, I trace its development through the lenses of the social and ask how to apprehend "modern" objects when they are less bounded by space than by knowledge and where to place the social within such a construction. In the following section, I analyze the implications of this rethinking through a discussion of the interconnected points among three key terms: the remnant, the social, and the assemblage, to use Paul Rabinow's term (1999: 3). Taken together, these terms delimit the spaces of modern objects that are cobbled together from partialities but nevertheless partake in more enduring sets of structures. In a subsequent section, I return to the field to discuss the gap between the social of the field and the way that the participants themselves saw the venture industry as an object beyond the immediate apprehension of their everyday activities. From this I draw a parallel in which the doing of ethnographic fieldwork may not readily index the knowledge produced in the ethnographic text. But this limitation can be productive in facilitating a more accurate reading of the topology of the objects at hand and so affording the anthropologist opportunities to fashion new diagnostic tools. As I will suggest in conclusion, the fracturing of a phenomenon—here termed the ethnographic object—into distinct domains produces a problem of inadequacy in the tools already at hand (in this case, the colloquial concept of the social), an inadequacy that itself produces an impetus for innovation.

This essay is based on fieldwork conducted in 2001–2002 and again in September 2006 on the venture capital industry in South Korea. As a participant observer, I worked for six months in 2001 as a special assistant to a venture firm in Teheran Row, a densely packed, gleaming street at the heart of Seoul where most of the venture firms were located. In fact, my apprenticeship had begun a year earlier when I served as a research assistant to a business professor at Rice University who focused on risk analysis. Then, for four months in 2002 I worked as a venture capital associate, an entry rank, after which I was transferred to the Mergers and Acquisitions team, before I quit the firm to continue interviewing various actors in the industry full-time. Although my routine at the firms differed only in that I was given time off to interview people, I was not an employee. I feared no reprisal, nor did I have deep-rooted stakes in the firms' success or failure, and I was therefore an "outsider." However, I learned the rudimentary skills that these firms used to examine data and events. This became the basis for understanding the language and the logic of the venture industry in South Korea and, from this partial view, for analyzing the larger rubric of the circulation of venture capital.

Before the Field and Already There

My dissertation project was born out of curiosity prompted by the Asian Currency Crisis in 1997–1998 and Korea's responses to it. During the summer months of 1997, the American media's concerns about the Crisis carried like the sound of a Greek chorus that shares in the pathos but not in the consequences: upholding the moral order, chastising the transgressions, but remaining apart from the center of the action (Pollack 1997; Gerth and Stevenson 1997; Arnold 2006). However, as it engulfed presumably robust economies such as those of Korea and Hong Kong, threatened institutions far removed from Asia or the currency market, and touched people who had believed themselves to be insulated from the chaos, the Crisis brought to the fore the reach and density of the pathways that joined these ostensibly discrete domains.[8] At the same time, the evident scale of damage inflicted legitimized the category of the global as an analytical unit, however contested the concept remains, and underscored the idea that this greater context issued from an underlying process not yet fully grasped.[9]

The Asian Currency Crisis surprised economists and governments alike[10] and for a short period strengthened the hands of those who critiqued what Stephen Green, a political economist, has called "the epistemological confidence of the modern risk order" (2000, 10). Modern financial trade methods are built from the works and methods of mathematics, a discipline as revered as any for the rigor of its epistemology. For these events to have taken so many by surprise, though some claimed prescience, hinted at the limitations of financial technology, namely quantification, in apprehending the dynamic of the system it engineered: Is a system built from rational parts necessarily rational as a whole? The question suggested the weakening of the epistemic certainty of quantification, if only for a moment, and put forward the possibility that devices derived from mathematics may be fallible after all.[11] However, this doubt was soon overshadowed by an argument that laid the blame on the policies of the affected countries

---

8. The *New York Times* published series of articles covering the Crisis, which can be found at http://www.nytimes.com/library/financial/asiamarkets-index.html.

9. For a wonderful list of articles and speeches on the Currency Crisis, see http://newton.uor.edu/Departments&Programs/AsianStudiesDept/general-crisis.html. For the timeline of the Crisis, see http://www.washingtonpost.com/wp-srv/business/longterm/asiaecon/timeline.html.

10. For example, the Working Group on Discourse, Dissent, and Strategic Surprise from George Washington University issued a 2006 report on the political insecurities aroused by the "failure to anticipate and prevent" the Crisis, calling it a "strategic surprise" (Institute for the Study of Diplomacy 2006, 1).

11. A school of economics known as behavioral economics has emerged as an alternative to the neoclassical model based on the rational market and has gained wider readership as the result of failures in the market (see, e.g., Thaler 1994).

and presented the Crisis as an unfortunate but rational expression of the collective knowledge of the market participants.[12] The potency of critique, fragile to begin with, waned as the improbable distension of the American stock market/ Internet bubble squeezed out any dissent against the necessity of moving toward financial capitalism. That eventuality, however, lay somewhat ahead of the time of the Crisis, and while this sense of fragility lasted, doubt had its day.[13]

The Crisis upended yet another established fact. One moment Korea was the world's eleventh-largest economy, and the next it was enduring what President Kim Young Sam described as the "bone-carving pain" of economic loss (Pollack 1997). It was a sharp reversal. In 1996, the Organization for Economic Coordination and Development, a club of industrialized nations, had admitted Korea to its ranks based on the country's wealth. Merely a year later the government requested a historical level of emergency loan, US$ 55 billion, from the International Monetary Fund, the financier of last resort. Large conglomerates, the sturdy engines of Korea's industrial growth, proved fragile, as one after the other, six of the thirty went into bankruptcy protection (Beck 1998, 1018). Massive layoffs followed, leading to suited but jobless men sitting at train stations, killing time before returning home. These losses exposed Korea's present as fragile and its future as unpredictable, a condition that led to what was more a lament than a question: How could forces unseen take away in such a short time what had taken two generations to build?

And yet, talk of a Korean venture boom began to circulate in late 1999. After the initial shock, the economy had made an unexpected, quick turnaround. By September 1999, the government had paid back the bulk of its debt to the IMF and was orchestrating a rapid growth of the previously nonexistent venture capital market through tax subsidies, investment guarantees, labor law reforms, and other such steps (International Monetary Fund 2001; Baygan 2003). Domestic newspapers carried stories of venture *yulpoong,* a Korean word for typhoon. University students across the country created venture *dongaris,* academic activity clubs, to become entrepreneurs. Movie stars married venture capitalists, a sure acknowledgment of their social desirability. Contrasted with the chaebols, rhetorically shunned as "old Korea," the venture market was riding high on the slogan of the new, receiving fevered interest from sources as diverse as Korean

---

12. For papers from the perspective of the rational market, see http://faculty.washington.edu/karyiu/Asia./papers/AsianCrisis.htm.

13. Despite this apparent consensus, the question of the certainty of quantification lingered in debates about technique (Toporowski 2000; Peter Coy et al. 1998 http://www.businessweek.com/1998/38/b3596001.html). This doubt, it seems to me, reflects a more general concern about failures in modern sciences (Fortun 2001; Miyazaki and Riles 2005).

housewives, foreign venture capitalists, and Michael Jackson.[14] At the same time, venture capitalism in the industrialized world was touted as the next great leap forward.[15] Held out as a way to climb up and keep up, it was credited with restoring hope to a confidence-shaken nation by offering "vision," a neologism for a bright and promising future.[16]

These events were bewildering to witness: What had happened? What was happening? As a practical matter, how did the nascent venture market in Korea function? Admittedly the very breadth of my curiosity betrayed an economic innocence (I was not even able to define then what "what" represented) and reflected a tradition in which an ethnographer, ideally, lets the field surprise her. In striving for this neutral stance, or at least openness, Mary Black urges that anthropologists "should not go to the field armed with specific questions to which they intend to find the answers but with an open ear for responses to which they intend to find the question" (Black 1963, 1347). Fieldwork so practiced has the tenor of an inductive process of discovery in which the purposeful ignorance of the anthropologist becomes the "measuring device" to categorize native knowledge as "he attempts successively more correct behavior and tests his knowledge of the cultural rules by constraining informant responses" (1347). The substantive content of fieldwork remains undefined, resistant to pre-design, precisely due to this inductive bent (cf. George Marcus in this volume) and due also to the inherent limit of the ethnographer's control and knowledge. As Marilyn Strathern points out, anthropology as practiced begins with "the unpredictability of initial conditions"—that is, not knowing what will happen when and why—from "the viewpoint of the observer" (1999, 44).

To what extent, then, is this lack of shared expertise between the ethnographer and the interlocutor productive? Contemporary expertise thrives on specialization and production. In the disciplines of economics, politics, and area studies, various branches of expertise on the whys, whats, and hows have formed a lattice

_____

14. In "Losing His Grip," an article written for *Vanity Fair*, Maureen Orth reported the following: In May 2000, Tim Nelson of the *St. Paul Pioneer Press*, upon hearing that Jackson was taking "the helm of a $100 million Korea-based venture fund that will invest in entertainment-oriented Internet companies," listed nine other Jackson projects and asked readers to guess which ones were "actually in the pipeline." His answer: "All of them! Every one! Coming soon to a vacant lot near you!" (Orth 2004).

15. For a comprehensive view of the logic of American venture capitalism, see Gompers and Lerner 2004.

16. In a 1999 speech to commemorate the 54th anniversary of national liberation from Japanese colonialism, Kim Dae-jung (1999) described the economic future this way: "A leap to become a first-class economy in the 21st century requires the growth of knowledge-based industries." In contrast, the large domestic conglomerates, the beneficiaries of the past industrial policy, are identified as the "the most problematic element in our economy," the element that stands in the way of the challenge he poses to his listeners, "to become new intellectuals."

of discourses so thick and immense that comprehending this landscape, let alone clearing the space for another perspective, seemed doubtful at best. For starters, there was the discourse on the Internet's capability to remove scarcity; on the revival of the Korean economy; on the venture market's dual use of calculable and unknowable risk; on the social nature of its operations. The list was "undisciplined," meaning that it adhered to no discipline in particular. Such a reading strategy promised loss of focus and specialization, an issue Ely Devon and Max Gluckman address in *Closed Systems and Open Minds: Limits of Naivety in Social Anthropology,* where they argue that each discipline must maintain its boundaries and stay "naive" to other expertise to prevent this very outcome (Devon and Gluckman 1964, 158–262). Well taken as their point is, the expertise on the objects called Korea, developmental economics, and venture capital differed from the expertise they cite, such as that of the sociologist and the psychologist. In the Korean case, the expertise structured the understandings and actions of the market participants: what to do, how to do it, and how to recognize its effects. The Korean venture market, in other words, was being shaped by "reflexive performativity" (Kaplan 2003, 49) in which the participants enact certain types of economic logic while monitoring success or failure of their actions, a process similar to what Pierre Bourdieu calls "objectification" (see Graeber 1996, 7). If successful, the participants recognize their limits and, to correct this, adopt and enact what is not immanent to their domain, thereby seeing themselves anew in an altered environment. Given this structuring role of expertise, I began my apprenticeship among the books, newspapers, articles, Internet sites, and lectures on venture capital, Korean economics, and other things—some of the materialities of the venture market in Korea. Thus, the field began by my seeing the connectivity (see Jim Faubion in this volume) of these dispersed pieces. This formulation, however, presented the problem of how to approach the social, even if a remnant, in my ethnographic project.

Remnants: In Their Dispersions and as Materials

An enduring source of inspiration, Max Weber's imagery of the iron cage of capitalism condenses an argument about the progressively coercive nature of rationalization that fractures a more organic and integrated life world into distinct and logically independent domains of calculability and efficiency (Weber 2002). The iconic imagery belongs to a tradition of casting modernity in its various modalities as a process of alienation and extraction from an earlier natural state (Faubion 1988). Building on this broad historical narrative, Ulrich Beck (1992),

Anthony Giddens (1991), and Ian Hacking (1990, 2006) among others have pointed to the growth in the number and variety of experts as further evidence of this fracturing of knowledge into discrete domains, thus denaturing the subject into areas of competencies. In this analytical vein, knowledge is broken down into its various elements, leaving various participants holding on to partialities that perhaps, like Humpty Dumpty, cannot be "put together again"—remnants, if you will.

Remnants in the repertoire of ethnographic inquiry draw from a long-standing and diverse, but largely implicit, history. Durkheim, for example, proposed that individual facts reveal the interlocking logic of a presupposed totality called society (2006). Marcel Mauss rethought the project of society from the organizational principles of the temporal sequencing of the gift and its excess capacity to carry something of the giver, thus identifying social relationships in the transaction between value and personhood (1990). From yet another perspective, Claude Lévi-Strauss proposed a system of cognitive and cultural mythemes as the ground of a past holistic integrity of a common, but drifting, origin. These varied canonical works show how the principles of a system have an honored place within the thinking of anthropology and highlight their role in providing the analytical vocabulary adequate to the task of analyzing social systems and, by extension, the totalities of the discipline's boundary, in the study of culture (2001).

Conversely, remnants are the antipodes of a system, their presence often signaling a whole in need of (re)construction. More widely, remnants have also been understood as diacritics of modernity in their evocation of a lost past, no longer available to us whole and unbroken: Lévi-Straussian mythemes certainly function in this iconic fashion (2001). In compensatory fashion, such totalities as "culture" and "system" emerged as analytic objects precisely at the moment when many once embedded objects were being wrested from their more "natural" state to be reassembled in different configurations. The classic strengths of anthropology, especially during its golden age spanning from early to mid twentieth century, have lain in the capacity to reconstruct a stable whole by bracketing the Saussurean "drift" evident in *parole* (Saussure 1983).

Of course, this short synopsis condenses, for the sake of argument, the great breadth of works that moved beyond the confines of the closed system, including those of Immanuel Wallerstein and Eric Wolf, and glosses over the intense debate on the nature and stability of knowledge and practices within the cultural sphere (Wallerstein 1979; Wolf 1982).[17] Perhaps the integrity of the whole was only

---

17. The concept of system possessed great romance even in the early 1990s when I was an undergraduate student in anthropology. The graduate students, being apprenticed in the great Chicago

ever comprehensible ideal-typically. My purpose here is merely to point out the extent to which structuralism integrated disparate facts into a single continuous interpretive cultural framework, a rather astonishing accomplishment, if now mostly fallen into disuse, and to note that structuralism became the last dominant theoretical framework of systems theory within anthropology. Of course, the once dominant concept of systems theory has come under much pressure and is itself a remnant of its former hegemony, although the question of whether its decline has been due to the changed nature of culture or the flawed heuristic assumption of stable social reproduction is yet to be settled.

In response to this critique and decline, recent formulations have disregarded—with such important exceptions as Luhmann (1995)—even the heuristic assumption of a system.[18] After all, the watchword of the recent wave of ethnographic work is situatedness and thus the partiality of knowledge. Situatedness, which posits a particular perspective, underlines the impossibility of an omnipresent view, and the origin of my own project bears out the axiom that anthropologists are already embedded within the knowledge systems they analyze and thus must limit their claims to a privileged perspective (Riles 2004; Strathern 1999, 2004). The drivers of this trend are both external and internal: the world has produced new technologies—cultural and mechanical—redrawing the form and process of the givens, and thus the language of systems gives way to the language of partialities and connections.

But giving up the omniscient view has produced new dilemmas. As a result, and as opposed to the whole that they once implied, remnants now have a more ambiguous status, pointing not so much toward the system as toward a particular sort of alienation and confusion over the present state of things. The range of phenomena identified as evidence of the globalization of markets and production has brought these questions to the fore. Because globalization is represented as an abstracted logic of the market as well as the effect of that logic in the affairs of material and symbolic production, an interest in systems is revitalized under another rubric, one that avoids the stability implied in the former articulation of the system. In a revival of this strain of analysis, the struggle with remnants and the partiality that they now imply has a currency in several different domains within anthropology. In fact, "partiality" has become a central trope in raising the contemporary question of knowledge as an issue of limit. Knowledge is not

---

tradition, began their professionalization with mandatory courses called, if memory serves, Systems I and II.

18. In elegiac mode, George Stocking in his *Delimiting Anthropology* reflects upon how the "boundaries of a boundless discipline" were formed by the greats among the early American and British anthropologists (Stocking 2001, 303).

only becoming information, as Latour and Woolgar (1979) have argued, but also has a limited efficaciousness, marked by "gaps in form" (cf. Riles 2000, 161). In this line of analysis, such a limit sets the parameters for further innovation, as the knowledge regime pursues newly imagined alternatives.

The place of the social within the process of disembedded technological innovations has been analyzed from various theoretical perspectives that have worked around the uneasy tension between the two (Granovetter 1985; Granovetter and Swedberg 2001; Ong and Collier 2005; Zaloom 2006). These works respond to the changes in structures that Paul Rabinow, following Michel Foucault, has broadly termed technologies (Rabinow 1999; Foucault 1972, 1986). Common to these approaches is a shared perspective on the problematic of measuring and analyzing the fracturing of the whole into various pieces, the remnants of a system. With these developments, the ascendancy of partialities can be noted in the quiet popularity of concepts that imply a temporal limit on durability, such as the concept of the assemblage, which accordingly has production rather than reproduction as the center of its significance.

Part of the usefulness of the concept, then, lies precisely in its denoting a heterogeneous materiality—part structure and part event—which has deep resonance in science studies but also in anthropology. The term "assemblage," which Rabinow (1999)clearly articulates in *French DNA,* seems to have gained a wider currency after the fall, or rather the falling apart, of the postmodern. This latter theoretical sensibility produced works on heterogeneity and collage as the dominant modality of nonlinear cultural production. Arising out of a strong dissatisfaction with the trope of the collage and the consequent rethinking of modernist concerns, the concept of the assemblage provides a stopgap measure to allow the to-and-fro between structure and emergence that now marks the contemporary problematization of culture. The drawback of the concept of the assemblage is that it can be a weak metaphor, but evocativeness seems to be its strong suit (see Thrift 1999). While not providing a firmer theoretical ground for thinking through the problem of the open system that now engages social science, the concept of the assemblage signals how important unstable cultural objects have become. Ephemerality, explicitly evoked in calling up the assemblage, is an index of contemporary anxiety about impermanence even in the face of such imposing and enduring structures as those of power and economy.

Assemblages thus register contingency as the mark of a contemporary open system in which the norm is not reproduction, but the production of new objects, on which its survival and growth depend. Things—machines, for example—fall apart; it is in their nature to do so. In contrast to the more agnostic notion of the place of the social in the ambiguous usage of assemblages, a body of work now known as Actor Network Theory (ANT), developed by Bruno Latour, Michel

Callon, and John Law, posits two methodological conditions: 1) the equalization of the human and nonhuman, and 2) the resulting heterogeneity of elements in the production of the world (Latour 1987, 2007; Callon 1998; Law 2002).[19] So far, ANT has proved to be especially attractive to science studies as a theory readily married to the variegated materiality of the scientific domain, in which objects, and forces sometimes invisible to the human and largely separated from human agency, such as gravity, create part of the network within which action can be initiated and through which it can be known. The body of work known as ANT is currently made most intelligible within the context of social science studies; the latter seem to capture vital aspects of the making of meaning and experience, that of the agency of true others, like machines and natural forces, as illustrated in Law's analysis of building airplanes and the interaction among many materialities (2002). This focus on "making" extends to looking at economic processes in which analysis proceeds from examining forms analogous to economic rationality and not in opposition to it.

From this perspective, the concept of the assemblage and ANT share some aesthetic ground. However, the assemblage and ANT as methodological frameworks differ in subtle but important ways. As George Marcus and Erkan Saka note, the concept of the assemblage easily lends itself to "a more rigorous characterization of a network in which nodes in the larger system can be called upon to form temporary lines of communication and process" (2006, 5). Thus, the assemblage married to the network is one expression of a larger structure, an object that cleaves closer to the notion of structure than to uncertain ephemerality. However, as I suggested earlier, the advantage of the concept of the assemblage might be its very vagueness, as it leaves open the idea of a relation among things, positing them as contingent and heterogeneous (Rabinow 2007).[20] Contingency, Rabinow seems to imply, calls upon experimentation and play as its methodology in contrast to taking the found "epistemologies" as given in Faubion's critique of ANT's orientation found in this volume.

To underscore this very openness of the assemblage, I have co-opted and shifted the meaning of "aggregate" from economics to represent the complexity of assemblages that do not seem to exhibit linearities of relations between part and whole and that are observable only in part. An "aggregate" is understood as a composition in which the logic of the part is not equivalent to the logic of the whole and is thus disjointed from immediacy. For my purpose, an aggregate is a

---

19. In this equalization of the human and nonhuman, ANT as a body of work claims to sidestep the classical problems of individual/society and agency. For the sake of brevity, I will bracket this discussion here.

20. I am grateful to Kim Fortun for suggesting this line of thought.

specific type of assemblage, which "can refer to a subjective state of cognition and experience of society and culture in movement from a recent past toward a near future (the temporal span of emergence); or it can refer to objective relations, a material, structure-like formation, a describable product of emergent social conditions, a configuration of relationships among diverse sites and things" (Marcus and Saka 2006, 3). Let me stress here that aggregate is not necessarily a thing in the world but can be called upon based on the ethnographic question. The aggregate assemblage broadly defined is a temporal and emergent object 1) whose elements have no predetermined and so only a contingent relation to one another, and 2) whose temporality is of indeterminate duration. An aggregate, then, is a type of assemblage that exhibits a nonlinear relation among diverse elements, which then raises the question of the centrality of "the social"—and presumably Black's model of the unschooled anthropologist—as the anthropological method of measurement.

The admittedly schematic overview I have outlined here serves to highlight the issue confronting the ethnographer before he or she enters the field about what she will count as data and how. In different ways, the metaphors for the anthropology of the now—Rabinow's assemblage (1999), Strathern's partiality (1991), Faubion's connectivity (in this volume), Marcus's multi-sitednes (1998) and Maurer's laterality (2005b)—invoke the question of what objects, subjects, processes, pathways, and even systems are deemed "ethnographic" in the enterprise. Common to all these projects, then, is the opening up of the question about the connectivity of heterogenous things, in the fundamental sense, in which their "countability" is left open rather than closed. Recent debates and conversations among various theoretical and methodological perspectives cannot be understood without reference to this question of discreteness and permeability of domains in their different paths of dispersion. What I suggest here is that the social, too, has become a remnant, and thus mobile, and so might serve as the material for new kinds of aggregates—but then again, might not.

Being There and Not

At this point, I turn to my activities in the field, which—as in classic ethnographic accounts—comprised long periods of boredom occasionally punctuated by events that broke the monotony. The humdrum tone of this genre becomes even more pronounced when placed within the confines of an office, whether that office is in Seoul or Houston, as the routine hardly varies. For the duration of the field year, daily life was uneventful, mostly repetitive, taken up with fulfilling the immediate requirements of my supervisors or other tasks that needed my attention. In the matter of "doing" ethnography, most of my time was spent interacting with people at the firms, learning the things that they had to learn, doing the things that they had to do, unwinding after work as they did. The experience vacillated between fun and frustration, but the transparency of the activities surprisingly occluded the relations and situations not immediately apprehensible or grounded in the social. This reflected a more general dilemma faced by the venture participants themselves. I describe such activities here to demonstrate that insight into the nature of venture was not readily extractible from the "doing" of fieldwork in the social milieu.

While employed at the venture firm, I woke up in the morning at 6 a.m., squeezed into the Seoul subway with another million or so commuters by 7 a.m., and reached work by 7:30 a.m. Entering the high-rise, I was greeted by the door-man and by employees from other venture firms occupying different floors. We all came into the office around the same time, went to lunch at noon, and left at the same late hour—this constituted a workday. Upon arriving at the office, I taught an hour-long high-level business English class for the firm and then set to work on documents and helped with ongoing deals. Along the way, I translated business texts, snacked during the daily ritual of the four-o'clock break with the very few female knowledge workers employed by the firm, and participated in meetings for the firm's regional and global partnerships. I also went along on company-wide retreats where drinking beer and eating barbecued meats seemed less like work than fun. Often, I would take a short leave to conduct interviews at other firms.

At the venture capital firm, the rhythm repeated itself. I went into the office, looked at papers in my file, browsed through the English and Korean newspapers to mine important facts, translated the letters of intent or terms of agreement from Korean into English, went to lunch, reviewed applications for investment, wrote up reports about various technological sectors of investment interest using LexisNexis databases, and participated in meetings. Different place, same rou-tine. Eventually I came to know well the rhythm of Seoul life and understood the micro-shifts in the mood of the city. Working there is not for the weak-hearted: even after the long day, I went to the gym with my co-workers (we acted in con-cert), went to dinner, then returned to work, and often later went out for drinks to unwind. Social life revolved around the firm and paralleled the intensity of office life. Certainly, it was a busy schedule.

The problem was that, given the nature of my ethnographic question, the gulf between the actual construction of the everyday in the office and the implied structuration taking place as an effect of the everyday was wide and sometimes ungraspable. In early 2000 when I applied for funding for the project—research into the newly established venture capital market in Korea—the market was in ascendance. But a few months before my departure for the field, the cumula-tive value of technology firms in the stock market decreased by some 30 percent (KOSDAQ 2001). This crash was, in retrospect, the first mark of an implosion in the venture capital market in Korea, but at the time the volatility was seen largely as a correction process inherent in an infant industry that had been bloated by the rapid entry of uncompetitive firms. This optimistic interpretation proved to be wrong, and the recognition of failure slowly seeped into the market as I worked in the field.[21]

My experience suggests that the aggregate is not directly observable through a full participation in the making of it. The transparency of the day and the emergent system being set into motion by the adoption of a new financial technology—and the gap between the two—led to an intensification of my thinking about the nature of knowledge and practice in ethnography. What if the sociality of the office was a remnant of the architecture of knowledge that had created the structure of a system, not apparent to the knowledge worker who dealt with one miniscule piece of the implied but never realized whole? What if the work of the office and the logic of the ethnographic object were related, but elliptically so? What if the tension between the ethnography of the senses and the abstraction of numbers was irresolute *here* in this project?

This is not to suggest that the social is not important sui generis. For an eth-nographer, social ties can give initial access and also solve many a knotty problem when working in several contemporary arenas. In both instances, I was able to procure a series of interviews through the use of weak links with a partner at each firm of interest and later ask to intern at that firm as a participant observer. Indeed, such links signify the pathways through which social networks can be tapped and utilized (Granovetter 1973). More important, Korea's intense social life, including the drinking culture, provides a locale where intimacy and the rationality of the market place are toggled. Many employees practically live in their offices.[22] This sociality has bred an expectation that much business will be conducted outside the office in such (gendered) places of leisure as golf clubs, saunas, and drinking salons. These expectations are not necessarily false; from my own observations, leisure activities cement relationships, catalyzing affect into productive bonds. Social relations can be harnessed to facilitate the exchange of more "honest" information, undercutting the official numbers that most dismiss

---

21. By the time I left in August 2002, the only news generated from this sector was the series of bribe and fraud scandals involving prominent venture businessmen—and they were men—and government officials.

22. During the periods of my fieldwork, people put in an average of over fifty-five work hours per week, which included Saturdays. Although the Noh Mhu-hyun government proclaimed Saturday a holiday at the time, many companies still require their employees to come into work on the weekend.

as suspect, and thus are part and parcel of the activities of business. Participants are adept at transforming social relations into knowledge that may be leveraged into economic capital. However, among the venture capitalists I knew, these social practices were inadequate in significant ways. One lawyer for the venture capital firm put it this way: "You can get some deals done by knowing someone, but you can't know what's coming down the road through that." In other words, participating in these social activities and relations could not bridge the gaps between parts and the emergent whole that are characteristic of an aggregate. This became a problem for the Korean venture people, whether they were on the financing or the venture side. Part of the problem lay in the rapid changes in the domestic economy itself, specifically in the allocation of such financial structures as credit, spread among various economic agents such as consumers and banks.

At the time of my fieldwork, this was especially true. The venture capital industry in Korea, although operating since 1981, never had noteworthy success or economic presence prior to 1997 (Bayan 2003). This placed it in the vulnerable position of any young industry during unstable economic times, a vulnerability it had itself helped generate. There were many unsettled questions: whether the government was going to prop up the venture market through further capitalization of the stock market for technology; whether the weak financial infrastructure of second- and third-step venture capital markets would develop as a response to market pressures; whether the laws that governed the definitions of venture and venture capital firms—and thus their eligibility to receive preferential treatment and money—would change. Thus, among the venture capitalists I knew, the anxiety to keep close watch on the rapid turn of events and the fear of the cost of partial knowledge were intense.

For example, soon after the rise of the venture industry in Korea, the banks introduced consumer credit for the first time, a move that transformed not only the means of payment for goods but the structure of the domestic economy as well. The savings rate went down twelve percent from one year to the next and the percentage of the household income debt (seventy-three percent of total GDP) rivaled that of the United States (seventy-nine percent), an event that signaled the decrease in funds for investment activities, including venture (Lee and Crotty 2001). All the pronouncements by J. P. Morgan Chase and Fitch Ratings that proclaimed the consumer sector sound aside, the collapse of LG Credit, amid rumors of other pending failures, due to payment delinquency, dealt a fatal blow to the venture capital sector, because the drag on the domestic economy meant fewer investment activities and lower prices on the KOSDAQ. With these developments, many of the smaller venture capital firms and venture firms simply disappeared.

A second source of instability lay in the globalization of venture capital, which made the industry sensitive to events and trends abroad. As my earlier discussion of modernity brought into view, contemporary objects are segregated into disparate domains that may not be mutually accessible. In fact, my apprenticeship at the venture capital company was cut short as a result of the shifting of resources within the firm itself. With the venture industry winding down, a new consensus had emerged: the rate of return possible in China now exceeded that in Korea.[23] Already anecdotally China was one of the largest targets for international venture capital investment. However, due to Chinese laws that stipulated that all investment had to be partnered up with domestic companies owning at least fifty percent, some venture capital firms in Korea had decided to confine the nature of their business activities to mergers and acquisitions, activities suited to funding matured companies rather than start-ups.

Among the venture capitalists and participants I knew, the firm-level perspective was only one small part of apprehending the industry as such. The stated role of venture capitalists in their interaction with their collaborating venture entrepreneurs is social in nature, using that modality of relations to offset the weaknesses of the structure of governance (i.e., overseeing by the capitalists) and the possible weaknesses in the managerial experience of the entrepreneurs. Yet, in moving from a firm-level to an aggregate perspective, I have highlighted how these claims about the role of the social occlude the larger concern with the shape of the industry as a whole and the final, most important end of its investment activities—profit. Profit was pitched to the vagaries of the aggregate in a way that was disconnected from the much-touted role of venture capitalists as advisers: one thing (the social) did not lead to the other (knowledge of the venture market).

And the people I worked with had similar questions in relation to my own work. In late spring, some time after the evening of bonding with which I began this essay, one of my co-workers, Lee, took me aside after the noisy four-o'clock snack. Wearing a quizzical, almost pained look, he asked me, "What are you doing exactly?" "Doing" here referred both to my professional career and to my specific project of researching venture in Korea. Anthropologists still have the time-warp reputation for researching bones and primitives and thus are themselves viewed as exotics within the humdrum world of contemporary life, especially in the corporate world. To find me there in the office, sitting in front of the computer or going to work part-time at the venture capital firm, confused

23. In 2005, Korea had become the single largest investor in China, beating Japan to that title (Kim and Mah 2006).

many of my companions. They knew that I was an anthropology student and I was there for an anthropological project, but could not extract from my activities the nature of my work. After I had transgressed their expectations by showing no interest in what they considered to be the differences that marked "culture" (e.g., shamanism), many of my observers—and I was being watched—were puzzled about the nature of my diacritical domain of anthropological knowledge. I suspect that they pegged me as a quixotic and lazy sociologist—since at least sociologists study modern institutions—who just wanted a job in Korea after her "research." For them, "research" was marked by some distinctive set of practices distinguished from the everyday, but my behavior flowed into the familiar to the extent that research was no longer an apt framework for understanding it. Really, they wanted to know: What kind of an expert was I? What kind of research involved working at a job like any other employee?

My initial answer, that I was studying the venture industry as an anthropologist, proved inadequate as it defined only the general problem of anthropology, not my particular project. Thereafter, my answer to them was more specific: that I was seeking to find empirical data to test the idea of risk as an index of a changing notion of modernity in Korea. I argued, in English, that cultural critiques have led anthropology to an empiricism in which going beyond the limits of any ethnographic object does not lead automatically to the social but sometimes to an abstract numerological world by the way of other disciplines.

Indeed their confusion about the nature of my work mirrored my own about them and their work. For these venture capitalists and even venture firm entrepreneurs, the social practices of the everyday comprised a discrete area of action, in which the social could not always be transformed into knowledge. Instead of understanding this as a failure of the integration of doing and knowing, I reimagined it as a problem natural to contemporary practices, in which the whole is a reconstruction from dispersed points of various objects, knowledge, and relations. In this way, the questions posed by my former colleagues reflect my own, and they remain as yet questions and possibilities, a remnant of a field that still shifts its shape both in my analysis and in the world.

More an Appendix than a Conclusion: An Ethnography of Connectivity

In the words of cultural historian Mary Poovey,

> To move beyond the language-based theories that have dominated critical inquiry in anthropology for the last few decades, and to integrate theory more effectively into a methodology that collects and uses

various kinds of evidence, I think we need to form alliances with practitioners in the social and natural sciences. As far as I know, practitioners of these disciplines also need to develop more sophisticated methodologies, but, whereas humanists need better tools for collecting and managing (nontextual) evidence, social and natural scientists might need more theoretically informed analytic paradigms. Theory and practice must somehow be brought together so that the construction of theoretical paradigms draws more closely upon observable evidence. (2003, 440)

Here Poovey expresses an optimistic view of ethnography as a science that "collects and uses various kinds of evidence," an apparatus geared toward the productive questioning of historical and literary problems through the authentication of observation. Thus, she advocates rethinking methods predicated on "language-based theories" in favor of the evidentiary process of science, all the while implying the analytical productivity of doing so. By no means is this turn a move toward crude empiricism. Poovey is, after all, a theoretician well acquainted with the construction of naturalized objects in the world, such as numbers and facts, whose history reveals the cultural work that went into erasing their very historicity (see Poovey 1998). What she seems to be implying, then, is the need for new tools in light of evolving theory, to reorient attention from theory to method. In such a reading, tools can be upgraded or discarded as the objects of the inquiry dictates, the way methods often are in science.[24] Put this way, Poovey's concern with evidence converges with the larger debate outlined here about the range and limits of ethnography.

Like Poovey, I suggest deploying tools of science; empiricism in this sense means openness to the possibility of the limitation of the social as an ethnographic method. This requires attention to different ways of being and acting, not only embodied but also enumerated and assembled from many types of objects and processes. By no means am I advocating a displacement of the social, but I want to suggest an opportunistic relationship to it as a suit of strength, a contingent relationship rather than a necessary one.

The implication for anthropology is perhaps minor. After all, anthropology is more than simply ethnography, and ethnography itself can be elasticized to encompass fantastically diverse projects and questions. And ethnographic doings have evolved far beyond using the social as the main source of data. However, I suggest a more careful consideration of how the nature of the objects and subjects

---

24. Neuroscientist Sebastian Seung stated (2006), "Most advances in science have not been theories but in our ability to measure things." The twinned logic of science, induction and deduction, is not abandoned, but methods are privileged.

of our analytic curiosity necessitates an inductive attitude toward method as well as toward the object of study.

When I was in Korea, I was confused about what constituted method. Faced with the limits of relying on the social as a method, I cleaved to the constructs of my interlocutors, the numbers and logics of venture capital, soaked in the affective framework of nationalism. However, what became clear after a time is that, as well as a way of measuring, method is also a way of constructing the objects to measure, now part of anthropological common sense but not quite part of the field's common tools. For this project, the method, then, required expansion to include heterogeneous objects, subjects, and processes, connected by the field, an unstable object itself, partly located in the immediacy of the face-to-face social and partly in capital flows, theories, structures, and discourses.

Anthropology, George Marcus once said, apprehends the emergent before what emerges solidifies into structures, and the messiness of such an endeavor is its very virtue (personal communication). Fulfilling Mary Black's dream, and mine, of knowing the world through curiosities, to become the "good anthropologist," who "finds her way through it," as Jim Faubion (in this volume) succinctly characterizes the dilemma, seems to call for embracing the vulnerabilities of locating one's project, and oneself, in the not knowing of the "connectivity" (Faubion again) of what is encountered. Yes, it is a return of sorts to the beginning, to the naiveté so valued by the Greats. After all, remnants remain, and they become the materials from which another object emerges.

Acknowledgments

This article is dedicated, with gratitude, to Jim Faubion and George Marcus, both teachers of divergent methods but shared purpose. Many thanks, also, to Kristin Peterson, Lamia Karim, D. J. Hatfield, Hiro Miyazaki, Annelise Riles, Jong-bum Kwon, Katherine Moon, the two reviewers, and Markus Deulks for all the ideas they so generously shared with me.

3

ON THE ETHICS OF UNUSABLE DATA

Jennifer A. Hamilton

That the conditions of contemporary anthropological fieldwork have changed seems at this point axiomatic although the precise dimensions of these conditions remain up for debate. And, as Marcus and others have compellingly argued, it is not simply the "field"—as a primary site of data collection—that has changed; the circumstances under which anthropological research, scholarship, and pedagogy are generated have also shifted (e.g., Marcus 1998, 2008a). My contribution here is to outline some of the issues, challenges, and problems I encountered during doctoral fieldwork—especially in terms of the generation of what I call *unusable data*—and to describe how these were ultimately productive in terms of the dissertation and in the shift to my postdoctoral project. Juxtaposing what I considered to be my highly problematic dissertation fieldwork with my more recent incarnation as a professional anthropologist highlights some of the norms and assumptions that differently shape apprentice and professional ethnography.

I am not attempting here merely to repeat a narrative of triumph over adversity: a phoenix (my dissertation) rising from the ashes of some great conflagration (my doctoral fieldwork). Rather, my purpose is to critically engage the following problem: namely, that while the data of my fieldwork did not form the substance of my dissertation, it is nevertheless the case that the dissertation and the book that followed could not have been produced without those data and that experience. Even more important, my postdoctoral ethnographic work would have been impossible.

Contemporary fieldwork conditions are fraught with certain kinds of questions usually defined as ethical—how to protect vulnerable research subjects, how to establish and maintain appropriate relationships with research communities, how to integrate the concerns and interests of your informants in your research and writing, how to fulfill the often mind-numbing bureaucratic requirements of institutional review boards while nevertheless remaining committed to an ongoing process of ethical negotiation with your informants. There are a variety of ways to answer these questions and, as the extensive literature on the subject suggests, such questions and their answers are often context-specific, dependent on a variety of factors and constraints. While routine in their prevalence, such questions (as well as the novel ones generated in the ever-shifting terrains of fieldwork) nevertheless require continuing energy and creativity on the part of the ethnographer. I suggest, as others have before me, that these ethical endeavors are not separate from, nor are they simply incidental to, the practice of fieldwork. What has come to frame the practice of ethics as well as ethical practice is not only itself worthy of anthropological investigation, but also forms a key part of the practice of ethnography (Faubion 2001b).

What is the notion of *unusable data* in this context? I am not referencing data that simply weren't useful. I would venture an absolute here—every ethnographer and every field project produce data that aren't useful either because they aren't relevant or interesting or because they simply don't fit into the broader ethnographic or analytical schema. What I mark as distinct here are ethnographic data that *could not* be used precisely because of the conditions under which they were generated. That is, they could not be used explicitly in the mode of thick description, or as examples of key social processes, or as concrete articulations of broader analytical problems. Yet, I will contend, they form a central part of the ethnographic endeavor.

An Ethnography of Indigenous Justice: Doctoral Fieldwork

> A critique is not a matter of saying that things are not right as they are. It is a matter of pointing out on what kinds of assumptions, what kinds of familiar, unchallenged, unconsidered modes of thought the practices that we accept rest.
>
> —Michel Foucault, "Practicing Critique" (1988)

Throughout the 1990s, the development of culturally specific justice initiatives in Native North American communities became a way not only to express dissatisfaction with the contemporary conditions of a limited and discriminatory justice system but also to historicize these conditions in the context of a colonial past. Thus, discourses of indigenous justice operated as moral critique, and cultural difference was the primary idiom used to express it. My dissertation project was originally concerned with how indigenous legal concepts, especially as they pertain to criminal justice matters, were being defined and used in urban contexts among First Nations and American Indian peoples living in the Northwest. Seen largely as a return to traditional forms of justice that existed prior to the imposition of colonial laws, indigenous justice had become an especially rich area for many indigenous groups seeking political, economic, and cultural autonomy from the nation-state. Not coincidentally, justice programs had also become important alternatives for statist governments grappling with the expense of the criminal justice system, discriminatory rates of incarceration for indigenous peoples, and issues of indigenous self-determination.

My doctoral fieldwork was in many ways quite traditional in terms of both its substantive focus (indigenous peoples, law) and its neo-Malinowskian methodological orientation ("go there" and "just do it" ethnography). Specifically, I went into the field in 1999 to investigate the postcolonial emergence of culturally specific justice practices among urban indigenous peoples in Vancouver, British Columbia. I was particularly interested in the ways in which claims to culture and justice were deployed in legal spaces and in the tension between the cultures of recognition and feminist activism.

I moved from Houston to Vancouver. I did volunteer work (at a legal services organization and an Aboriginal feminist activist organization). I sat in on government meetings and law classes. I had informal conversations. I interviewed informants. I did archival research. I wrote fieldnotes. I walked around. I rode the bus. I took dance classes four times per week to help mitigate my fieldwork-induced paranoia. While it seemed that I had a clear object of study—Aboriginal justice in the city of Vancouver—it was not at all clear how I was to study it. My grant proposals had explicitly outlined my methodological plans, and I followed these plans, all the time attempting to remain flexible and open to new research opportunities.

Of course, what became apparent is that doing (or attempting to do) *in situ* ethnography among people more or less loosely affiliated—through bureaucratic conventions, welfarist programs, spatio-legal practices such as police surveillance, kin relationships, multiculturalist policies, and indeed my own ethnographic gaze—posed a series of conceptual, methodological, political, and ethical challenges. These included attempts to constitute an object of study beyond "the community" that could account for the complex configurations of kin and political associations, funding networks, and governmental structures as well as attempts to determine how best to conduct research in an area and among peoples who have a long and often fraught history of association with

anthropologists. This latter history, especially in the context of Canadian anthropology among First Nations, has produced conditions wherein the normative
expectations of anthropological advocacy are quite strong and the absence of
explicit advocacy is considered suspicious. Further, while the object of study itself
seemed increasingly diffuse and difficult to grasp, I nevertheless felt as though
something was happening, but that something seemed beyond my specific methodological toolkit.

What happened in the field? Well, it seemed, not much. I conducted a series of
unproductive interviews about indigenous justice in which my informants either
gave me party-line responses to questions—responses I could have scripted
myself before having done the interview—or told me things off the record. I
attended a number of government meetings in which particular bodies fulfilled
particular functions. Disappointingly, as a nonaffiliated anthropologist, a "cultural outsider," I was not permitted to attend any of the several pilot healing
circles under the auspices of the now-defunct Vancouver Aboriginal Restorative
Justice Project (VARJP), nor were there any publicly available transcripts of these
sessions. In some ways, such constraints were a matter of course. I had entered
the field fully expecting to have limitations on my access to various people and
places; white doctoral students in anthropology, especially those coming from
obscure universities in exotic locales like Texas and with no clear local connections, tend to provoke a certain level of suspicion. Nevertheless, the specific
dimensions of access in the field did not follow any discernible pattern, and I was
often baffled by where I was and wasn't allowed to go. The healing circles seemed
an especial blow because I had imagined them as key interpretive sites—my very
own Balinese cockfight, if you will.

I heard whispers about what had happened at such healing circles, yet these
were always followed by "but don't tell anyone that I told you" or "you didn't hear
that from me." And, in the small world of First Nations community organizing
and activism in Vancouver, aggregation wasn't possible and simply anonymizing
informants would not have been sufficiently protective. Further, while my access
to more "official" events was either limited or proved unhelpful in terms of data
collection, people were sometimes willing to tell me what they thought about
this issue or that person, so long as I didn't write about it.

I grew increasingly frustrated with the methods available to me. Other graduate students had stacks of tapes, data that need to be transcribed and mined for
their cultural meanings. My own experience reflects a growing problem with the
"interview" in certain contexts; I could predict with great accuracy what people
were (or were not) going to tell me before I ever went in. At one point, in a scenario that became all-too-familiar during the course of fieldwork, I found myself
sitting in an interview with a low-level bureaucrat, my informant nervously and

repeatedly checking my tape recorder as though keeping an eye on it would prevent any unintended and potentially hazardous revelations. As he answered my pre-scripted questions in a pre-scripted way, it became clear to me that I could have crafted his answers myself, begging the question as to why I had made numerous phone calls, left multiple messages on voicemail, and traveled downtown on yet another dismal Vancouver day to do an interview with someone whose demeanor toward me ranged from apathy to discomfort to barely disguised irritation. Why, indeed—other than to say that I had done an interview, done something.

What is clear to me now is that the conditions under which the interview took place, and the conditions which enabled it to take place at all, were central both to "the field" I was seeking to understand and to the then-nascent questions I was attempting to formulate. One of the things that became increasingly apparent was that I circulated in some way that *mattered*. The subjects of my research sometimes saw me as a means to articulate claims of authenticity and to critique the claims of other local groups competing for recognition and funding. For instance, in later revisiting my notes, I was reminded that after attending a community-level meeting, I was seen by said bureaucrat standing outside the building talking (well, gossiping) with one of his colleague-adversaries. After weeks of failed attempts to set something up, I was given a card and invited to make an appointment, a hard-won victory that reflected not rapport in the Geertzian sense, but a kind of *rapport-lite* in which my presence was recognized, tolerated, and accommodated. But this rather common fieldwork phenomenon hardly seemed the stuff of great dissertations—it seemed trite and hardly worth noting (see Geertz 1973b). Further, to chart my own circulation in this complex field would have required betraying confidences and potentially undermining the work of local organizations. The latter was of real concern in the thorny political context of British Columbia wherein indigenous claims to rights and resources are almost always subject to challenge by its discomfited settler populations.

During fieldwork, I was particularly caught up in the feminist politics of restorative justice, both by virtue of my own inclination and training and my (albeit marginal) participation in a local indigenous women's activist organization. Members of the latter group were strong critics of restorative justice as it was developing in the indigenous context of British Columbia, but also more globally. In particular, they expressed concerns that were becoming increasingly prevalent among activist-feminist organizations including that such initiatives failed to pay attention to broader structural inequalities such as sexism and racism and that such programs would ultimately, and dangerously, focus on a certain class of violent offenses: those that fall under the category of violence against women and children (domestic violence, sexual abuse, and so forth). While these concerns certainly mirrored my own, they nevertheless seemed but a point of departure for a dissertation project, not something that could form the core of it. Further, a mere description of the oft-cited "tension" between multiculturalist policies seeking to recognize indigenous rights within a framework of justice *and* feminist critiques of patriarchal-colonial models of culture was insufficient to account for the complex circulation of people, capital, and ideas in this historical moment.

Informant discourse in some ways repeated earlier modes of both statist and anthropological discourse, particularly in terms of the culture concept, certain conceptions of identity and postcolonial critique. Thus, despite my attempts to get at the specifics of "culturally specific justice initiatives on the ground" and to examine "how justice discourses circulate in multiple spheres," I was caught in a discursive field that in some ways was all too familiar because it was circumscribed by my own academic/activist discourse. And it was an academic/activist discourse that seemed increasingly paltry to me throughout the course of fieldwork, although it wasn't until I was writing the dissertation that I began to grapple with this inadequacy in any kind of full way. What became apparent is that restorative justice works in complex and contradictory ways, but as Bill Maurer reminds us, "the complexity of the present cannot simply be grasped by invoking that complexity and leaving the description and analysis at that" (2004, 4).

But how to account for the complexity that created the first government-sponsored indigenous healing circle in the province of British Columbia for a white Catholic bishop accused of sexually assaulting indigenous women, or that that enabled healing circles convened for young disenfranchised indigenous men to make amends to their "corporate victims" (the Royal Bank) under the rhetoric of "community healing"? Further, how was I to move beyond my knee-jerk sense of outrage at such events, especially when they seemed simply a reinforcement of the status quo in postcolonial Canada?

In my estimation, by the end of my time in Vancouver, I had amassed a mound of unusable data. As my fieldwork time wrapped up and I prepared to leave, I thought of the entire experience as a personal failure. I became convinced that I would return to Houston for dissertation write-up with nothing much to say. Moving between the twin modes of outrage and bafflement, I worried that I would end up making arguments that I could have made prior to going into the field although perhaps with greater subtlety and more illustrative anecdotes. I have since learned that this kind of crisis is familiar to many apprentice ethnographers, but I reference it here because I think my own methodological assumptions profoundly shaped my experience in ways that were occluded at the time.

Despite being conversant with various modes of anthropological critique and aware of important shifts in our anthropological understandings of ethnography,

I think as an apprentice ethnographer I was nevertheless methodologically attached, albeit unwittingly so, to an older formulation of interpretive anthropology, expressed here in traditional Geertzian fashion: "The essential vocation of interpretive anthropology is not to answer our deepest questions, but to make available to us answers that others, guarding other sheep in other valleys, have given, and thus to include them in the consultable record of what man has said" (Geertz 1973a, 30). When I started, I intended to investigate, describe, and analyze ("place in broader context") these emergent justice initiatives. I wanted thick description. Yet moving in such a politicized environment wherein anthropological knowledge mattered in a way that, while not unexpected, was nevertheless fraught presented a series of difficulties to the apprentice ethnographer, especially because of my focus on *doing work, gathering data*—what I thought I was supposed to be doing. In other words, I was so focused on doing fieldwork (and on the accompanying frustration and difficulty) that I most likely missed other opportunities including attention to the richly ethnographic problems I was having.

In his discussion of "Ethnographic Emergences," Maurer points out that ethnographers, especially those who study novel objects and emergent formations, find themselves in challenging positions because often their traditional claims and analytical modes have been picked up by their informants in ways that closely resemble, if not mirror, anthropological frameworks (Maurer 2005; see also Holmes and Marcus 2005; Riles 2006). I was rather unsettled when I found what I identified as my own critical "insights" about indigenous justice not only reflected in activist discourse but also echoed in unexpected ways in government rhetoric and policy documents.

I saw something emergent, in particular the ways in which indigenous difference—indigeneity—in legal contexts was shifting in response to micro- and macro-level phenomena. Yet I was incapable of responding in the field in the way that Maurer prescribes: "an anthropology of emergence that is not content to settle for mere descriptive adequacy but that uses its objects to unsettle anthropological claims to knowledge" (2005, 4).

Unusable Data as Problematization

It is at this point that I would like to return to the concept of unusable data and the problem I briefly outlined in the introduction. My dissertation work was not, at least in a more traditional sense, ethnographically rich. Or at least it was not rich in the sense I imagined it. I did not end up using any interview transcripts. References to fieldnotes are infrequent and often oblique. I have no illustrative anecdotes that neatly encapsulate particular issues or give a full sense of the site (although I will note here for posterity that my first day of fieldwork at the provincial courthouse involved a too-close encounter with human fecal matter—read what you will into that). Nevertheless, the dissertation and the book that followed could not and would not have been written without these *unusable data* and the fieldwork experience that accompanied the collection of these data.

But how did such unusable data come to matter in the dissertation, to shape an orienting series of questions, to enable the exploration of particular phenomena? Or, to put it more bluntly, why and how do I insist on their centrality to my project and suggest their importance to the practice of contemporary ethnography itself?

A key part of contemporary anthropological research is the continuing theoretical-methodological exploration of the ever-malleable potentialities and limits of ethnography (e.g., Biehl et al. 2007; Ong and Collier 2005). Part of this exploration has included elaborations on Foucault's concept of problematization and the possibilities it offers to anthropological projects (and indeed to the project of anthropology itself) (see, e.g., Faubion 2001b; Rabinow 2005). According to Paul Rabinow, Foucault conceives of problematization as "the ensemble of discursive and non-discursive practices that make something enter into the play of true and false and constitute it as an object of thought (whether in the form of moral reflection, scientific knowledge, political analysis, and so on)" (Foucault 1984; cited in Rabinow 2005, 43). It is not, Foucault warns, "the representation of a pre-existent object nor the creation through discourse of an object that did not exist," but rather a dynamic process motivated by uncertainty and loss as a "result of difficulties in our previous way of understanding, acting, relating" (Foucault 1984; cited in Rabinow 2005, 43). The appeal of problematization as an analytical mode is that it allows ethnographers to move beyond a strict positivist/constructivist dichotomy, facilitating instead the charting of what James Faubion calls "a constellation of points of reference" (2001b, 89). Further, problematization allows for an explicit articulation of a "specific type of relationship forged between observer and the problematized situation" (Rabinow 2005, 45), one determined neither by a specious objectivism nor by a truncated reflexivity that never seems to penetrate the analysis that follows.

What I want to propose here is that my unusable data formed a key part of "a constellation of points of reference" that enabled the articulation of a particular problem, what I ultimately called "indigeneity in the courtroom." And, beyond the specific data themselves, the conditions and rationale of their unusability were part of this larger constellation. Thus, the unusable data generated in the field were in some ways transformed through the process of problematization.

"Like a Cockfight with a Court Stenographer": Indigeneity in the Courtroom

> Any assessment of the adequacy of a particular course of field-work...always hinges on the contribution to the resolution (if not the solution) of the questions that the fieldworker sets out to explore or encounters as he or she proceeds.

—James D. Faubion, *The Shadows and Lights of Waco* (2001a)

What was clear to me from my fieldwork experience is that politically progressive policies and programs did not necessarily result in a progressive politics. This is hardly a novel or startling revelation, but through the course of fieldwork and dissertation writing, I noticed that "the politics of recognition" in Native North America, especially in the realm of law, had particular logics but often very contradictory results. I became increasingly interested in the conditions of possibility that allowed for the emergence of *indigeneity*, of *indigenous difference*, as such a powerful cultural category at the end of the twentieth century. As Elizabeth Povinelli argues in *The Cunning of Recognition*, postcolonial political subjects are faced with a series of often contradictory impulses and forces operating on them, and indigenous subjects in particular must overcome this contradiction, this impasse, in order to satisfy the conditions of recognition. Povinelli's critique allows "for the possibility that liberalism is harmful not only when it fails to live up to its ideals, but when it approaches them" (2002, 12–13). This insight helped me to "move beyond the outrage" and allowed rather for an examination of what Povinelli calls the "intercalation of the politics of culture with the culture of capital" (2002, 17).

While I was in the field, I was following a series of contentious legal cases in addition to my daily fieldwork, cases involving land and resource claims, treaty negotiations, free-market valuation of indigenous property, and indigenous healing circles for white Catholic bishops. With the exception of the last case, any connections among these cases and the specific questions of justice I was pursuing did not seem especially strong. In fact, I began writing a paper about an odd property case in Vancouver that I initially imagined as a piece separate from the dissertation. Yet, as I worked in parallel—on the article and the dissertation—I began to note connections in the underlying logic that motivated these phenomena. It is at this point that indigeneity itself emerged as a problem, as the line that linked a constellation of points. Indigeneity mattered in legal settings in a way that was not present thirty or forty years before. Indigenous legal subjects were materialized in some contexts, but not in others.

Law, then, was the conceptual nexus through which the foci of my dissertation came into connection with each other. Law was both social phenomenon
and research imaginary; a "semi-stable" point of departure, one which articulates
"points for intersecting levels of analysis as well as intersecting persons or groups"
(Landecker 2002, 1). Law generally, and legal documents in particular, thus became
for me a broader way for organizing and interpreting what I had observed "on the
ground." It worked almost like a topographical overlay that *disciplined* (in multiple senses) both the excesses of fieldwork and the literal absence of usable ethnographic data from traditional fieldwork methods. As Hannah Landecker notes:

> law is a relatively stable conduit between multiple sites. Law is rea-
> sonably stable and wonderfully documented, like a cockfight with a
> court stenographer, a place for the formal stylized discrete accretion of
> norms, conventions and taboos, and their challenges. The precedents,
> formal analogies and metaphors by which law makes decisions on the
> present—or the novel object—on the basis of particular pasts is a for-
> malized abstraction of many of the shifts and negotiations that anthro-
> pologists would like to track. (2002, 1)

Ultimately, the dissertation—and the book that followed (Hamilton 2008a)—
focused on the problem of "indigeneity in the courtroom": When and how does
indigeneity in its various iterations—cultural, social, political, economic, even
genetic—matter in a legal sense? When does it not? (By indigeneity, I mean not
the specific ontologies and epistemologies of peoples living throughout Native
North America, but rather the political, economic, and legal articulations of
indigenous difference and the discursive and material effects of these articulations
in postcolonial settler nations.) In a way, then, I was fundamentally concerned
with the making of certain kinds of subjects, especially in the realm of the legal.
The point I want to stress here is that the specific questions that emerged in the
frustrations and seeming failure of doctoral fieldwork and in the process of dissertation writing were fundamentally informed by an ethics of unusable data.

From Indigeneity to Ethics: Postdoctoral Fieldwork

**This suggests that it is necessary to treat the intersections and gaps
between disciplines as its own ethnographic zone, to observe how
particular actors make claims for themselves and their disciplines
through and against disciplinary accounts and the borrowing of one
another's methods.**

—Annelise Riles, "Anthropology, Human Rights, and Legal Knowledge" (2006)

Following graduation in 2004, utterly convinced that my dissertation would linger, collecting dust on a shelf at the Rice University library, I was looking to define a new project. A friend of mine who worked as a bioethicist called to tell me about a job opening at Baylor College of Medicine, a prestigious medical school located across the street from Rice in the Texas Medical Center. In her phone message, she said there was a project starting, something about "Indians and genetics," and that I should call about it right away. To make a long story short, I was hired soon after to work on an NIH-sponsored project entitled "Indian and Hindu Perspectives on Genetic Variation," a project tasked with engaging "members of Indian communities in the Houston metropolitan area to elicit their perspectives on genetic research and the International HapMap Project."

I must confess that my original interest in the project came from the mistaken belief that the NIH-sponsored project concerned *American Indians* as opposed to people from the Indian subcontinent (yet another Columbus-inspired moment of confusion). Nevertheless, after hearing about the specific dimensions of the project and recognizing the opportunity to get paid well to do interesting research, I signed on. For two and a half years, I was officially a "Senior Research Coordinator," a kind of ad hoc postdoc (but with slightly better pay and terrific medical insurance) with "some" administrative duties, although the nature of that "some" was something that I constantly negotiated.

In addition to the ethnographic dimensions of the project, "Indian and Hindu Perspectives on Genetic Variation" was also tasked with collecting blood samples from Houston-based Gujuratis for the HapMap, an international public endeavor that proposed to map human genetic variation among different populations in an attempt to provide researchers with a tool to uncover genetic causes for common diseases as well as to identify individual responses to therapeutic interventions. The HapMap was premised on the (not uncontroversial) idea that meaningful genetic variability exists among populations and that this variability is linked to human health and disease in significant ways. Some have argued that HapMap is the successor to the very controversial Human Genome Diversity Project (HGDP) of the 1990s, another project intended to map human genetic variation, but one which has been subject to trenchant critiques including widespread concerns about the "ethics" of such a project. Thus, "ethics" has been an integral part of the discourse surrounding HapMap from its inception, and it is in this milieu that ethnography itself lands smack in the middle of a complex structure of expectations: ethnography and its role in "consulting members of the community" about the ethics of human genetic variation research in general and the ethics of blood collection more specifically. The larger question that remains unanswered (and, to a certain extent, unasked) is for what does ethnography come to stand in contexts like HapMap research?[1]

I was hired as a professional anthropologist, more specifically as a professional ethnographer—as someone who *does* and *has done* ethnography. Beyond the collection of project-specific ethnographic data, I treated my job as an ethnographic enterprise from the beginning, especially in terms of teasing out some of the relationships between professional bioethics and anthropology in the context of big science. In a contrast with my apprentice fieldwork, however, I stayed in Houston. I was paid to work. I sat in on meetings and classes. I had informal conversations. I interviewed informants. I did archival research. I took fieldnotes. I walked around the medical center. And, while I no longer had time to take dance classes, the fieldwork-induced paranoia was virtually nonexistent.

My point here is that the ethnographic techniques I deployed in my postdoctoral project were quite similar to those I deployed in my doctoral project. Yet this ethnographic experience was fuller, the questions were better, the data were richer, the writing was easier. What changed? Beyond the substantive shift in focus, beyond a kind of predictable maturation, what distinguishes my current ethnographic orientations, practices, and experiences from earlier ones? And what can a juxtaposition of these very different fieldwork contexts reveal about the norms, the assumptions, and indeed the expectations, that differently shape apprentice and professional ethnography?

My postdoctoral project is in some senses a study of ethics experts and the constitution of ethical expertise within the framework of big science. But it is also a project about the ways in which ethnography and ethnographic expertise are being picked up in nonanthropological contexts. In particular, how does ethnography encounter ethics and how is it deployed in a way that, I would argue, is supposed to make the practice of ethics more accountable, more rigorous, more *ethical*? Unlike *Indigeneity in the Courtroom,* my postdoctoral research is very much a work-in-progress. Because this research is still more or less unfolding and its main foci are still being defined, I include here brief sketches of three related projects still in preliminary stages as examples of how I am approaching these questions.

Project One: Revitalizing Difference in the HapMap

In this first iteration, I have been pursuing ethnographic research on the HapMap and its bioethical formations in a project called "The Vitality of Difference."

---

1. For a beautifully rendered discussion of some of the dimensions of cross-disciplinary collaborative work on this project, see Deepa Reddy's chapter, "Caught! The Predicaments of Ethnography in Collaboration" (chap. 4, this volume).

As this title indicates, I focus on the production and mobilization of difference—especially but not exclusively racial difference—at the nexus of large-scale gene mapping and human disease research. I explore how categories of race and ethnicity are configured as biologically meaningful and therefore as having important diagnostic and therapeutic implications for population health. My project centers on the questions why and how, and to what effect, human difference—including understandings of race, ethnicity, ancestry, genetic variation, and population—has come to occupy a central place in our current understandings of health and biomedicine, particularly in the intersecting fields of population genetics and population health. I further explore the ways in which racial difference is made viable through appeal to an ethics and a pragmatics that attempt to reorder difference along more politically palatable lines.

Project Two: Ethical Practice, Ethical Substance?: Ethics and the Politics of Human Genetic Variation Research

This work explores processes by which new translations of value are created, especially those that apply to the production, circulation, and configuration of *substance* in a broad anthropological sense. What kinds of agents, knowledge, and expertise are mobilized around translations of value? What kinds of scientific and social logics about the essential substances of human nature and personhood underlie various kinds of scientific knowledge production? Specifically, this work traces the emergence of certain forms of ethical practice in the controversial area of population genetics. It asks how certain practices and processes are newly translated as ethical around the collection of genetic substances in the realm of human genetic variation research.

The role of ethics and what constitutes ethical practice became prime sites of negotiation in the aftermath of the HGDP, which in part sought to collect biological samples from "vanishing" and "isolated" indigenous populations to use as points of reference for mapping the evolution of humankind. Indigenous and other activist groups vehemently objected to the HGDP, arguing that it was potentially exploitative of both individuals and communities. That opposition precipitated a major shift in the role of ethics in population genetics research. This work traces some of the ethical innovations that emerged around the HGDP controversy and demonstrates how these have been translated in more recent human genetic variation research projects including the public International Haplotype Map and the private Genographic Project (sponsored by IBM and National Geographic). It then examines the effects that such translations have on the meanings of genetic substances themselves in the politicized contexts of such endeavors.

Project Three: Ethnography, Ethics, and Culturally Appropriate Informed Consent

In this third work, I explore the ways in which traditionally anthropological/ ethnographic methods have been revalued and reconfigured in the context of research ethics, especially in the context of its quintessential object: the informed consent document. Usually conceived as a document that explains in writing the risks and benefits of a particular research program to potential participants, informed consent has become ubiquitous in all areas of the academy. Informed consent, in both its idealized and practical forms, has long been subject to critique, anthropological and other. Anthropological critiques, in particular, have often focused on the serious limitations inhering in traditional informed consent documents and their accompanying practices. For instance, what are the underlying epistemological assumptions that motivate conceptions of just who the "subjects" (or objects) of research are? How is it that informed consent documents are marked by an abstracted temporality that extends the boundaries of consent beyond the possibility of informed decision making and thus rely on a truncated sense of the *it* that is being consented *to*? Other disquieting aspects of traditional informed consent include the absence of meaningful consent in instrumental and legalistic documents and the potential for informed consent to practices to mask embodied processes of negotiation and perhaps coercion. Because of such concerns, many social and cultural anthropologists and indeed many research participants treat informed consent as a necessary evil, as exclusively instrumental in nature, and thus as separate from "research" itself.

While I must confess to feeling certain sympathy toward such critiques, it is by now axiomatic that the research process in general, and ethnographic work in particular, cannot be so easily compartmentalized. Thus, as an orienting framework for this work, I juxtapose my critical orientation toward such documents (as cursory, instrumental, and overly formalistic) with my own ethnographic participation in an NIH-sponsored collaborative project, one of whose goals is "to develop culturally appropriate educational materials, research-recruitment strategies and informed-consent instruments." I do not mean to construe these positions as inherently contradictory, but rather as potentially productive, as a moment wherein the production of "culturally appropriate informed consent" can be explored within the context of the production of anthropological knowledge. With careful attention to how ethnographic knowledge and methods are used and produced within the context of seeking "culturally appropriate" informed consent materials for community-based genetic sample collection, I explore larger questions about the nature of the ethical and its relationship to the ethnographic.

I argued earlier in this piece that the configuration of my postdoctoral research would have been impossible without the problem(atization) of unusable data that I confronted in my dissertation research. Because of the substantive differences between them, I am often asked to explain the relationship between my dissertation project and my current research. The easy answer is that both focus on how and to what effect concepts of difference function in powerful institutions. The real similarity, however, is a methodological orientation that approximates Foucault's problematization: a process of creative articulation that explores relationships among formalized ethics, anthropology, and the life sciences as "a constellation of points of reference." Precisely because of their unusability, the data in my apprentice project necessitated a different kind of critical-ethical relationship to the associated processes of fieldwork and of post-field ethnographic writing. A course of recovery forced me to ask a different set of questions and to begin to envision indigeneity as something more than and beyond questions of rights and recognition; in other words, I was compelled to articulate indigeneity as a *problem*. When I began working on the ELSI-HapMap Project, the problematization of bioethics and the life sciences was my point of departure, rather than simply focusing on questions of scientific accuracy and the internal consistency of the ethics of informed consent.

The substantive areas of inquiry in my apprentice project (indigeneity, law) seem rather different from those of my postdoctoral research (human genetic variation research, ethics). But as Faubion reminds us, "In a less conventional understanding of the project, what we might be seeing is often an extension and elaboration of the parameters of the same question pursued, because it must be pursued, in other places than those of its previous pursuit" (chap. 7, this volume). Attention to unusable data and the problematization of "indigeneity in the courtroom" led me to a concern with the "vitality of difference" in the fields of ethics and human genetics (see, e.g., Hamilton 2008b).

In response to my observation that fieldwork this time around felt like a much easier and much richer experience, one of my mentors remarked to me that this was not simply a result of being in an easier site; rather, she told me, had this current project been my dissertation project, I would have felt "equally lost." In reviewing my early fieldnotes from 2004 for this chapter, I can track my own somewhat conventional anthropological struggle to make sense of my surroundings, to become fluent in the languages of my informants (molecular biology and bioethics), and to immerse myself in the unfamiliar professional culture of a medical college. More important, however, I can track my attempts to avoid a kind of distracting frustration with the rhetoric and methods of bioethics as well as a cynical knee-jerk reaction to sweeping and unproblematized scientific claims. I also became wiser to the seduction of outrage. Although less fraught on a daily basis, the debates surrounding the HapMap and human genetic variation research more generally are nevertheless deeply politicized, especially in terms of their relationship to issues of race and racism, intellectual property, scientific research and "benefit-sharing," and commercialization and commodification. This new wisdom certainly doesn't preclude critique, but rather insists that a critical account of the social emerge from a place other than mere outrage and further that it extend to include "an accounting for the enmeshment of the observer and the observed, together with their mutually reinforcing, yet oftentimes incongruent, knowledge formations" (Maurer 2005, 4).

Acknowledgments

My thanks to participants in the "Turns and Folly in Apprentice Ethnography" conference at Irvine in 2006, especially to George Marcus and Jim Faubion for their support throughout. I am also indebted to Hannah Landecker, Chris Kelty, Jacob Speaks, and Deepa Reddy for their continuing collaboration and conversation.

4

CAUGHT!

The Predicaments of Ethnography in Collaboration

Deepa S. Reddy

The Field in Pieces

> **Then lunch with a fellow and talk—about what?—In the afternoon: I lay down for a quarter of an hour, and started work—*bwaga'u* business. At about 5 stopped, was fed up. Excited, impossible to concentrate. Ate pineapple, drank tea, wrote E.R.M., took a walk; intensive gymnastics. Gymnastics should be a time of concentration and solitude; something that gives me an opportunity to escape from the [blacks] and my own agitation. Supper with a fellow who told me stupid anecdotes, not interesting at all.**
>
> —Bronislaw Malinowski, *A Diary in the Strict Sense of the Term* (1976)

In this and other passages from Malinowski's posthumously published diary, the lore and allure of *in situ* fieldwork dissipate variously into a sense of meandering boredom, agitation, irritation, preoccupation with other fascinations, work, the need for escape. Such narratives about the field and fieldwork, and there have been many such since Malinowski, render even the most mythic conceptualizations of ethnographic fieldwork incoherent—not without meaning, that is, but disjointed, comprising parts that must be methodically arranged to be made sense of. With "villages" and "communities" now either dissipated by their own transformations within nation-states or rejected as questionable projections of wholeness by anthropologists, it seems less and less possible to speak of the field in a single breath, as a single place to which the lone anthropologist travels to undergo his/her rites of professional passage. So I am interested here in the "field" as an almost random assemblage of sites that come into coherence through the processes of fieldwork itself: the field as deterritorialized and reterritorialized, as it were, by the questions brought to bear on it in the course of research. This process necessarily entails much movement, as much between physical locations closer or farther apart as between ideological positionings or frames of reference (as I call them). Tracking this movement, understanding the relationships between sites, one's own positioning within each, and the demands placed on the ethnographer coming-into-being—these, I believe are the means by which the field is made, quite alongside the objects of study that it yields then to ethnographic attention.

To explain this further in what follows, I use the example of my most recent ethnographic work on a NIH/NHGRI-sponsored "community consultation" project to research "Indian and Hindu perspectives on genetic variation research" in Houston (henceforth the ELSI-HapMap project, ELSI being the acronym for Ethical, Legal, and Social Issues in genetics). I reflect only in passing on first fieldwork simply because the links between my prior work on women's activism and identitarian politics in India and the ELSI-HapMap project are tenuous, at best. The topics were radically different, to be sure, but more: while I chose and crafted my dissertation project, going about it in some fairly traditional ways, ELSI-HapMap in some senses chose, identified, and pinned me. The "just do it" directive I instinctively followed in first fieldwork was grossly insufficient for the second, and was replaced by a highly organized and constantly vetted method—not so much because I wished it so, but because that was what being an anthropologist at the interface with science and medicine seemed to demand. ELSI-HapMap forced a rethinking of what ethnography entailed by having to explain what ethnography wasn't—or, conversely, of having to explain its possibilities at the outer edges of other disciplinary approaches. Quite possibly I could not have done this were it not for the prior experience of first fieldwork, but ELSI-HapMap was also a "first" in its way. Through it, by becoming an anthropologist among bioethicists and geneticists and social scientists interested in the study of "science" in motion, I learned of anthropology anew: of the "classic model" and all it was expected to produce, and of "how the authority of the discipline as craft comes to live on" (Marcus, this volume) almost in spite of the discipline itself. ELSI-HapMap was my means of "looking back" on ethnographic praxis, of finding the "anchor of lore in practice" while in the thick of collaborative research with the biosciences (Marcus, this volume). In this sense, a reflection on my second project seems far more pertinent to the themes of this essay and of this volume than an account of the movement from first to second.

My role in ELSI-HapMap was largely pre-written—with some flexibility and room for innovation, but still largely given, and drawing my expertise as Indianist specifically into the frame of a bioethics initiative. Not only because this is urban anthropology par excellence and Houston is a vast, sprawling metropolis with a large and diverse Indian community, then, but even more as a result of the framing of this research as interdisciplinary and collaborative, the field seemed already in pieces: a bric-a-brac assortment of people, institutions, interests, ideologies, skepticisms, locations, and expertise all forced into specific modes of contact with one another. And the field demanded piecing together via various prescriptive collaborative means, all toward an end—"understanding Indian and Hindu perspectives on genetic variation research"—that was at once crystal clear and frustratingly unfathomable.

The narrative below follows the evolution of this project with an eye to marking the disjointed character of the field and fieldwork that then calls for particular kinds of professional collaboration: indeed, gives older models of "community studies" a new lease on life and pressures particular kinds of "classic" ethnographic praxis into being. Collaboration in this context is both enabling and limiting, I suggest, but is nevertheless the overriding means by which a heavily deterritorialized and disjointed field is paradoxically given a (rhizomic) coherence of a kind, and new objects of ethnographic study acquire definition. Ethnographic "method" comes into being somewhere in the interstices of such a field in pieces, a product of interlocking expectations generated of *and* by anthropology. It is the emergence of such method alongside its ethnographic objects out of a bric-a-brac terrain jointed by the mechanisms of collaboration that I explore.

The Inherited Field

The charge of the ELSI-HapMap study in Houston, as I have often described it to Indians in Houston, is fairly straightforward. The NIH would like to collect blood samples from 140 Indian Gujaratis to add data (and presumably depth) to an already existing Haplotype map, which is a strategized cataloging of human genetic variation.[1] The original "HapMap" was compiled from four sets

---

1. The International HapMap Project (http://www.hapmap.org) is a collaboration among scientists in Japan, China, Nigeria, the United Kingdom, and the United States, formally launched in 2002. It goal is to create a haplotype map of the human genome, to describe common patterns of human DNA sequence variation. Differences in individual bases of the DNA sequence are called single nucleotide polymorphisms (SNPs or "snips"). Sets of nearby SNPs on the same chromosome tend to be inherited in blocks, and their pattern on this inherited block is known as a haplotype.

of samples collected internationally and named thus to indicate their sources: Yoruba in Ibadan, Nigeria; Japanese in Tokyo; Han Chinese in Beijing; and CEPH (Utah residents with ancestry in Northern and Western Europe). To these originary four were to be added a longer list that included samples from African Americans in Oklahoma; the Luhya in Webuye, Kenya; communities of Mexican origin in Los Angeles; Denver (Colorado) metropolitan Chinese community; Tuscans in Sesto Fiorentino, Italy; and lastly Gujarati Indians in Houston. The relationship between the different data-gathering phases of the HapMap project has never been entirely clear; in fact, the project was announced to be complete in October 2005, making the data that we were at the time yet to collect from Indian Gujaratis a supplement, at best, to the completed HapMap. In any event, the Houston project has benefited from being last in line by having the flexibility to precede any request for blood samples with a full two years of ethnographic inquiry—much longer than the time allowed any of the other constituent projects, as the urgency to collect samples had almost entirely lifted.

But what was this period of ethnographic inquiry supposed to achieve? This being a "community consultation" initiative, the objectives were, all things considered, clear. We were to consult the Indian community in Houston over the question of their participation in HapMap, tracking everything from their understanding of genetics to their interests in genetic and biomedical research, from their decision to participate (or not) in the creation of "culturally appropriate" informed consent documents, and the nature of the returns they might expect for having contributed vials of blood. The reasons why the NIH/NHGRI would support such extensive community consultation is of course a story in its own right that deserves more attention than I can afford here (although I will return to this theme a little later in the essay). Essentially, community review is a means to better anticipate and so circumvent the sorts of controversies that have dogged other blood sample-collection initiatives, the most notorious of which was of course the Human Genome Diversity Project (HDGP). In some ways a direct heir to this contentious past, the HapMap project frames itself as an ELSI initiative, meant to focus first on the Ethical, Legal, and Social Issues raised by research in genomics, meant not to presume the unilateral support of communities and to

---

Blocks may contain large numbers of SNPs, but only a few "tag SNPs" are sufficient to uniquely identify haplotypes in a block. Such reasoning makes it possible to reduce the number of SNPs needed to examine the entire genome from 10 million common SNPs to 500,000 tag SNPs. Genome scans that seek to find genes that affect diseases will therefore become both more cost-effective and efficient. The International HapMap Project itself does not attempt to correlate genetic variants with diseases, but to make information about variation available to other researchers who may then carry out disease-specific research programs. All samples are stored at and distributed from the Coriell Institute in Camden, N.J.

move forward with sample collection only with some clear sense of community consent. As such, the project has a history that is quite independent of anything specifically Indian—but always the aura of possible controversy, the sense that things could go terribly wrong if procedures are not followed, the right questions not asked. The task at hand, under the watchful eye of the Institutional Review Boards (IRBs) involved, is nothing short of risk assessment and potentially also that of fire-fighting.

Here enters something called "Culture" with a capital "C": Chinese Culture, Mexican Culture, Masaai Culture, Indian Culture, the Culture of a definite People. I should note that not all the HapMap community review projects included anthropologists, and not all placed particular emphasis on the collection of ethnographic data, but there was a definite "Culture" with which to contend, nonetheless. This concept was both intimately familiar and strikingly alien to me. I knew and recognized it, of course, as the presumed object of ethnographic research: variously a source of fascination, a demarcation of difference, a cordoned-off territory, a thing to revere, contemplate, catalog, or champion. But here also was Culture *operationalized* (Kelty 2004) by ELSI, rendered into a usable something that is then amenable to deployment as a guide for procedural ethics in genetic research. And I, it would appear, had been recruited not as independent observer but as facilitator of the process that was to investigate culture and render it a workhorse for bioethics, with the beneficiaries being (my) community on the one hand, and researchers on the other.

I will have more to say about my positioning between groups and their respective interests below. For now I want only to note that the ELSI-HapMap project gave me a role in the operationalization of culture, as an interpreter-translator of Indian ideas into usable material for ethics that could, say, filter into informed consent documents so as to "appropriately" inform, or hurt no cultural sentiments in the research process. My assigned role was that of cultural broker in a transactional chain that led from something called "community" to something called "genetics."[2] Certainly, this was unlike any role I had ever been handed before, as I was being called upon to put culture (and my cultural expertise) to "good" use and, as I would quickly discover, also harness my position as an area academic for the betterment of *my* community. The fact that I am Indian was not incidental to either role. Quite the contrary, it had a use-value, a (presumed) closeness to both "culture" and "community," with the very position of the native

---

2. And not just my role, to be sure: each of us involved with the ELSI-HapMap study in Houston played broker to greater or lesser degrees. This said, my "ethnic background" shaped my position in ways that set my discomforts and commitments somewhat apart from others in our group, as I am about to suggest.

anthropologist taken to set the objects of classic ethnography into motion—this time not merely for the sake of ethnographic understanding, but rather in the specific interests of ELSI.

In short, the inherited field turned me, and everyone else in our research group, into cultural producers of the very kind whose work I might otherwise have been interested in scrutinizing.[3] For how else might we have completed the task of generating interest in genetic research (and our study in particular), perhaps producing educational materials or just generally keeping the community informed about the project? How would we, in all good conscience, staff booths at community events and recruit volunteers for interviews and focus groups without communicating some sense of the worthiness of our efforts? The choice was between being invested and being disingenuous, and neither was a comfortable position, for if one allied me wholly with ELSI research or pitted me straightforwardly against it, the other entirely masked my professional affiliation and commitments. Perhaps being overly sensitive to the comments of colleagues who somewhat disparagingly named HapMap the unfortunate successor of the Human Genome Diversity Project, I was also acutely affected by the atmosphere of deep skepticism that prevailed among many (although not all) scholars engaged in the social/ethnographic study of science—for whom any truly ethical position vis-à-vis genomics would have to be a skeptical, critical, and distanciated one. Chris Kelty (this volume) notes a certain anthropological predilection for exclusivity, the avowed professional interest "in remaining anthropologists rather than joining in and becoming part of their field" for the sake of maintaining "critical distance," which I would argue has considerable impact on shaping the field.

Indeed, our own wariness as researchers involved (implicated?) in the ELSI-HapMap study cannot be underestimated in this regard. Ours was a project steeped in what Mike Fortun has called an "ethics of suspicion," an anticipation of everything going awry especially when genetics are involved (Fortun 2005). This was a formulation we quite embraced, in NIH/NHGRI workshop presentations about what concerns and risks we *didn't* find among Indians in Houston, in our own insistence that the sampling phase of the research *would not* proceed without active community involvement and support, even in the assessment that our findings (such as a healthy regard for Knowledge) were "anticlimactic," as my research assistant Corrie Manigold once described them. From this perspective, there were significant risks involved in taking on more-or-less close, rather than

---

3. Indeed, we were each interviewed by Jenny Reardon for her own NSF-sponsored research, entitled "Paradoxes of Participation: The Status of 'Groups' in Liberal Democracies in an Age of Genomics," in June 2006.

obviously distanciated, roles within the ELSI-HapMap project. The field that unfolded was thus a polarized one overdetermined by critique in which ELSI research was exactly as James Watson imagined: a move to preempt the critics (cited in Fortun 2005, 162).

So there are two meanings of the word "caught" as the title of this essay that are both relevant to understanding the field and its formation: the sense of being embedded in a nexus of relationships that each makes its own demands, but also *found out,* caught red-handed with hands in cookie jars as it were, taking the multiple demands seriously, allowing ethnography to become a tool in the hands of other interests that are properly the objects of critique, and then needing to explain the undoing and redoing of ethnography's and one's own complicities within these schemes. The point is not so much that ethnography can be professionally risky business, but that the terrains in which it is produced and in which it acquires meaning are many and can hardly be avoided, and that an accounting of the demands of each of these is what pressures research into existence. The inherited field positioned me, with not much apparent wiggle room, on the one hand in a research community comprised of bioethicists, physical anthropologists, population geneticists, legal historians, and sociologists and, on the other, amid a "community" comprised of various and sundry religio-cultural organizations, and of course the people running these organizations from diverse personal and professional backgrounds. Because I found myself the point of articulation between these two loosely defined "groups," much more so than my colleagues for being both Indian and Indianist, the sense of divergent commitments to divergent sets of interests (on both sides) made the work consuming, both personally and professionally. I longed frequently for Malinowski's pineapple, tea, gymnastics, and other comparable modes of escape.

Collaboration as Method

This distinct sense of discomfort generated by a particular kind of positioning within the field alerted me to what I have come to see as a characteristic of the field itself: its disjointed nature, its sometimes overwhelming sense of being a collection of segments—places and positions and commitments—disconnected and therefore in need of ethnographic grounding. I had encountered such a field before in my dissertation research, in tracing expressions of Hindu political identity from middle-class Hindu homes to political party offices and media debates, ethnicist rhetoric becoming a resource for new critique and refashioned feminist identity in the spaces of women's groups and broadly Left politics in India. No position, in no place, was entirely comfortable for me as (Indian, Hindu, middle-class, upper-caste, even NRI or non-resident Indian) anthropologist; being in any one involved a level of complicity, with all the ethical heaviness that complicity inherently implies.[4] Within the frame of my "first fieldwork," I sought to link a series of sites that were engaged in rather heated debate with one another, in states of mutually reinforcing outrage, as it were—but that linking was an after-the-fact means to make an argument and thus to render the field analytically intelligible (cf. Hamilton, this volume; Reddy 2006). In other words, it was not a precondition of fieldwork itself, and it made my apprentice fieldwork extraordinarily burdensome, pressing me to become a veritable contrarian, as Jim Faubion once remarked. The field in pieces was an exacting place to be, as each site demanded allegiance, to greater or lesser extents, and tolerated deviations only marginally. Within this there were models of collaboration, to be sure: the Women's Studies Research Center Anveshi's "Law Committee," which brought together scholars and lawyers with a shared interest in indigeneity and human rights, and the Women's Resource Center Asmita's creation of spaces in which women with different needs and different interests could meet and work and interact, to offer just two examples. But there were as many other possibilities of collaboration that were foreclosed, thanks to impenetrable histories of difficult personal relations and differences in political approaches, so much so that any account of women's activism in the city, including my own, was subject to more or less stringent critique. Negotiating different sets of expectations, demands, and politico-scholarly positionings was not merely impossible in first fieldwork, it was professionally risky business: I doubt very much that I could go back now to Hyderabad, should I want to, to pick up all the threads of my dissertation project with equal ease.

In the ELSI-HapMap work, too, there is a series of very distinct sites that come into dialogue with one another. By this time in the history of genetic research, however, heated criticisms of sample-collection had given way to a set of procedures that replace the charges and dilemmas of complicity with a methodology called "collaboration" that shapes fieldwork. Let me clarify. Collaboration here is not so much the possibility of working jointly with informants and interlocutors (cf. Lassiter 2005a, 2005b), although that is never precluded, but is at once a recognition of disciplinary distinctiveness, specializations and expert cultures, a form of professionalism and a method by which to tackle matters that straddle the boundaries of science, ethics, culture, legality, religion, and more. Collaboration does not appear in our grant application as an explicitly rationalized research strategy, nor is it a recognized "method" of ethnographic research. By

---

4. The ethnographic literature on such uncomfortable alliances suggests that such experiences are not exceptional. See, for instance, the essays in the 1998 (7:2) issue of *Science as Culture*, guest edited by Kim Fortun and Todd Cherkasky.

the time of our research, however, it is a presumed strategy of turning disciplinary "pluralism into a strategic resource" (Fortun and Cherkasky 1998, 146): of hitching different forms of expertise to a single carriage and therefore training each, in more or less significant ways, to make sure the carriage does ultimately get pulled. Differences matter here, far more than commonalities, although they must somehow be aligned to become meaningful means to larger, predetermined ends. The identity of fieldworker as contrarian, which had been so useful in situating myself in the fraught fields of Indian feminist activism and religious politics, was unnecessary here, even counterproductive. What mattered far more now was disciplinary particularity, the recognized value of disciplinary difference.

The unease of recognizing, valuing, and committing to labor across disciplinary difference (all of which Fortun and Cherkasky see as inherent to collaboration) has at least one important methodological outcome that I want to highlight here. I have occasionally been struck at the relief with which anthropologists sometimes approach one another at consortium gatherings or other interdisciplinary meetings as though discovering long-lost comrades in the embattled fields of expertise, the given designation "Anthropologist" apparently obviating all intradisciplinary differences in approach and training. By identifying Anthropology as the key to "Culture," and thus as *the* discipline to bridge the social and the biological sciences via the conduits of "ethics" (cf. Marcus 2002a), collaborations between the biological and "human" sciences also generate "Anthropology" to the extent that they generate certain specific expectations of what Anthropologists exclusively *do*. For one thing, as I have said above, Anthropology is charged with operationalizing knowledge about Culture. But how is it that Anthropologists are to gather their data so as to preserve the uniqueness of their contributions? Not so much through interviews, which are common to other disciplines, not so much through other forms of face-to-face contact with people, but primarily through something called "participant observation." The method seems to require both much justification and no explanation at all: How quantifiable data will be extracted from "hanging out" and naturalistic observation, how bullet-point ends will be met by such meandering means certainly bears spelling out. The method itself, however, as somehow self-evidently a form of "cultural immersion" seems to require little further rationalization. In this, "participant observation" becomes virtually synonymous with "fieldwork" in Anthropology, a pithy, catch-all phrase to capture the uniqueness of ethnographic method and, indeed, of Anthropology itself. It also becomes (oddly) a sort of disciplinary defense, a sign of the value and the esoteric impermeability of the discipline that protects the Anthropologist's place at the collaborative, not to mention financially lucrative, tables of ELSI research. It becomes the reason for the collaboration and simultaneously the means by which ethnography produces value for ethics in science. If collaboration as methodology generates some of the connective tissue between the diverse disciplines brought into dialogue through ELSI research, then, it does so also by generating select tropes that come to stand in for what ethnography concretely *is*.

Here I should add that few other community consultation projects made such room for "participant observation" in their research protocols. Indeed, other anthropologists I met at NIH/NHGRI-sponsored workshops on community consultation remarked that we were lucky to have had even such support for ethnographic method in our collaborative exercise. In most other projects, focus groups and interviews represented primary modes of data collection. Qualitative research, broadly conceived, stood in for ethnographic fieldwork, involving ethnographers simply as skilled practitioners of qualitative research techniques. Even focus groups—a methodology employed in market research far more than in classic ethnography—become ethnographic by association with the qualitative. Anthropology and its practitioners are yet again transformed in accordance with the needs of ELSI research.

The object of research, it bears restating, is given and clearly so: understand community perspectives on genetics (for the sake of capturing risks and needs), develop "culturally appropriate" recruitment strategies, develop "culturally appropriate" consent documents, and—almost as an afterthought, although a hugely crucial one—collect 140 blood samples from Indian Gujaratis. With an apparently definite "Indian and Hindu" Culture in play, the outcomes of this research for the NIH/NHGRI are anything but elusive. Anthropology in this context is an instrument, a stepping-stone, the means by which to mobilize Culture for the sake of (bio)ethics and then in the interests of Science. And, precisely as a means to some other nonanthropological end, the means of ethnography, which are its *in situ* methods with their qualitative emphasis, are far more important than its modes of, say, analysis, which also could be said to give the discipline its unique stamp. The collective labor of collaboration at this stage of research is not primarily to establish the NIH/NHGRI's goals, which other collaborations (such as that of the HapMap Consortium) have already established. The collective labor of collaboration at this stage is primarily to establish the means by which these goals are best achieved, and to implement these, with sometimes less, sometimes more emphasis on ethnography itself. Anthropology is reduced, as a result, to its classic fascination with "Culture" as object, and to its classic method in the form of "participant observation," its qualitative emphasis. In short, Anthropology is expected (largely) to perform either a prior or distilled version of itself.

It is not a coincidence that such oddly classic formations as "Culture" and "participant observation" become the emblematic of a fetishized ethnography precisely as "culture" (as object of study) and field methods have been filtering through successive decades of disciplinary transformations. Nor is it a coincidence, I think, that "Culture," as a definite association with a people, comes to be methodologically mobilized within the HapMap project alongside the category "populations," which the International HapMap Consortium recognizes as scientifically valuable but culturally quite imprecise (2004, 469, Box 2). This is not to critique HapMap as much as it is to recognize that outmoded ideas of ethnography, "the way we *don't* do things any more," exist as a normative, even prescriptive, means to rein in other objects (like genetics) that are obviously and simultaneously in motion. "Collaboration" as the modus operandi of research done in such a framework necessarily generates stultified expectations of ethnographic praxis and makes Anthropology instrumental to the large promises of "world health" (International HapMap Consortium 2004, 474) while simultaneously yielding itself to new ethnographic inquiry. "Collaboration," too, like culture, is itself everywhere these days, itself a bit "too feel-good, too friendly a notion for the commitments, fights, and compromises that anthropologists frequently make in order to pursue some kind of conceptual innovation," too weak a word to describe the entanglements that are by now thoroughly commonplace in cultural anthropology: entanglements of complicity, responsibility, mutual orientation, suspicion and paranoia, commitment and intimate involvement, credit and authority, and the production of reliable knowledge for partially articulated goals set by organizations, institutions, universities, corporations, and governments (Kelty, this volume).

And yet it is precisely the friendly feel-good quality of the term that renders collaboration a stable methodological tool to "break up a problem into identifiable, exclusive chunks" that could, but don't necessarily, pave the way for "conceptual and theoretical work" (Kelty, this volume). Whether any conceptual and theoretical work in fact ensues, or whether collaboration is limited to what Kelty identifies as simply "coordination" is of course a separate question. One way or other, collaboration becomes the neatly coordinated way in which we *do* now do things; the messy and multiple entanglements of "collaboration" are fresh material for fresh ethnographic reflection, beyond the strict purview of collaborative method itself. The conceptual and methodological tools may be worn, outmoded, or weak for ethnographic purposes, in other words, but their utility is not lost in cross-disciplinary exercises like ELSI-HapMap, which serve then to bring new ethnographic objects into view. The operationalization of ethnography points, fairly ironically, into new ethnographic terrain.

But what exactly is my work beyond the operationalization of ethnographic knowledge? What does it mean to make HapMap an object of study, encrusted and contained as it is by worn-out notions of ethnography? The grant applications

I wrote as a doctoral student seeking funding for dissertation research compelled me to articulate responses to such questions at the outset. All the pages submitted for NIH review, by contrast, defined NIH goals and made those mine for three years, but configuring any ethnographic goals beyond was a separate task. As clear as my objectives were, as clearly defined as my methods, my own tasks were ill defined. Recognizing this fact in advance, the associate dean at my university asked me once if the HapMap research was really to be considered "research" for my own purposes; would it yield publications? I rationalized that it was all about positioning, buying myself access to a field that would invariably yield at least some research products. But, again, what was this field? And what did I plan to study in it?

Before I address these questions, however, I need first to tackle my given object of study, the "community," and a second mode of collaboration that also brings the disjointed field and its objects into better view.

"Community Consultation" as Collaboration

As with "culture," here again in "community" was a concept both intimately familiar and overwhelmingly alien: on the one hand, an object with presumed coherence, a focus of ethnographic expertise and, on the other, a group as diffuse and disparate as the city of Houston itself, a "beguiling linguistic fiction" with vague and elusive referents (Comaroff 2005, 127). Our relationship as a group of researchers to this "community" was given in the form of a methodology known as "community consultation." The community was to be engaged or consulted over issues related to genetics in order to discern risks, possible harms, and expectations of returns in advance of sample-collection. We were to investigate the following: (1) so as to establish a "Community Advisory Group" or some equivalent body to serve as liaison between the community and scientific bodies: Who speaks for the Indian community? Where are the sites of authority, how are authority and voice ordered? And (2) so as to assess interest and risk and manage both: What were the expectations of researchers and the entire process of sample-collection? "Community," presumably already intelligible in all its depth to anthropologists, especially native ones, was now to be made navigable for the sake of Ethics of ELSI.

"Community consultation," to offer only a cursory summary here, gains force and spurs further debate as a consequence of pressing demands for group/collective recognition, sovereignty, and identity, which "transform the context and substance of population genetics research" and in this way "help define what the 'principled conduct of research' might mean in practice" (Brodwin 2005, 148).

Community review has really only one foundational premise: that communities have a crucial stake in their futures and in their representations and therefore need to be at least aware of and ideally involved in research that involves them. This definitive premise emerges largely as a result of prior encounters between researchers and community, but is consolidated in the furor over the Human Genome Diversity Project, an international initiative to collect blood samples from select indigenous communities to anchor understandings of human evolution. Groups targeted for sampling sharply criticized the project for its biopiracy and biocolonialism, further demanding a role in defining research agendas, interpreting the facts, and acquiring the right to the (monetary) benefits of research itself. The overwhelming response to the HGDP as a globalized iteration of the politics of recognition rendered Human Population Genetics forever "politically vulnerable," as Paul Brodwin has remarked (2005, 148, 169), from that point on. The premise of community review, I wish to highlight here, is a particular response to this deepening sense of political vulnerability.

Community review—in other words, a prior notion of *community* and the premise for *review*—comes into our ELSI project in Houston, then, as a prepackaged preemptive move in anticipation of political assault. In this, it defines the nature of my contact with Indians in Houston and guides the sorts of questions to be addressed with them. Its mode is wholly representational, which is to say that participants must on some level identify with the principle of representation: the fact that some groups/cultures and some (genetic) populations and some views are underrepresented, and that efforts such as ours are meant to address these historic imbalances. So also does community review very nearly expect the communities in question to see themselves as politically vulnerable.[5] Ethics then can help negotiate the vulnerability of researchers, on the one hand, and the vulnerability of communities, on the other, by bringing these into dialogue: you tell me where your rights begin, so that I can determine where my nose ends, to reverse the popular dictum.

Not only is this model of ethics culturally and historically specific, it is also procedurally overdetermined. Virtually all our decisions as researchers were subject to IRB scrutiny. Confidentiality and consent needed to be explained over and over. Paperwork needed signing. Documentation of all sorts, from meeting minutes to mileage to assiduous quantification of "participant observation," needed generating. Decisions about from whom to collect samples needed to be made—Indians resident in Houston, who had had opportunities to participate in the consultation, or Indians visiting Houston for regional Gujarati congresses

---

5. But not too vulnerable: Native Americans were deliberately not selected for sampling because of their overwhelmingly critical response to the HGDP (International HapMap Consortium 2004).

with no prior knowledge of the community engagement phase of our work? Did the distinction matter? The infrastructures of ethics, precipitated in community review which was itself premised on a sense of political vulnerability, were the obvious and not-so-obvious guides to just about everything we could do.

The individuals with whom I met and interacted generally understood little of this background. Only those who had themselves been professionally involved in addressing health or other disparities among Houston's diverse racial/ethnic groups identified readily with the premises of our work. Most others variously ignored the consent documents, dismissed them as "legal mumbo-jumbo," or saw them simply as the constraints under which we (researchers) had to operate. The questions we were asking seemed valuable, but rather irrelevant to "the community"—a fact which was borne out by the reluctance of some institutions to lend our efforts time and support: "it's not that genetics isn't important," I was sometimes told or shown in so many polite ways, "it's just that we are not doctors. *Our priorities are different*"[6] (cf. Reddy n.d.).

On the other hand, there was also a model of "collaboration" actively advanced by many with whom I spoke. Less theorized than "community consultation," to be sure, there was nonetheless a discrete set of expectations that derived from a recognition of my position within the ELSI-HapMap group and that were therefore brought to bear on me and my work: sing at the temple, help organize the health fair, help organize community events, attend said events (held with relentless regularity in Houston), lend support to various and sundry cultural initiatives, become a "torchbearer" for the establishment of an India Studies program at the University of Houston (I was sent a poster mock-up that named me as one such), and more along similar lines. This was not collaboration as professionalism or interdisciplinary harnessing of differences, but collaboration as volunteerism, personal favor and personal commitment to something still abstractly assembled as "the community." Here, however, the concept was less anthropologically inflected, a much more straightforward reference to "Indians" as a diasporic group within the United States. And the pressing need for this community in diaspora was not so much representation, especially at a moment when Indian institutions, organizations, and activities are all but commonplace; Indians have

---

6. Of course the comment that "we are not doctors" assumes that only physicians would be interested in the outcomes of genetic research, an interesting perspective in its own right that is, oddly enough, well in line with the emphasis of the International HapMap Project on health-related outcomes. And the comment ignores the number of Indians who are themselves physicians in Houston alone, not to mention the clout of the AAPI (American Association of Physicians of Indian Origin) nationally. The simplest reading is that the comment is intended to limit further conversation, but it also points to the disjuncture between "community" and "genetic research" as entities that come to be allied only within the context of community engagement studies.

run for political office (in Sugarland, Texas, and elsewhere), and most measures of advancement indicate superlative progress. Certainly, there was almost none of the political, or for that matter cultural, vulnerability on which "community review" so centrally depends for its rationale. Rather, the pressing need—the vulnerability that impels action, as it were—was much more for links to be maintained with Indian cultural traditions, all the more as newer generations are born and grow up outside India, and for "Indian culture" (that construct again) to be somehow merged with mainstream American life.[7] Indeed, my own participation in the HapMap study gained meaning and value precisely because it fitted this mold: something done for the betterment and development of "the community." And because I was already so positioned, it followed logically that I should then contribute ever more for the sake of that abstract goal.

The expectation of service (for the community), I have argued elsewhere, itself rationalized community participation in our study, whether in its ethnographic or sample-collection phases. Giving time or blood was tantamount to serving some greater community good, in other words (cf. Reddy 2007). The fact that this expectation extended to me was logical, of course, and its pressing nature made me acutely aware of the distinctions between the two models of collaboration in operation here: one a "paid mandate" (which would after three years be neither paid nor a mandate), the other wholly voluntary, based on ethical commitments to communal ideals; one rooted in a history of research violations and controversies, the other moved by the imperatives of diaspora; one invested in the reformulated and procedural "Ethics" of ELSI, the other invested in ethics quite incognizant of ELSI.

Both sets of collaborations were deeply invested in such concepts as "culture" and "community," but for purposes that were quite at odds with one another. Not only was I made aware of the two divergent models of collaboration, I was also pressed closely between them: asked to give of my time and my energies beyond the demands of professional and paid obligation, and asked for a commitment to things Indian in a way that the ELSI project was just not framed to

---

7. So in recent years cultural performances of music and dance put on by students and local artists have become regular offerings at the Miller Outdoor Theater in Hermann Park, a statue of Gandhi now towers over an odd assortment of busts of Latin American figureheads at the Rose Garden, and the local Kannada organization organizes yearly seminars in collaboration with the Museum of Fine Arts Houston, inviting the participation of scholars from Europe, India, and all around the United States. The initiative to establish an India Studies program and/or Chair at the University of Houston is also in the same vein. Finally, we received much praise from community representatives for organizing a Grand Rounds Lecture at Baylor College of Medicine and the Methodist Hospital, on Gandhian ethics of nonviolence and medical practice. The wish clearly was that discussions bringing Indian ideas into other, non-Indian contexts and encouraging the interaction of "community" with "academia" would continue.

incorporate. My community—mine because I did identify with it and because it claimed me, in turn—disregarded entirely the "thirty percent" quantification of my annual participation on our grant. Instead, I was reminded that most people who really contributed to community development did so after they were done working ten-hour days. And, having been hired on the ELSI-HapMap project as an Indianist, precisely for my close ties to the Indian community, and being the only Indian in our research group, suffice it to say that I felt obligated to build and maintain the very ties that I was presumed to have. I felt crushed between two sets of expectations, two registers that each claimed culture and community in divergent ways, and above all by the demand that anthropology as discipline would have the ready-made means to link these meaningfully.

What did it mean to return the benefits of genetic research to the Indian community in Houston? For us, as researchers, the moral imperative to "give back" flowed logically from our own responses to the fallout of the HGDP and from such wider movements as resulted in the Declaration of Belém, which effectively instituted the principle of redistributive justice as central to any kind of ethical prospecting research.[8] So it was obvious that something needed to be returned for the favors of time and blood, but what? We were not collecting samples for commercial use, so there was no question of royalties flowing back, even if geneticists down the line might have generated royalties. In any event, Indians are not in need of community development projects or communal toilets or schools, but instead frame their priorities in terms of needing to foster ties to "Indian culture" and to bring this into the American mainstream. What was needed was not the return of monetary benefits, but the return of work, effort, time, and above all identification with the community's notions of culture: presentations on genetics at the Meenakshi temple, presentations articulating Gandhian principles with medical practice. As an anthropologist and as an Indian, I saw it as necessary not merely to document, but also to incorporate, these priorities and the conceptions informing them into our research. As an Indianist with my own proclivities, I found it difficult to live up to such expectations, especially when they demanded an overwhelming focus on Gandhi (at a time when stringent critiques from some quarters have perhaps bolstered allegiance to Gandhian precepts in others). As a paid researcher with the ELSI-HapMap group, I recognized the impossibility of asking colleagues for participation beyond the time-allotments given in our research protocol, or beyond the mandated three years of our grant's term. The

---

8. And not just to prospecting-based research, either: witness the ways in which companies as ubiquitous as Target and Starbucks also make the idea of "giving back" central to their "ethical" business practices.

expectations of community far exceeded the capacities and parameters delimited by our study.

The Double Bind of Genres

The deterritorialized field unraveled, then, into a series of expectations manifested in distinct sites: multiple commitments to multiple publics, each quite important, each quite inescapable. The parameters generated by the ELSI-HapMap project were those of a classic double bind—in which my commitments as an ethnographer to the community I was studying were implicated as much as my commitments as an Indian to the community to which I belonged. Even so, the means by which to navigate the double bind were not straightforwardly to be found in the company of Anthropologists. Why?

Here, again, were two additional sets of expectations to consider. The notion that "science is political" has become virtually axiomatic in social science discourse, an all but predictable conclusion that seems nonetheless to foster the "ethics of oppositional critique" of which Mike Fortun has written (2005, 161). The prevailing ethos of critique within the discipline had a profound bearing on the directions of my work, as I was soon to discover. The orientation of HapMap being in some ways undeniably political, given its heritage in controversies like the HGDP, how could I ignore this or even set it aside, no matter how apolitical the Indian community's own positions on the issues of ethics in genetics were? What was the nature of the choice I was making, and what was its rationale? Such were the questions posed (not unkindly) to me at a panel presentation made at the Society for Cultural Anthropology meetings, for my paper had been written in the voice of an Indianist. This was one additional set of expectations brought to bear on my work by an audience of none other than Anthropologists. Here was, among other things, an atmosphere of deep skepticism about science and genomics, and there was no circumventing it; it was the given framework of everything, it seemed.

By contrast, I wished for a useful means by which to take stock, say, of the "ressentiment" that not only marks much of science studies writing (Fortun 2005, 164), but also characterizes the responses of at least some geneticists to analyses generated via an increasingly privileged ELSI research. If critique was the overriding framework guiding analysis, then there seemed the need to admit its multiple manifestations. Was there a way to reasonably account for the frustrations of geneticists over, for instance, the centrality accorded "race" in science studies writing? How could one avoid presuming, implicitly or otherwise, that if the scientists designing genetics research were only "more humanistic, more ethical, more responsible, or had better values to begin with, we wouldn't be faced with the 'implications' that justly preoccupy our attention" (Fortun 2005, 164)? What did it methodologically and conceptually mean to demand that geneticists be more humanistic, more ethical, and more responsible? Not unrelated were the "well-meaning," anti-racist motivations of HapMap organizers and other scientists as phenomena with which to reckon, as Jenny Reardon has done in her writing on the HGDP (2004), but not merely as oddities or apparent contradictions. And, finally, I wished for a way to incorporate the so-called emic and the seemingly anticlimactic Indian apolitical affirmation of the inherent value of "science" into an analysis of ELSI-HapMap itself. Not taking such views into account would have been tantamount to suggesting, on the advice of fellow Anthropologists, that the very ethnographic perspectives I had documented were naïve and ill informed for their apolitical orientation, at worst, or that they belonged in a separate "cultural" register, *not* amenable to integration with "mainstream" thought, at best. The choices delineated by the prevailing modes of critique within the discipline seemed untenable even as they defined the very framework of any possible research based on ELSI-HapMap.

As the lesser of two evils, I gravitated somewhat defensively toward retaining my commitments to "community," to India studies, and to my ascribed identity as Indianist. But the problem of segregation dogged me still. With the fields of science and technology studies and the social studies of science now well instituted as "areas" in their own rights, where did the older "area studies" models fit in such reformulated intellectual terrain? The "Indian and Hindu" perspectives that the ELSI-HapMap research sought would no doubt have made for an interesting addition to the annals of bioethics, but only as a segregated chapter with not much more "value added" than that. Retaining too closely the identity of an Indianist in the company of scholars of science seemed to run a similar risk: here, too, my work might be of interest to Indians and other Indianists, but beyond those audiences, it would be largely an interesting chapter on "Culture" added to the annals of science studies, another model of giving to add to the existing mixes. So the challenge in this struggle over genre, it seemed to me, was not merely that of navigating the binds precipitated by ELSI-HapMap, but that of learning to speak to the different audiences within the discipline of anthropology itself, as also to the distinct professional and intellectual compulsions these groups represented. Subject and object (or area) demanded integration, all the more since ELSI-HapMap tied both together within the framework of its expectations.

Arthur Kleinman makes a distinction between moral processes and ethical discourse, where the moral is a dimension of practical, localized engagements with specific social worlds and the ethical is abstract, principle-based, a debate over codified values, the space of (bio)ethics itself (Kleinman 1998, 363–65). For the "moral" community represented by Indians in Houston, blood is largely and unproblematically a possession but a wholly alienable one, to be freely given for an easily identifiable "greater good" represented by genetic research. For a community of scientists, particularly bioethicists and those others allied with bioethics initiatives (including anthropologists), blood is an abstract but ethical problem, one which marks out a terrain fraught with anxiety, the perpetual threat of controversy, and all the attendant legal/institutional protections and precautions. Kleinman sets out then to "develop the case for *experience*," arguing that "the concern with ethical discourse far predominates over an orientation to moral experience" and that his own professional positioning prepares him for such an approach (Kleinman 1998, 373).

What I have tried to demonstrate in this narrative, however, is that it was harder by far in the context of the ELSI-HapMap research to make the same choice. It is a significant comment on the current predicament of anthropology as a discipline that we find ourselves allied with both sides on questions like that of blood sampling: as ethnographers who discern the contours of practical, localized engagements with specific social worlds, and as ethnographers working within the scaffoldings of established bioethics projects (such as the HapMap), who track abstract debates on codified values lifted from some local contexts and brought to bear on others.

Even further, I mean to suggest that we find ourselves caught in between the "subject" and "area" pulls of the discipline particularly when called to be Anthropologists in the prescriptive "ways we don't do it any more." Area specialty, of course, often remains crucial to ethnography for professional identification and on the job market besides. But despite that, it also runs the risk of becoming a niche identification in an age where any exclusively "area" approach to ethnography is not only dated, but is also diffused by the predominance of the more topically driven, interdisciplinary approaches in cultural studies, science studies, and the like. The case for "moral experience" that Kleinman builds, which is centrally the case for immersed local, cultural engagements, is therefore both valued and marginalized within the discipline ironically in much the same way that "Indian and Hindu perspectives" are valued and marginalized in wider conversations about bioethics in genetic research. Shifting from one collaborative context to the next, ethnography has perforce to deal alternatingly with the shifting values of its objects of study.

The double bind of genres, the sense of being caught in between multiple and divergent sets of expectations precipitated both by specific projects and the social science study itself, seems increasingly emblematic of the character of fieldwork, and seems increasingly to define the parameters for any analysis that can then logically follow. Something called "ethnography" is perpetually undone and redone, and as a result, fetishized, protected, or freely reinvented. Ethnographic "value" is thus forever in the process of being translated, reconstituted, recirculated; ethnography is made up as one moves through collaborations and the various sites that give it meaning. Not only does the ethnographer become a cultural producer in his/her own right, but ethnography, too, becomes both by-product and end-product of such endeavor.

Between Thick and Thin

The by-products of the ELSI-HapMap work (the press releases, the statistical data, the synopses of "community perspectives") are of course end-products in their own right and of a different order than the anthropologically desired ends of such research in which I am—we are all—observers *and* the things being observed: participant observation with a vengeance, I dare say. The ELSI-HapMap project, it should be said, too, internally tolerates little methodological bricolage. This is an NIH-funded initiative that allows latitude but demands rigor of the kind that quite plainly produces data that is of PowerPoint clarity, intelligible to diverse audiences of medical practitioners and researchers. As rich as the ethnographic data generated are, as useful as the analysis is, these do not obviously speak to audiences other than social scientists. The richness of the data works somewhat against the stated goals of the project, ironically enough. Snowballing subject recruitment techniques, or even the multi-sited method that follows a thing, a metaphor, a plot/story/allegory, a conflict (Marcus 1995) may be increasingly commonplace or quite unquestioned in the course of ethnographic field research. Such methodological strategies are, however, red flags for other audiences with more positivist leanings, to whom anthropologists also must speak with greater than anthropological authority. Failure to do so is not just the failure of research-mandated collaboration, but forecloses any hope of releasing "anthropology" from its given, prescriptive forms and making it more broadly relatable to medical/basic science research. So, within the project, method is consistently vetted, means to particular ends specifically chosen and justified to IRBs, funders, physical anthropologists, medical anthropologists, and ourselves alike. Method simply cannot be made "out of a rhetoric of circumstance" (Marcus 2002b, 198)—not because ethnographers have such expanded freedoms to experiment but as a result of specifically devolved conditions of constraint.

Method is another story entirely, however, beyond the deadlines, mandates, and regulations of the ELSI-HapMap project. Here is ostensibly free terrain where predetermined methodologies are both scarce and sparse, not least because it is difficult to devise both questions and method to encase a project that already possesses both questions and method and in whose execution one is primarily (and currently) involved. "In classic ethnography," George Marcus has written:

> thickness was a virtue, thinness was not; in multi-sited fieldwork, both thickness and thinness are variably expected, and accounting for the differences in quality and intensity of fieldwork material becomes one of the key and insight-producing functions of ethnographic analysis. This accounting for the variability of thickness and thinness of ethnography is the most substantive and important form of reflexivity in multi-sited projects. (2002b, 196)

Not just to account for variability, I venture to add, but (reflexive) mechanisms to track thick and thin, to track the transformations of thick into thin, are equally key to stitching together a field inherited in disciplinary pieces. Movement into, out of, and in between collaborations in multi-sited research is such that meaning is neither uniform nor stable. "Culture" described thickly as a "stratified hierarchy of meaningful structures in terms of which twitches, winks, fake winks, parodies, rehearsals of parodies are produced, perceived, and interpreted" (Geertz 1973a, 7) must be filtered, distilled, and reduced for HapMap into a thinner-by-far version of itself. And yet, HapMap is thick with its own negotiation of "science" and "ethics" that begs documentation tailored to particular outcomes: defining new approaches to population genetics, or new ethnographic objects. Sites are not either thick or thin, but produce meaning and demand coherence by configuring thick and thin to meet given ends.

Really, I am searching out a praxis that takes stock of the fact that field sites (and the ethnographers who encounter them) exist simultaneously in multiple forms: even as "the field" unravels into a series of nodes and pathways and signposts pointing both ways at once, it retains the coherence of collapsed bits and pieces—that often seem anything but logically whole to the interlocutors within. Sarah Strauss, reflecting on her work on yoga as transnational phenomenon, observes that she certainly could have written a "traditional" ethnography, but in so doing "would also have failed completely to represent the Rishikesh which I experienced, knowable only within the context of movement and change" (1999, 189). She's right, of course, but one wonders if her comment would apply just as well for those who are ashramites or *sadhaks,* and come to Rishikesh for other kinds of study, in search of a place that coheres and endures and whose enduring coherence is precisely tutelary. In my own work on caste, too, I've grappled with the fact that while ethnographic theory now can slash essentialisms with ease, these very discounted formulations of stabilized identity continue to be power-fully central to Dalit political discourse (Reddy 2005). The variation of thick and thin seems roughly coeval with such variations in the demand for coherence and meaning that remains stable, at least until the next movement into new disciplin-ary or conceptual space.

"But isn't this just the distinction between the 'etic' and 'emic' of classic anthro-pological theory?" someone asked at my presentation at the Society for Cultural Anthropology meetings in 2006 (which my colleague on ELSI-HapMap Jennifer Hamilton, also a contributor to this volume, and I collaborated to co-organize) in which I analyzed data as Indianist but in that analysis left out any mention of the outer encasings of HapMap. I take the question as a prompt not so much to choose between etic and emic, or between "traditional ethnography" and eth-nography "knowable only within the context of movement and change," but to bring these differentiated frames into conversation (as I have tried to do in an essay on blood, based on our engagement with HapMap: see Reddy 2007). It is an awkward task, at best: How does one neatly draw together an apparently straight-forward commitment to science and the value of knowledge with, for instance, the (rather too damningly) critical suggestion that Indians were selected as a HapMap population precisely because they were not likely to oppose its ends—to produce what Jennifer Hamilton once called a HapMap of the "ethically com-pliant" (personal communication)? How would I, as link between community of researchers and community of Indians, convey this unsettling possibility to my interlocutors or otherwise take it into account?

Such questions notwithstanding, what method emerges from the overlap-ping contexts of collaboration must necessarily undertake the awkward task of stitching together the differentiated and opposed terrains of collaboration—or the terrains opposed (paradoxically) only in the context of collaboration. What are the sites that demand coherence? What sort of coherence is it and how is it enacted, "produced, perceived, and interpreted"? How do subject and object, topic and area interact and what does their interaction yield to analysis?

The point is not just that a new ethnographic object comes into view and that that object is HapMap itself. The point is also that the diverse array of col-laborations on which HapMap (and a good number of science studies projects like it) is built yields an equally diverse array of expectations and commitments, professional, personal, and variously political in nature. Each of these needs to be negotiated; each of these demarcates a set of parameters that constrain, but also crucially define, the possibilities for ethnographic method and analysis. Each of these needs to be dialogically linked to track an elusive "culture" as it sometimes stands still, and sometimes refuses stable definition.

Recoding the Field

> Every rhizome contains lines of segmentarity according to which it is stratified, territorialized, organized, signified, attributed, etc., as well as lines of deterritorialization down which it constantly flees. There is a rupture in the rhizome whenever segmentary lines explode into a line of flight, but the line of flight is part of a rhizome. These lines always tie back to one another.
>
> —Gilles Deleuze and Félix Guattari, *A Thousand Plateaus* (1987)

The metaphor of the rhizome, thus far buried, bears some unearthing in conclusion. Collaboration, to my mind, has a distinctly rhizomic flavor: it contains lines of segmentarity from which it derives form and by which it is driven; so also does it rely on and produce a field of multiplicities; it contains the mechanisms for deterritorialization. And yet, as lines tie back to one another, the collaborative exercise necessarily oversees the reconvergence of directional vectors. Dualisms are meaningless, but restratification is always imminent.

The value of the metaphor in closing lies particularly in the suggestion that the field for the ethnographer is disjointed not only prior to collaboration, but by the successive arrangements of collaboration itself. The labor of recoding is, then, guided in no small measure by the expectations, commitments, and parameters generated by the collaborative exercise: in the case of the ELSI-HapMap, the history of ethical violation that generates funding for "ELSI," the methodology and rationale for community review, the IRB oversight, the demands made of anthropology. What room there is for innovation—and there is this room, more so in our study for the presence of three anthropologists at the table—is nonetheless guided by the ways in which we are each called upon to be ethnographers within the frames of ELSI research: a function of positioning, expertise, and other professional considerations besides. Method comes into being, incompletely and never entirely perfectly, in a field defined by such limits.

The rhizomatic character of collaboration is also evident in the fact that it has no real conclusion: such work as ours in the ELSI-HapMap project ends almost arbitrarily when funding runs out (although the Coriell Institute, where the samples we helped collect are housed, provides some funds for continued contact with the Community Advisory Group) and quickly becomes "preliminary data" for new R01s (perhaps the most sought-after category of NIH funding) and RFAs (Requests for Application) to the NIH. The speed of Science, and especially of such futuristic technosciences as genomics, makes it always-already a moving target for ethnography—whose own "unbearable slowness" (Marcus

2003) is such that the catalytic powers of collaboration are quite necessary to retain Science as a viable object of interest. The lines of flight are many, and demanding of pursuit across a field in so many thick and thin pieces. Ethnographic praxis is both subject and object in this landscape, interminably caught in collaboration.

Acknowledgments

Research on which this paper is based was part of an NIH-NHGRI study entitled "Indian and Hindu Perspectives on Genetic Variation Research," conducted in Houston from 2004 onwards. My thanks go to our research group in Houston— Rich Sharp, Janis Hutchison, and particularly Jennifer Hamilton—for all the explicit and implicit conversations about our chance collaboration; also to George Marcus and Jim Faubion as ever for rich feedback and the opportunity to articulate the methodological issues that the ELSI-HapMap project in Houston has raised. A version of this essay is soon to appear in the inaugural issue of *Collaborative Ethnographies* (2008, forthcoming).

5

THE DRACULA BALLET

A Tale of Fieldwork in Politics

Nahal Naficy

**Politics is made up of two words, "poli" which is Greek for "many,"
and "tics," which are bloodsucking insects.**

—Gore Vidal, *The Best Man: A Play about Politics* (1960)

**Sorry, there is no way to talk about politics and to speak of beautiful
shapes, elegant silhouettes, heroic statues, glorious ideals, radiant
futures, transparent information—except if you want to go through,
once again, the long list of grandiose ceremonies held by various
totalitarianisms which, as we are all painfully aware, lead to the
worst abominations. The choice is either to speak of monsters early
on with care and caution, or too late and end up as a criminal.**

—Bruno Latour, "From Realpolitik to Dingpolitik or, How to Make Things
Public" (2005)

Based on my fieldwork among fellow Iranian scholars, writers, and activists in
Washington, D.C., in 2004–2005, this is a story about the terror of intimacy and
the intimacy of terror. It is meant as a reflection on fieldwork as collaboration—
and its dark side. It is not so much a matter of the anthropological colonization
of the native as rather something with a touch of the reverse. Yet, perhaps at the
end everyone in this story remains colonized in his or her way. This is all the more
uncanny in a place such as Washington, the formal seat of the Land of the Free in
which every street, every crossing, every Other has gained in the light of the
War on Terror the haunted, spectral quality of the Secret, the Dangerous, the
Insidious, and the Seductive. In addition to the ever-present perception and
anticipation of a creeping element of evil, the analogy of Dracula helps evoke the
tensions and sensations of an intimately and terrifyingly transformative kiss on
the neck, perhaps a certain incarnation of what James Faubion terms "connectivity" in this volume, "standing between the still perilous Scylla of going native and
the now phantasmatic Charybdis of declaring positively Other the native that
one always already somewhat is anyway."

Although, as Faubion affirms, a great divide between Self and Other is no longer analytically plausible for today's "good" ethnographer, at least not as securely and definitively as it used to be, I found a tension between what I call different mechanisms of making sense to be central, rather inescapable, in my relationship with my interlocutors. With my historian, sociologist, political scientist, writer, translator, human rights activist, NGO director subjects-friends, I not only shared my nation and expatriation but also my passion and profession as an observer, recorder, presenter, and interpreter of human social experience; and yet, our modalities and machineries of perception and presentation of what we shared were significantly different. The real site of cultural encounter was, thus, this interpretive terrain and the "material data-making (and consequently, scale-making and world-making)" practices that we each employed as "expert knowledge practitioners" (Kaushik Sunder Rajan, personal communication). Their end products were databases, memoirs, online libraries, voters' guides, or news letters, and while as an ethnographer I worked with and for them at times, in voluntary and paid fashions, it became increasingly evident that I was not there to produce the same kinds of knowledge as they.

For one thing, let us be reminded that this was the American capital throbbing with post-9/11 terror and thrill of information for war and war without information. Iraq was invaded in search of weapons of mass destruction, of which none were found, and many fingers in Washington were pointing at Iraqi exiles such as Ahmed Chalabi as responsible for providing incorrect information to further their own agendas. It was suspected that America was now looking for Chalabi-like figures from among Iranian exiles who would benefit from providing information, true or false, that would support America's fear and readiness to go to war. For some of my interlocutors, who had tried for years in exile to open the world's eyes to the atrocities of the Iranian regime and the urgency of international help for its removal, this was prime time to address America. Of course they had no intention of providing false information, nor was a full-fledged war desirable in their eyes. Nevertheless, they appreciated the demand for information, of the kind that they were well positioned to provide, in the American policy nucleus as well as among the general public, the middle-aged white ladies who now passionately read and discussed any books about life in Iraq, Afghanistan, or Iran in their midday suburban book clubs. All of a sudden, these countries were present not only in policy forums and meetings and documents in Washington but on the Charlie Rose Show and Oprah, even on the Weather Channel. To my interlocutors, this was a golden opportunity. To their critics, of which there were many and most of whom were quite harsh, my interlocutors were "personification[s] of native informer[s] and colonial agent[s]" described in an 1835 decree by a colonial officer that Hamid Dabashi cited in his *Al-Ahram* article, "Native Informers and the Making of the American Empire": "We must do our best to form a class who may be interpreters between us and the millions whom we govern, a class of persons Indian in blood and colour, but English in taste, in opinions, words and intellect" (Dabashi 2006). But there were others of my interlocutors who used the same fertile ground to plant seeds of policies of a different kind, offering Washington their advice as "Middle East experts" against the perils of anything short of good-faith diplomatic engagement with Iran. They, in turn, were accused by my different-minded interlocutors and their American supporters of being minions of the Islamic Republic, protecting its sovereignty and its international image.

In such a turbulent time and place, I found it nearly impossible to conceive of speaking publicly about Iran without being accused of having received either a neo-con Dracula kiss (if I said anything about human rights abuses or limitations imposed on women) or an Islamic Republic Dracula kiss (if I said anything about the achievements of women parliamentarians, lawyers, activists, or filmmakers inside Iran, for example). Of course one could subscribe to a polyandrous ethic and remain faithful to multiple realities despite the charges of moral adultery leveled by one or another group, but the fear remained that even so one would never know what the sound-bite machinery of Washington could take from what one said and what it was capable of doing with it.

The transformation of the descriptive into the prescriptive, of the material for contemplation into the material for action, often seemed inevitable, unprompted, and unbeknownst to the speaker. For me, this undesirable and involuntary transformation became the creeping element of evil that I constantly tried to escape during my time in Washington, where my opinion as an Iranian in America who was familiar with both languages and cultures and was earning a Ph.D. in social science studying other Iranians in America familiar with both languages and cultures and earning (having earned) Ph.D.s in social science was almost as much a hot commodity as many of my interlocutors were themselves. As an ethnographer, it became my aspiration and my labor to produce knowledge that would be essentially useless for the policymakers while still of interest to us anthropologists by choosing from the "abundance of details and microevents" that Aleksander Hemon calls "the ephemera, the nethermoments" as opposed to the "fireworks of universal experiences, the roller coaster rides of sympathy and judgment" (Hemon 2002, 41).

Here I am making a case not against the possibility or desirability of anthropologists in general having an impact on policy; far from it. Rather, I am pointing out new dimensions of "speaking" in the Quaker call to Speak Truth to Power and of "representation" in "Can the Subaltern Speak?" (Spivak 1988). I am, however, also acknowledging different conceptions of rank and power, in speaking with our interlocutors, even when language (one wishfully thinks) is not the problem. What kinds of productive conversations can we engage in with our interlocutors today, productive for us and productive for them? My tale of field-work here will present two examples, a dinner-table conversation followed by an unexpected heated argument. They portray my engagement with what George Marcus calls in this volume and elsewhere "epistemic partners," even if the partnerships in question were sometimes vexed. I regarded my interlocutors as my friends, of course, but I often experienced my partnership with them as one with *rivals* or *doubles* at best, like shadows that haunt one another and crowd one another's discourse with uncomfortable accents (Bakhtin 1982).

I recognized myself, people I knew, and some of our experiences in some of the data my interlocutors produced (such as in Azar Nafisi's *Reading Lolita in Tehran* [2003] or in the human rights database that documented victims of human rights abuses in post-revolutionary Iran), as will my interlocutors recognize themselves, people they know, and some of their experiences in some of the ethnographic data that I have produced. We have each represented the other, and perhaps there is a certain level of discomfort in the way that we each find ourselves represented. It might have something to do, in my case, with my general perception that any act of representation is always inevitably an act of creation; that there are no categories, only categorizations (see Goodman 1978), and I cannot help but find in my interlocutors' various acts of observing, recording, and analyzing, as well as in mine, remnants of that modernist impulse to impale. Like a lepidopterist. Or like Vlad the Impaler. My tale of fieldwork here manifests in rather gory detail the tensions and sensations of finding oneself trapped in the categories that somebody else has made. The irony is by no means lost on me that the ethical, ontological, and epistemological challenges of that situation are every bit as relevant to human rights and policy activists such as my interlocutors as they are to anthropologists such as myself.

These intimate conversations (the one at the dinner table followed by the heated argument) are central to the point I am trying to make with regards to the nature of my "connectivity" to my interlocutors, even if they reveal less than flattering "secrets" of our relationship and the darker side of our collaboration. Marcus invokes Michael Herzfeld's concept of "cultural intimacy" in another context in this volume, but it also works here. My interlocutors and I recognize that we share such intimacy, rather ruefully as we may, while perhaps wishing to hide it from those foreign to our intimate sphere (Herzfeld 1997). My greater fear, however, has been not the gaze of the foreigner but this intimacy itself, not the excess of distance but the lack of distinction, not so much the "rueful self-recognition" as the possibility that I might not be able to recognize myself at all the next time I look at myself if I become too intimate with my interlocutors, if I, were such a thing possible, *understand them too well* (Herzfeld 1997). It is, at core, a terror of intimate transformation, of speaking with their accent, of Faubion's Scylla and Charybdis. As Dracula casts no reflection in the mirror, it is also the terror of becoming (,) that other monster. And so here is my tale:

I have always had a certain fascination with the phantom and vampire folk, so when I heard that Count Dracula himself would be performed in a ballet at Roslyn Theatre, just across Potomac River from my field in Washington, I decided that going to the ballet was the most appropriate gift I could give myself for my birthday, which happened to be on a Saturday. October was coming to an end and the fall foliage was fantastic, phenomenal, in full color. There was even something blood-like, a biting intensity, about it all. Naturally, I decided to take a walk through Georgetown, across Key Bridge, and over to the theater in Alexandria, Virginia. I was in a contemplative mood.

While walking, I received a call on my cellular phone from my interlocutors at Human Rights Organization (HRO). They just wanted to know what my plans were for the day. It appeared to them rather odd that I should be spending the gorgeous fall afternoon of such a significant birthday as my thirtieth going to a matinee Dracula ballet all by myself. They suggested that I have lunch with them on the way and then, if it had to be, walk with them across the bridge to the theater. The lunch was something Italian or French, something with only the most expensive and exquisite tomatoes, olives, cheese, bread, and wine to be found in Georgetown markets. But the ballet, well, we never quite made it there. The walk took us longer than I'd expected, and something that happened while walking made us forget about our destination, or we simply no longer cared. We had an argument.

It was no more than a mutually well-intentioned argument, really, but by the end of it I was feeling so dirty and violated and so robbed out of my essence that I knew we, my interlocutors and I, had hit yet another true milestone in my field and that, thankfully, I was going to have material for at least one more dissertation chapter. Not that it has to be that way, but perhaps I suffer from some kind of writers' narcissism when I think that the only stories worth telling are those that have touched me deeply personally. I still aim for my reader's heart (even though not necessarily to break it, for I'd like to believe, from my own rather vulnerable position, that there is still plenty of anthropology that is worth doing besides Anthropology That Breaks Your Heart) (see Behar 1996), and I've heard you cannot get there lazily or cleverly by circumventing your own heart. I think of myself as a site and instrument of fieldwork. But let me be unapologetic about the way I select which stories from my field to tell; there is only as much selection (and arbitration) here as there is involved when we form theoretical arguments and outlines of the topics to address. We write to provoke; to provoke thought, we shall hope, but also to provoke emotion, for what we deal with happens to be a human field. We also write to find and form coherence, but to "make sense" can also be to make manifest the striking soul and secret of the everyday, this shock of recognition, this epiphany in the Joycean sense, that may come as a distraction to our ostensive purpose.

The night before my birthday, I had been invited to have dinner with the HRO founders and a long-lost relative of theirs who was visiting from out of town. The relative, a young woman around my age, was born to an American mother and an Iranian father, one of the HRO founders' cousins or second cousins or something—something twice- or triply-removed or whatever. Her parents had separated soon after her birth, and she was raised by her mother in America while her father had gone back to Iran and then, after the Revolution in 1979, resettled in Europe. The young woman wanted to learn about the beloved mystery that was her father, his family, his country, his religion, anything that could help her know him better. As we sat around the dinner table, chatting away about her father as the HRO founders remembered him (he had been a funny and resourceful guy, if it should matter), about their scattered families and mine, about Iran before and after the Revolution, it came up that I was actually born and raised in Iran and had gone to college there as an English major. This fascinated the young lady and prompted her to inquire about what it had been like for me, for Iranian women in general, to go to college, to study English literature of all things under the Islamic Republic. "Because, interestingly," she said, "I just recently picked up this book, this Lolita in Tehran book that everybody reads and talks about these days, and frankly I find it so monotonous and depressing that I don't think I'm going to be able to finish it." Then, "Was it really that bad?" she wanted to know, looking at me as if looking for a more scenic shortcut to understanding life for educated women her age in Iran. One that didn't pass through James and Austen and Fitzgerald and Nabokov (she didn't seem very literary) and didn't, if at all possible, involve little girls raped by dirty old men who posed as their guardian angels.

For those of you who might not know the book, Azar Nafisi's *Reading Lolita in Tehran* revolves around an informal gathering (part private English literature class, part experimental women's studies workshop) held in 1995–1997 at Nafisi's home for some of her best female students after she quit her job as professor of English at one of the top humanities colleges in Tehran owing to its repressive policies. The book draws connections between the lives of these young women under the Islamic Republic and the books they discuss: Jane Austen's *Pride and Prejudice* and woman's choices, Henry James's *Daisy Miller* and the fundamental opposition of totalitarian mindsets to ambiguity, F. Scott Fitzgerald's *Great Gatsby* and the power of dreams, and, of course, Vladimir Nabokov's *Lolita* and the sobbing of a twelve-year-old who after hearing of her mother's death came to her forty-some-year-old molester in the middle of the night, because, "You see, she had absolutely nowhere else to go" (Nabokov 1955, 147).

Meanwhile, the book also chronicles the events before, during, and after the Iranian Revolution as they unfold for the author, who joins the Confederation of Iranian Students Abroad (Marxist-Leninist opposition to the Shah; 1960–1975) briefly while studying for her Ph.D. in English at the University of Oklahoma in the 1970s, returns to Iran, Ph.D. in hand, on the eve of the Revolution in 1979 to teach at Tehran University, and immigrates to America with her husband and two children in 1997 after eighteen tumultuous years of teaching and not teaching and teaching again, by force or by will. All in all, *Reading Lolita in Tehran* is a story of women, choices, fundamentalism, opposition, totalitarian mindsets, ambiguity, power, dreams, sobbing, death, molesters, nights, and having absolutely nowhere else to go. Well, actually, it is about a place to go, an otherworld, an Antiterra (a phantasmagoric planet parallel to Earth that is the setting of Nabokov's *Ada* [1969]), a refuge in literature, about which, in a *Washington Post* article entitled "The Republic of the Imagination," Nafisi says:

> We know that fiction does not save us from torture or the brutality of tyrannical regimes, or from the banalities and cruelties of life itself. […] But we do know that, when confronted by utter degradation, by confiscation of all that gives life its individual worth and integrity, many instinctively go to the highest achievements of mankind, to works that appeal to our sense of beauty, memory, harmony—those that celebrate what is humane, those that we consider original works of the imagination. (Nafisi 2004)

Which brings us more or less to where I wanted to go when faced with the long-lost relative's question, "Was it really that bad?" I was getting ready to talk about the celebration of what is humane, harmonious, beautiful, and adorned with tender memory in the midst of the banalities and cruelties of life (and so in a way implying that, no, I guess it wasn't that bad; not necessarily depressing, and certainly not boring) when one of the HRO founders cut in and informed the guest delightfully that I, too, had been a student of Azar Nafisi's. The young lady turned a few shades of red before she could stutter: "Oh no, I didn't mean to suggest that your teacher was depressing or boring…or her book…or your life in Tehran…or you…." I laughed and said it was okay a million times. It was awkward.

Considering the awkwardness of such encounters and the controversial politics surrounding the promotion and reception of *Reading Lolita in Tehran* in America, I did my best to avoid any association with the book or its author in public. Despite my wish, however, there were moments when those who knew about my connection to the book felt that they could no longer resist the urge to present me, for the sheer excitement that it could produce or the added urgency or poignancy to whatever case they were making. For the aforementioned HRO founder, the dinner party presented one of those moments. She was a woman with a singular unbending sense of mission, of course, and she was always making a case. Frequently, close friends and relatives and admirers, of whom she had quite a few, brought to her attention that her tone was a bit too much like that of a prosecutor in a court of law and they were exhausted by her application of "due process" to all aspects of their lives, being constantly questioned by her and asked for proof and evidence as if they were criminals. Accountability, she said, that's all I'm asking for. If you said you loved her, which came naturally as she was exceedingly lovable, she would look straight into your eyes as if you were out of your mind and enumerate, in a most charming way, your deeds and words in the past twenty or forty-five or eighty or however many days (for some this would be years, but I didn't know her that long) that in her mind contradicted your claim, leaving you seriously pondering even the morality of your emotions. You felt you needed a better-prepared file, and perhaps the right to an attorney, next time you had to appeal to her with a case of the above proportions. We friends and relatives and admirers were all in a way taken and taken aback by her agility and vigilance, and strove for a certain precision around her that is normally alien to emotions. Or to life outside the human rights database, whatever that was.

At forty-five, this HRO founder whom I call Shirin saw her life as the database for which she missed vacations and sleep and received no salary, and she often joked that she would one day end up in it as a victim. She felt abused by all the demands that the database imposed on her time, her finances, her home, her relationships, her nerves, her health, and her safety; and yet every bit of her was drawn to keep on going, documenting abuse, hoping that it would all pay off one day. As she said, she had a "worm" inside her that ate at her and forced her to pursue what she was doing despite its toll on her. In my mind, she was one of those extraordinary individuals who have what it takes to make a life (and I'm not saying a living) out of taking care of the dead, making sure that they each had a page in the database, a picture, a story, a list of rights that were denied them, and a personal touch (like how one loved soccer and the other was a chain-smoker, based on what their cellmates or relatives had said) that made them human and alive in the eyes of the reader. Obviously, she cared.

The other HRO founder repeatedly remarked, this Shirin, she is a born litigator, now only if she stopped litigating on me! There were, of course, movies and museums and brief love affairs and walks and talks (you could always count on talks around Washington about some conflict in one part of the world or another) in Shirin's life outside the database, and then there were dinner parties, but as I hope I have shown, the nature of these dinner parties was such that they were hard to distinguish from the life of the database and Shirin's unbending mission to make a case. "This is about shaming the Islamic Republic," she said. "You guys don't see me get that way about a panna cotta recipe, do you?" She was a great cook and no, we didn't see her "get that way" about recipes or other things she was passionate about, except that things had a way of always inevitably being about the Islamic Republic in the end. In the life of a person with a mission, there is no such thing as a casual conversation.

Whatever the case, I didn't particularly care for the sensation of being encased, even if inside a trophy, as was the case in that particular dinner party the night before my birthday, and I tried to squirm out of that burdensome position. I told the young guest that I couldn't think of anything extraordinary to report about our lives in Iran. We were English majors, we read novels, we wore something at home and something else outside, we were unhappy with our bosses and sometimes with our siblings and especially had problems with whomever they married, we thought our parents had no clue what we were all about, oh, and that my family was kind of quirky and we had our own home-run chemistry labs and pottery courses and summer festivals and we read manifestos at weddings and there were plenty of people who found us odd, plenty who were better integrated within the society and plenty who felt much more miserable about their lives in the Islamic Republic than we ever did; that I had always wanted to get out somehow, but there were others who felt just fine where they were, I mean, not just fine, but fine with the struggle; called it life, called it their share, called it home and family and love despite all the limitations and frustrations; you know? Our guest gave me a smile of recognition in return and remarked that "in the end, I guess it is our common humanity that matters." Perhaps this all got too sweet for Shirin's taste, for she urged me to recount those other stories that I had told her, of aunts and uncles and relatives and family friends being executed, of cousins being born in prison and hiding and exile—but not even to mention the eight-year Iran-Iraq war (1980–1988) and the city bombings and the closing of schools and losing of classmates and living on rationed goods, for that would divert attention from the atrocities of the Islamic Republic and sound too much like any other war anywhere else. As if Iran was like anywhere else.

I said fine, and I gave my wide-eyed audience a chance at those other stories I tell every once in a while, of this well-lit room full of bloodied, bruised dead people somewhere on the second floor of some raided political organization where, some time between the ages of four and five, I remembered having clutched my mother's hand as she went silently from one body to the next, putting holy dirt out of a pouch under their tongues and tying their big toes together. For my audience's pleasure, I recalled a midday conversation about age with my cousin Salman over pasta, about me being five and him being six, my mother being thirty-five and his being thirty-seven, when my uncle came by on a bicycle to take me to my grandparents' where my pregnant mother and older sister had taken refuge after my father was arrested. I told them of the Revolutionary Guards that popped up on our walls like cats and walked on our carpets with their boots and searched my mother's books and journals with their Kalashnikovs as if they were dirty to the touch. I told them of the patrol truck that took my mother away and of my little sister screaming and running barefoot on the asphalt after her; then of my mother coming back one day when my cousin Salman and I were playing in the backyard and of her hugging me for several minutes with no words and no tears; of a fountain of tears opening up like a wound in my heart since then that is kind of hard to explain. Then of being stopped, at age ten, by the morality committee patrol for wearing a yellow dress under my uniform on the way to a friend's birthday party, and of the black dress that my grandmother changed into every time she heard of a relative's or family friend's execution and how one day it was her own son and daughter-in-law, then a son-in-law, then another daughter-in-law, and she didn't bother to change from black to anything else for years. I told them of this giant gray stuffed elephant that I had received as a present from my mother's best friend before she was executed and the very interesting gifts that I always received from relatives in prison, pen cases made out of shampoo bottles, little coin purses knitted from dental floss with straightened safety pins, hair clips made out of chicken bones and such. I was clearly on the right track to horror and nobody interrupted me. I must have stopped at some point by myself to take a bite or a sip of my wine, and we never picked up that topic again. In fact, I have no recollection of how the rest of the evening went. Maybe I had too much to drink.

I was informed only the day after, on our walk to the Dracula ballet, that I had had the audacity to go on by saying that I had left Iran not because of the horror stories I had just so elaborately recounted but because of a certain existential restlessness, some wanderlust or whatever, and that there were still plenty of women in Iran who were not willing to trade off what they had back home for my position as a forlorn foreigner. Apparently, I had sounded irritated for some reason and as though I wanted somehow to protect the Islamic Republic's reputation by saying that the decision to leave had been due to my own personal dispositions and not our impossible living conditions. Apparently, I had also added that the point of the Lolita in Tehran book was not for American women like her (the poor guest) to feel depressed for us but to become inspired by our courageous criticism of ourselves and maybe do the same with their own damned demons. I was told that our guest had become fairly flabbergasted and found herself at loss as to how to react to this encounter.

So what was it with me, Shirin wanted to know on the way to the Dracula ballet—why was I so defensive, so reactionary, so snobbish even? Was I by any chance, like most other Iranians she knew, concerned about looking bad in the eyes of the foreigner and had therefore resorted to such obscure musings about why I had left? "I mean, how could you be so blasé about the whole thing, acting like, eh, it was a mixture, like everywhere else; as if there was anything like here?" After all that I had observed at the HRO and all the many tragic stories that we had exchanged, how come I sounded as though I almost intentionally tried to hinder the fact that Iran needed to change?

"But why do you think I was supposed to make sure she understood that Iran needed to change?! Who was she, anyway?! Was this a press conference?! Was I giving policy recommendation?! No, the woman was asking me about my personal life in Iran and I was telling her about me, my personal life. I don't understand why you get so passionate and possessive about this. I mean, how is this your business?"

"How is this my business? This is exactly my business. The woman is a reporter in Ohio; her best friend works for CNN. I'm hoping to have them cover the story of the database once we go public. Do you know how hard we have to try to convince these reporters that the question of human rights in Iran is urgent and relevant, that the personal lives of ordinary people there are such a mess and that's what they need to pay attention to instead of the damn nuclear power and which of the baboons is currently the president? It takes just someone like you to ruin it, an educated, smart young woman to come out here and say that eh, it wasn't so bad, it isn't so bad for everybody. And you get this woman smiling and saying that, yeah, in the end it is our common humanity that matters?!"

"Oh, I get it. Of course you had a mission; what was I thinking? That this was just some innocent dinner party with me and your cousin? No, it's never just some dinner party. It's always some reporter or some funder or some policy-maker or some aspiring senator and you want me to boost your case so that everyone sees how nonsensical and idiotic and brutal ordinary lives are in Iran and why America should do something about it. But you can't stand what my personal life has been about. What is my life is your damn project. My personal life is nothing to you."

"Honey, it isn't about your personal life, don't you get it? When these Americans ask you about life in Iran, they are not looking for your existential problems and quirky family traditions and how you stole cookies out of your grandmother's jar. Your life, sweetheart, does not represent the problem that is Iran today; that's not what they are looking for when they ask you these questions."

"Well, then, I don't care what they are looking for. I happen to think that I am part of what makes Iran today and so is my life and my family and so are the stories that I choose to tell. I don't care how typical I am or my life is, or how ordinary or extraordinary, or what action my life story prompts, or whether it matches the other stories that other people with other lives have told these people. It's their job to put all these different things together and form an opinion; if they are too lazy or dumb to do that, I mean if they get confused by the fact that people in other places do not all live the same reality, that's not my problem. You are telling me that I can't afford to have a personal life that is odd and interesting and confusing like everybody else's; that I'm sentenced to have this box life, this case life that you can present. Well, I don't like that."

"What makes you think that people in Washington want to spend all this time hearing about how odd and quirky your family is, or how interesting you are, or how confusing reality is, or whatever? What makes you think there is ever that much time on Capitol Hill? Is there not one practical bone in your body?"

"But I'm not talking on Capitol Hill! See, here's the difference between us: I don't want to be on Capitol Hill, but you are there! You are always there! You don't say one word unless for its impact on policy; I turn pale when I hear policy. That's true, Washington needs people like you and probably any change in the present condition of Iran also takes people like you. That's why I shut up every time you guys have guests; because I don't want to come between your cause and these guys' ears. I just didn't think this was one of those occasions, because you said she was your cousin. Anyway, it seems that being me ruins your project; so maybe we shouldn't hang out anymore or maybe I should never speak, because obviously my life annoys you."

"Oh no, you can speak, of course you should speak, but you should make sure you contextualize your experience so people know that you are not talking about the people of Iran as a whole."

"Don't worry, I leave that to you guys to do, to talk about the people of Iran as a whole. I have no interest in the category. You think my life is irrelevant, fine. You go represent the life in Iran since you haven't been there even once since the Revolution...."

"Oh, I see what you are doing. You all do this; people who come out of Iran and think they know everything just because they lived there; like their experience is some kind of capital or something. Because we are in exile, you think we have no idea what is going on inside Iran. Well, for your information, we have spent the last twenty years, thirty years, while you kids were busy receiving nursing and potty training, following the news on Iran. I hurt in my guts when I hear that people in Iran have gone to the polls and voted for these guys yet again, and you didn't even know who your president was, because you know why, because your family provided you with this enclave where you didn't need to be bothered with the president, because you had your own labs and classes and festivals and your own alternative reality. You didn't live in Iran; you lived in the Naficy family. You don't get to come here and talk about what those people over there need."

"I didn't talk about what those people over there needed. I don't know what people over there or anywhere need. You spent your summers in the south of France; I'm sure you are much better qualified to say what people over there need. I've lived in Iran for twenty-four years, but my experience is irrelevant; actually my experience is not, because I did experience a lot of shit, a lot of painful stuff, but my narrative of it is somehow wrong, I just don't sound as tragic as I should for your project to work; I recall all the wrong memories. I'm just not as miserable. Not enough of a victim."

"Aha! And what is wrong with being a victim? See, here it is, this arrogant attitude again, this false pride, that for some reason you don't want to admit that you have been a victim. Somehow that's beneath you. But, sweetheart, you are a victim, you kids all are, we all are victims. I admit it; yes, they slaughtered our friends, they shattered our lives and families, they confiscated and destroyed our property, they ruined our friendships; for God's sake, you have had to see dead people at four, and what do you gain by denying that you were a victim? We cannot heal unless we acknowledge that we've been victims. We cannot set it right unless we admit that we've done wrong, and we've been done wrong to as well. But you are all for some reason trying to cover up for the Islamic Republic; just go ahead, love your oppressor, save your murderer's face, very typical Iranian thing, very typical Iranian thing."

Back when I was between the ages of four and twenty-four, my father thought I was irrational and my arguments bore no logic because invariably I would start crying in the middle of any intense conversation. He would become absolutely silent and refuse to continue the conversation with me unless I did away with the tears. That is why on my thirtieth birthday, in the middle of an argument about who I was supposed to be and what my life was supposed to mean, I became preemptively silent when I felt the tears coming. We had walked all the way across the bridge, descended to the riverside on the other end, and were now walking on a bed of dead leaves, bending every once in a while to avoid the tree branches, faces flushed with the heat of the argument and the chill of October air. The other HRO founder, who had not said a word yet (not that she could get any in edgewise) and had remained amazingly patient, attracted our attention to the migrating ducks on the river. They were nice, all right. Then I said: "You want me to get to my knees now and say that I've been a victim? Is that going to make it all better?"

Shirin said I was being melodramatic. She then put her hand on my shoulder and we started descending toward the end of our fight in the way that the best-intentioned fights end, by saying things like "I didn't mean to…" and "all I meant was…" and such. All I had meant, for my part, was that Washington was a state of mind, a diamond-shaped grid that organized every expression in a certain way according to what impact it could have on what was always already being made, a lepidopterist apparatus of sorts that trapped and pinned and formulated everything and everybody that came by fluttering innocently, or not so innocently, in its vicinity. It was an organization that my mind perceived as distortion, as if you were to rearrange a watercolor landscape painting according to its colors, all the whites in this square, all the blues over there, or according to its lines, all the straight lines in this square, all the curves over there. So I had lost my ability or desire to express:

> And I have known the eyes already, known them all—
> The eyes that fix you in a formulated phrase,
> And when I am formulated, sprawling on a pin,
> When I am pinned and wriggling on the wall,
> Then how should I begin
> To spit out all the butt-ends of my days and ways?
> And how should I presume? (Eliot 1971, 5)

As we climbed from the riverside up to the streets of Georgetown, I thought about how it all seemed as if I had gone to the field only to discover my own ailment, going there only to find my own internal rot. It did not escape me that that was what good ethnographic fieldwork has been expected to do ever since *Anthropology as Cultural Critique* (Marcus and Fischer 1986); but this cultural encounter was not so much between me as an Iranian and Washington as an American field, between me as an Iranian student in America and Iranian Americans, as between different modes of perception and representations of reality (what one could call culture, I suppose) that were not divided by nationality. The fact that I was technically a "native anthropologist," studying people of my own kind, even engaging, as it were, in some sort of collaboration with my subjects, did not result in immediate and unproblematic identification with them; neither did it grant me an exclusive insight into How Natives Think (cf. Lévy-Bruhl 1926). Ours was an encounter between different mechanisms of making sense, an encounter with similar terrorizing and thrilling erotics of *trans* (transfiguration, transition, etc., but also a state of "trans" as simply being in between two universes), as in any transformative encounter with the Other. As my "I" mixed with and tore itself apart from "I-ran" and "I-slam," I realized there was no Republic of the I that stood in absolute distinction from the Islamic Republic of Iran that violated me and housed me, owned me and disowned me at once.

Ironically, this all had to happen on my birthday, the day you celebrate your singular existence.

I had feared throughout my fieldwork becoming too much like my interlocutors. I loved them, for they treated me as one does friends and family, I wholeheartedly embraced their defense of life instead of a certain ideology, and I admired them for their vision, passion, and hard work. Yet, I had nightmares of waking up one day and not being able to recognize myself: What if I, too, thought of economic sanctions as furthering the cause of democracy in Iran? What if I, too, felt that regime change in Iran was more likely to come through people's consistent nonparticipation than their active participation? Already, I had heard a well-known scholar and political adviser start a talk by declaring, "I am a neo-con and I stand for the values of the Bush Administration," and continue by saying that we should teach the Muslims how to fish instead of importing democracy, and I had emerged smiling, with a notebook full of his words that I had found insightful and inspiring, with, to my horror, no trace of my usual cynicism and smirk at all the neo-con plans for fishing courses in the Middle East. What was happening to me? Was I kissed in my sleep by the hawks of Washington and losing my cynical anti-establishment blood and turning into a minion of the bloodsucking god of policy? Already, an ex-classmate of mine from Iran with whom I had maintained an amorously mildly suggestive relationship (he had asked for my permission to address me by my first name in his e-mails) had ended a wildly heated online chat series by calling me an amour of the Imperialists for my research which they could, indeed they would, use to further imbue the Muslim world with suffering. Was I a vampire already and didn't know it? Was I *one of them*? My argument with my interlocutor on that fall evening was a rather reassuring proof to the contrary, but then I had been accused of having become someone of another sort, more frightening to *them:* what my interlocutors at the HRO referred to repeatedly as the "agents of the Islamic Republic," the apologists who, even if they did not know it, saved face for the Islamic Republic.

We walked into an antique furniture store in Georgetown, one of the HRO founders' favorite places to hang out and pass time. We walked around in it aimlessly and pointed at this and that item. Shirin said I had good taste, which was surprising considering that I had grown up in the Islamic Republic. She rested her arm on my shoulder. Then we went to an Austrian café, as we were starved and exhausted, and they ordered me something very expensive, the name of which I could not even pronounce and I don't now remember. Then when I went to the bathroom and came back, they surprised me for my birthday with candles and a deadly cake called Death by Chocolate.

I died that evening, needless to say; and when the respectable ladies called me mid-morning the next day to see if I was planning to go to work on that day, I opened my eyes to a life that I thought had ended but that, my fieldwork in Washington proved, was only off to a new start in a new form: my life with the Islamic Republic.

6

THE "WORK" OF ETHNOGRAPHIC FIELDWORK

Lisa Breglia

The Work-Break Game

In *Toward a Formalization of Fieldwork,* Morris Freilich addresses the ins and outs of how to be a participant observer. Amid concerns for tailoring modes of participant observation to forms of data required and the cultivation of acceptance and rapport in the field, he describes "the work-break game":

> At certain times, and in certain types of situations, the anthropologist and some natives find it mutually advantageous to make believe that the anthropologist is not working, that he is indeed taking a break.... The rules of the game are simple: good moves are those which make the deception more believable; average moves neither help nor harm the deception; and moves which are not permitted are those which uncover the reality of the situation. The latter bring to light, for all to see, that the anthropologist in reality *is working.*
>
> ... The anthropologist often finds himself in a dilemma: to achieve his research goals he constantly must be collecting data. However, in many situations it is extremely embarrassing to appear to be working. The anthropologist, like the natives, is ready to grasp opportunities to make such inherently embarrassing situations more pleasant. (1970, 533–34)

Rather than inventing the work-break game, Freilich is describing the intricate play of appearances that all fieldworkers engage in at one time or another. The smoothing-over of the "embarrassing" procedures of ethnographic fieldwork promised by the cleverly devised work-break game is only possible because of a tacit agreement between researcher and informant regarding the nature, aesthetics, and appropriate modalities of fieldwork practice. Thus the work-break game is not only cleverly devised—it is mutually devised.

Freilich's work-break game reveals the shared perspective among researchers and informants that ethnography constitutes a strange kind of work—so strange that its exact nature cannot be revealed as both parties share in misrecognizing the work of fieldwork. Meanwhile, the work-break game confirms that the ethnographer's interlocutors do indeed understand that fieldwork, in the traditional mode, has indistinct spatial and temporal boundaries. As a way of demonstrating acceptance of the ethnographer as a researcher, the interlocutors agree to play the work-break game, participating in the concealment of ethnographic labor initiated by the ethnographer (who must put away pen and notebook, or digital recording device). But loathe the ethnographer who plays the work-break game so well that "he" forgets it is one of deception and illusion, Freilich warns: indeed this researcher has lost his observational distance, given up the distinction between *researcher* participant observation and *human* participant observer and has "going, going, gone native" (1970, 530).

Freilich's work-break game screams of a (supposedly) outdated mode of positivist objectivism exacerbated by a rigid distinction between "us" researchers and "them" natives. Yet I find this scenario of the work-break still compelling for contemporary times. In exposing the work dynamics inherent in participant observation, Freilich is putting his finger on precisely what I see as one of the most crucial issues in any discussion of tradition, pedagogy, and innovation in ethnographic fieldwork: the concealment and agreed misrecognition of ethnographic labor. Freilich describes the work of ethnography as so odd, awkward, and even bordering on untoward that the researcher agrees to its concealment. Herein lies the focal point of my discussion. This compulsory misrecognition of ethnographic labor is infused into the standards and pedagogy of the Traditional Fieldwork Model, the formation of which we credit to Malinowski, and in the maintenance of which we are, now many generations on, complicit.

It seems to me that since the modern origins of the discipline, there has subsisted a distinct anxiety over what constitutes "work" in fieldwork. This is not exclusive to the ethnographer, but implicates the interlocutors, too, as a key component of rapport between the two parties is founded upon the mutual acknowledgment of the awkwardness or even inappropriateness of revealing—rather than concealing—the tools and techniques of ethnographic research. The anxiety and tension over the appropriateness of the work of fieldwork is intensified by having to face the (in)commensurability of ethnographic research with other kinds of work which are already naturalized in the fieldsite. As I'll go on to discuss in the case of my own apprentice research in and around heritage sites in Yucatán, Mexico, the proper tools and techniques of research belonged to archaeologists. In today's diverse and heterogeneous fieldsites, ethnographers face the ethical, logistical, and intellectual problem of mapping our own work modes and styles onto the complicated field of what "Natives" do, be it farming or gene-splicing.

At stake in identifying this problem concerning the work of fieldwork is the recognition of the ideological role and regulative norms of methods at work in the discipline and how they are reproduced through the traditional fieldwork model—one of the broader concerns of this volume. Our own participation in the concealment of ethnographic labor (revealed in Freilich's disclosure of the work-break game) is intimately tied to our understanding of standards and methods in fieldwork practice and the pedagogies thereof inculcated in the training of apprentice ethnographers. How would one teach ethnography, especially "methods" per se, to compensate for this problem? Is it possible that our past efforts to assemble a "toolkit" of methods have been remedial, retroactive attempts to address the problem of the blurriness of what constitutes the work of fieldwork? Is the traditional "Malinowskian" fieldwork model, rather than a historical, prescriptive model, merely a phantasm?

The Traditional Fieldwork Model: Revisiting a Phantasm

The impulse for the genealogical exploration of the Traditional Fieldwork Model that I take up in this essay is backgrounded by two related questions. First, why didn't the disciplinary transformation (perhaps revolution) from positivism to humanism offer a revamped fieldwork model? What's more, why didn't 1980s critique further articulate new fieldwork practice? Here I reflect on and reevaluate what I generalize as the Traditional Fieldwork Model—that hybrid and experimental assortment of research strategies, tactics, and modes of preparation—formalized as such and formalized as "off the cuff" that we typically associate with the Malinowskian tradition. The short form of this model involves basic guidelines for "being there": 1) extended *in situ* participant observation, 2) the engagement of local idioms, and 3) extensive reliance on multiple styles of interviewing. Knowing that fieldwork is also deeply intertwined with epistemology and methodology, the Traditional Fieldwork Model further involves 4) the creation of data, 5) the development and translation of a holistic sense of quotidian life, and 6) the image of holism as model for comparison. It is important to remember that these features are imaginatively based upon, rather than limited to, the actual practices of Malinowski in his fieldwork. Thus, the

Traditional Fieldwork Model is a phantasm that we ascribe to the particularity of Malinowski's fieldwork practice, the image upon which we build our agreement as to the standards of doing ethnography.

The critique of the Traditional Fieldwork Model is that much more difficult for its phantasmic quality. For ethnography, "critique" has meant only one particular kind of critique. It signals a trenchant, if limited, revamping of the modes, methods, and metaphors of representation: of the field, of the Other, of ourselves. Yet however clever, responsible, and necessary this was (and continues to be), it left in place and even further reified the Traditional Fieldwork Model. As technologies of representation continue to be thought of as second-order manipulations of firsthand fieldwork, the Traditional Fieldwork Model subsists and is sustained as the unassailable hallmark of ethnography.

What has since emerged from the critique is a somewhat artificial distinction between "research" and "representation." Perhaps this temporal, spatial, and epistemological distinction between research and representation has, for a time, served well. After all, the discipline needed its bulwark—fieldwork—to push through the crisis and emerge, as some might agree, more nuanced and relevant. As we take up the task of reassessing the Traditional Fieldwork Model, it is important to realize that research and representation go (and have perhaps always gone) hand in hand. Nicholas Thomas maintains a tension between the mutual entanglement of research practice and representation and their concomitant distinctiveness, asserting that "while ways of observing and ways of representing are often tangled up, and while methods admittedly constrain and influence forms of presentation, fieldwork and ethnography are separable" (1991, 307).

I, too, maintain the simultaneous entanglement and distinctiveness of "research" and "representation" in my discussion for both heuristic and historical value. My goal in this essay is to root out where conservatism subsists in ethnographic research practice. This goal is shaped and motivated by the element I am most sympathetic to in terms of the efforts of the 1980s critiques: the notion that ethnography has always been experimental. My efforts here are not, however, precisely akin to the experimental impulse of 1980s, in which "felicitous misreading" of traditional ethnography was employed in order to "draw out the underplayed, forgotten, or latent possibilities" already within "classic" forms (Marcus and Fischer 1986, 40). While felicitous misreading—undertaken as the interpretive project of poststructuralism—reveals the latent potentials vis-à-vis modes of representation, as critique it doesn't even begin to touch on fieldwork methods. I suggest here that throughout the past two decades of critique of/in ethnography, we have sustained a certain "misreading" of fieldwork practice—not in the spirit of critical reflection or revision, but instead as a kind of mystification of the contingencies and irregularities of fieldwork.

While the Traditional Fieldwork Model is really quite intricate and complex, we boil it down to "Just do it" or "Look, listen, learn"; as if all mannered preparation flies out the window when one enters the wild and untamed field. The "just do it" model is historically situated in ethnography's humanistic turn, offering and nurturing a post-positivistic breath of fresh air. Leave the kinship charts to rot away: just do it. All fieldwork is failure, and "misunderstanding" is the key to unlocking the native point of view: just do it. "Just do it" becomes discursively allied with the fall from positivism and humanistic understanding of the unpredictable dynamics of human creativity and diversity (in the mode of liberal pluralism) and methodological repetition without difference. The center of gravity for this reductionist and mystifying move is located in "common sense," as utilized by researchers navigating the messiness of the field and (if not somewhat contradictorily) the object of ethnographic study.

This discussion is my account of a still-developing reconception of the Traditional Fieldwork Model, grown from the experiences of my own apprentice fieldwork. I thus open with a description of an integral part of my ethnographic research in and around archaeological zones in Yucatán, Mexico. Conducting research alongside our disciplinary kin—archaeologists—shed a curious, if not uncomfortable, light on the issue of research labor: in comparison to archaeological fieldwork (namely, excavation), ethnography is, in the words of Diana Forsythe, "invisible work" (Forsythe 1999). The tools, techniques, and tangible data production of archaeological field practice contribute toward understanding archaeological research as a highly rigorous and specialized labor. This is recognized by the researchers themselves and by members of the local community, many of whom are employed as excavators and assistants for the project. As the mise-en-scène (condensed as "archaeological site") is shared with an ethnographer, the discourse of archaeology rules the day. The rigors of ethnographic engagement are generalized as "common sense," the enactment of ethnographic methodologies becomes "just talking to people," and our reflexively crafted data are, in turn, "what they say." As I'll describe below, this problem is not just specific to a personalistic clash between a "poaching" ethnographer and a team of archaeologists protecting their own turf. Instead, it has deep roots in how ethnographers ourselves conceive of and perform research in accord or ambivalence with the Traditional Fieldwork Model.

What are the larger implications of this apprentice experience for the pedagogies of ethnography? The "etic" perception of ethnographic practice as transparent, commonsense endeavor is far from unique to the particular conditions of my apprentice fieldwork. In wider scope, I believe this can be tracked alongside the changing conception of empirical knowledge in the social sciences that arose in the disciplinary disenchantment with positivism and turn toward humanism. Though the discipline indeed altered its notion of what constitutes empirical knowledge, our expectations for the kind of fieldwork practice that would produce this new form of subjective (as opposed to objective), contingent (as opposed to timeless and generalizable) and situated (as opposed to, as I see it, holistic) knowledge basically have not changed. How could this be? As my attempt to answer this perplexing question, I zero in on the precise location of conservatism that maintains the ideal image, if not the on-the-ground practice, of the Traditional Fieldwork Model—the concealment of ethnographic labor.

Apprentice Ethnography "in Ruins"

When I "went to the field," I had already been there for a long time—though not in the sense of the anthropology of "home" in which the researcher is already embedded in his or her fieldsite as an always already "native" subject. Rather, now I remember and frame my dissertation research with a focus on the intersection of three circumstances, all of which imperil the push toward innovation in the conduct and production of ethnography: 1) coming to the practice of ethnography from a theory-heavy interdisciplinary, Cultural Studies background; 2) researching within a heavily anthropologized culture area (the Maya area/ Yucatán, Mexico); and 3) sharing a space of knowledge production with disciplinary kin: archaeologists. I will relate my approach to the field as a practiced exercise in the utilization of uncommon sense.

The nature of my own fieldwork practice (and that of my subfield) took on high relief as I worked alongside archaeologists. For a period of time during my dissertation fieldwork, I played cultural anthropologist to an audience of academic researchers and local Maya residents in a seemingly transparent, yet complex mise-en-scène of fieldwork: an archaeological excavation site. For me, the "site" was almost paralytically overdetermined by the territorializing assumptions of archaeological science, the discourse on cultural heritage and the state. In a space zoned by the Mexican government, and mapped and gridded by archaeologists, and performed according to the predictable logics of tourism, the meanings of the site and the categories for the organization of this knowledge were rapidly ossifying. The only role for ethnography, it seemed, would be to articulate with already available categories. The site stood as a "ready-made" object of study, meaning that both appropriate methods and research questions stood inherent within it. As an ontological, epistemological, and pedagogical ready-made, the archaeological site easily captures the ethnographic imagination and conveniently informs the time- and place-bound shape of ethnographic research within its contours/confines. This is apparent in the growing body of ethnographic studies of archaeological heritage sites, which readily conform to a model whereby all ethnographic questions proceed from and are exclusive to the interests of archaeology.

Given the proliferation of archaeological materials in Mexico, one might conceive of the whole national territory as one big archaeological site. Yet whether by law or accident, only some become what Henri Lefebvre would call "beauty spots," or, as I like to think of them, points of intensification of scientific, state, and other interests (Lefebvre 1991). My dissertation fieldwork (2001–2002) was formed around the problematic of the production of Maya heritage and the development of archaeological sites in Yucatán and the interpretations, negotiations, and ambivalences of living Maya communities regarding this heritage (only sometimes expressed as "their heritage") in both its material and ideological/symbolic dimensions. In Yucatán, Maya archaeology and heritage sites are a major player in the everyday political economy of the region—given the growth and importance of tourism in Yucatán, and the key role that archaeological zones play in attracting international visitors to the Peninsula.

In the temporal space between the pre-fieldwork development of my project and the writing-up stage, interest in questions of the relationships between descendent communities and archaeological interpretation increased exponentially. Understanding how archaeologists conceived of field and local relationships pushed me into a reflexive position vis-à-vis ethnography. I did what they expected of an ethnographer while most of my research was perhaps not recognized as such. In the following section, I describe the arrangements by which I came to be invited to the Pakbeh archaeological project and the conditions of my research while in that association. What I was especially cognizant of seems to be a point aside from the concerns of this discussion: ethnographic labor. But as the conditions of my apprentice ethnographic research unfold, the relevance of what constitutes ethnographic labor in the field becomes a central issue in understanding both the conservative and potentially transformative elements within the Traditional Fieldwork Model.

In the first month of my fieldwork I met a well-known American historian of Yucatán. He asked me what my research was on, and I explained in short order. He smiled and left me with a single comment, "Oh…you're swimming upstream." Reserving my own perception of "studying up" to the ethnography of genetics labs, nuclear weapons research facilities, and sundry encounters between scruffy ethnographers and "suits," I did not realize what this really meant until I was invited by the co-director of the ongoing research project to join their team as an ethnographer who would work in the communities surrounding the excavation site.

The co-director's proposal to me was posed as applied anthropology: the project was specifically looking for a "development anthropologist" to facilitate the communication between the U.S. archaeologists and the local Maya residents. Project directors found this necessary for two reasons. The first involves questions of the legal rights as well as the ethics of the archaeologists excavating on the communally held agricultural lands of the site's neighboring communities. In the initial couple of years of mapping, excavation, and clearing of the site some "misunderstandings" had occurred between the archaeologists and community residents.

Specifically, the archaeologists' conception of the territory of the state-defined official "archaeological zone" of Chunchucmil conflicted with another territoriality which preceded the archaeological interest in the space: the land that is coterminous with the "zone" was already divided up into the agricultural lands of five different communities according to the Mexican land-grant (*ejido*) distributions of the 1930s. The project therefore was required by these communities to get access permission to work in the various ejidos, as well as contract laborers from the communities specific to the area of the zone in which they were working.

The second reason for the project's desire to bring in an ethnographer was to facilitate their plans for tourism development in and around the site.[1] Ambitious plans for an artifact museum, a "living museum" (loosely based on Colonial Williamsburg, in which local community residents would move out of their towns into the archaeological zones to demonstrate daily life practices of the ancient Maya), as well as other ventures required complex, ongoing negotiations between the project and community leaders in order to be carried out.

Averse to utilizing ethnography in such a capacity, I declined the offer. At the co-director's continuing interest, however, we returned to the negotiating table. I countered her offer with another, explaining that I thought the site would be an important place for research-oriented ethnography, making clear that I was neither an applied nor a development-oriented anthropologist, but a researcher whose agenda focuses specifically on the interfaces of archaeology and communities. I proposed a trial period during which I would do some background "straight" ethnography on the communities, not focusing exclusively on the archaeological project or its relationships. My project, I suggested, would be to establish the pre- and extra-archaeological context surrounding the site and its current development. In my primary site of research, the genealogy of Maya labor at Chichén Itzá, I had found that over one hundred years of archaeological work—which led to the area's becoming a major international tourism destination—had greatly influenced local conceptions of what Maya heritage is and how the site is inflected with varying understandings of the articulation of the ancient Maya

---

1. For a full explanation of the local meanings of heritage in and around Chunchucmil, see Breglia 2006a. For discussions of the project's efforts at practicing community archaeology, see Breglia (2006b) for an ethnographer's point of view and Ardren (2002) for an archaeologist's perspective.

to the contemporary world. In multiple ways, local residents utilize the site to make claims to this cultural patrimony that is simultaneously "theirs" and that of the Mexican state. Would this phenomenon express itself differently around a site that has only five years of archaeological work? The co-director wholeheartedly accepted my revised offer—"Yes, that sounds like exactly what should be done!"—and offered me a place to stay in the headquarters house. Two weeks later I was living and working in the Chunchucmil project, not as an official project member, but as a guest researcher.

But soon after I began, I found that exactly what was my "work" was an undefined area—not so much for myself, but for the other members of the project as well as community residents. I now turn to this question of the labor of anthropological research, drawing comparisons and contrasts between what archaeologists do in the field with the tasks, labors, and routines of ethnographers. I reference these ideas here in hopes of drawing connections between these characterizations of corporeal practices and questions of method and "data," moving toward destabilizing the Traditional Fieldwork Model.

The problem of labor commensurability was tangibly demonstrated in the obvious differences between the ethnographic and the archaeological workday. For archaeologists, official workdays (either five or six per week) were defined by a rarely variant schedule. Leaving for the fieldsite from the headquarters to begin at 6 a.m., project members returned by between 1 and 2 p.m., ate a group meal, and spent the rest of the afternoon engaged in one or more of the following activities: waiting in line for the bathroom, resting, pleasure reading, indoor work at the headquarters house, errands requiring travel to the next large town or to the capital city, or heading back to the excavation site, usually not to dig, but to catch up on taking notes or drawing profiles of the structural features which had been excavated. Almost everyone gathered again for the seven o'clock evening meal, and most were in their hammocks, even sleeping, by 9 p.m. This rigorous schedule is exacerbated by the climate of Yucatán, which is quite challenging even for people who have spent their entire lives there or archaeologists who come back to work season after season.

At least for my kind of research, 6 a.m. is not a particularly ethnographic hour. Thus, I began each day not measuring up to the archaeological work routine, waking up nearly an hour after the archaeologists had gone to the field: truly a series of Malinowskian mornings, as he relates in *Argonauts*:

> I would get out from under my mosquito net, to find around me the village life beginning to stir, or the people well advanced in their working day according to the hour and also to the season, for they get up and begin their labors early or late, as work presses. (1961, 7)

After an hour or so of language study each morning, usually in consultation with the archaeologists' cook and maid, I would bike to the excavation sites (often two or three in proximity to each other). I usually coordinated my arrival with the workers' morning break, at 9 a.m. I typically spent the break-time with the workers, often teaching English/Spanish/Maya equivalents and translations of words and phrases used at the scene of excavation. Most hired laborers were men, ages sixteen to sixty, from Kochol, a Maya town only four kilometers away from the archaeological site center. The same land upon which they were contracted by the archaeological project to work as seasonal wage laborers was their federally granted ejido land, where they were technically permitted to be carrying out cultivation (mostly corn). When break-time was over, I went back to work with them, either digging, hauling rocks, or looking for ceramic sherds or bone or obsidian fragments at the sifting table a few meters from the excavation area. With a tape recorder in a pocket and my notebook in the back of my pants, I used the time I spent working alongside the excavators to conduct conversations and interviews, some about the archaeological work itself, but also about the stuff of everyday life.

At the conclusion of work each day at the excavation site, I would heft my bike into the truck along with buckets, shovels, picks, and other tools and equipment and head with the archaeologists back to the house. Almost every afternoon, a sort of contest took place—a game that was the antithesis of Freilich's work-break game. The terms of the archaeologists' game required the explicit articulation of work rather than the concealment of one's research labor. The game was based on identifying who in the back of the truck was the dirtiest and what that person was doing today to get that dirty. In the final analysis, a discrete measure of work accomplished for the day was who embodied the highest ratio of dirt to sweat to produce the most generally awful appearance. I'm sure it goes without saying: I never won. I was not in the thick of archaeological work, and my body physically bore this sign.

The understandings of differing labor regimes, methods, and data I found to be embedded within other deep epistemologies of "the field," both spatial and temporal. Basically, it was articulated (understood more than dictated as such) from the outset that my field of research was based on the contemporary community—"contemporary" meaning at the moment archaeology comes onto the scene and "community" referring both to local residents and to the towns themselves. Thus, it was expected that the labor of my research would take place in a distinct temporal and spatial "site" apart from the normal workday at the archaeological site. It was unclear as to whether ethnography could take place in the space and time otherwise governed by archaeology. Ethnography was to happen "in the community," understood as the residential and public space of

Kochol proper. That I never appeared to be working on the archaeological site confirmed this turf distinction. Meanwhile, the residential community in comparison becomes an open field, free of archaeological coding in which archaeologists might develop both relationships and extra-archaeological projects outside of that which directly pertains to the scientific record.[2]

The temporal containment of archaeological work is thus matched by a spatial distancing as archaeological work proper is blocked off into discrete hours of the day, usually geographically tied to the fieldsite. Of course, this formulation is not nearly so neat with ethnographic research. In the Traditional Fieldwork Model, especially in the older, community-based model, when is a (good) researcher not doing ethnography? Is the whole time you are in the field doing ethnography? Also included in ethnography's problematic of temporality is the issue of coevalness—that we have to accept that the Other operates within the same temporal horizon as the researcher (Fabian 1983). Coevalness is not as simple as avoiding the use of the ethnographic present in terms of the technologies of representation operative within an archaeological site. What is archaeology if not specialized temporal knowledge, in this case, of the "Classic" period of Maya civilization (250–900 CE)? I would have just said "ancient." Certainly, one can't use common sense to understand social organization in an urban trading zone more than a thousand years ago the way that an ethnographer can (supposedly) understand "culture" just by heading over to a typical family's home in the village and spending the afternoon hanging about and talking.[3]

Working with archaeologists, I was quick to realize how hard they work, how precisely they gather their data, and how thoroughly they set about its interpretation. This doesn't compare well at all with perceptions of ethnography, especially because it is framed as a commonsense enterprise. While archaeologists labor in definitiveness and exactitude, ethnographers are turning toward contingency and ambiguity. While archaeology literally unearths tangible data destined to become part of an empirical record, ethnographic success is the attempt to reconcile

---

2. The study of local meanings of heritage and the impacts of archaeological development has now very quickly become a sub-subdisciplinary field called "ethnography of archaeology," and the publications resulting from my own research at Chunchucmil are featured among the "ethnography of archaeology" literature, though fewer cultural anthropologists than archaeologists are represented in this arena. Two examples of recent edited volumes show that archaeologists are active ethnographers in their excavation sites. Edgeworth (2006) is nearly exclusively confined to archaeology, while Mortensen and Hollowell (in press) offers a more balanced representation between cultural anthropologists and archaeologists with ethnographic perspectives on archaeology and heritage.

3. However, archaeologists equally run the risk of denying coevalness. Project members mixed temporal epistemologies in their pedagogic interventions with Maya site-workers, telling them "your ancestors built this," even when residents clearly expressed a nonaffiliation, that the ancient Maya were a different "race" of people (see Breglia 2006a).

ephemera with emergence.[4] In ethnography, the "messiness" of fieldwork is cele-brated. Yet this messiness is part of ethnography's insider discourse; it is an image that cannot survive the moment of transferal to an outside perspective. While our concept of the messiness of the field attempts to situate the complicities, complexities, and ambiguities of relationships and interventions, anachronistic standards of positivistic empiricism are still brought to bear upon it.

The deep incommensurability is exacerbated by the responsibilities of reportage. I think that ethnographers and archaeologists have different expec-tations in "coming clean" through their reporting. Archaeologists don't have to come clean about the dirty secrets of their project (misspent funds from questionable sources, exaggerated material evidence to support interesting and unique arguments about the site, tensions with local communities, etc.). What's more, archaeologists have the obligation to reconcile their findings not with those of ethnographers or the contemporary social contexts of their knowledge production, but instead with the archaeological record. The ethnographer has a different set of obligations. These are, in the spirit of the ethics and responsi-bilities of contemporary ethnography, to provide relevant, well-constructed, and theoretically sound, yet innovative, ethnographic productions. As an unspoken arrangement between the directors of the project and myself, I was often called upon to "come clean" at the dinner table. What did I find out about the people today? This was cause for much anxiety on my part, as, truth be told, I thought it not ethical to make the archaeologists privy to much of what was discussed both on-site and off with local residents, many of whom were highly critical of their project and suspicious of their intentions, especially those concerning tourism development at the site. The limits and dangers of the work-break game, as it had come to be played out on multiple levels, came into sharp and uncomfort-able relief.

A Pedagogy of Recognition

My apprentice fieldwork highlighted for me the possibilities of re-visioning ethnographic practice by taking seriously "outsider" perceptions and uses of ethnography—in my case, those of fellow anthropologists with whom I shared

---

4. Recalling a quotation that ends in a now very famous line, let us note that Malinowski was addressing the intangible data of ethnography in his preceding sentence, "there is a series of phe-nomena of great importance which cannot possibly be recorded by questioning or computing docu-ments, but have to be observed in their full actuality. Let us call them the imponderabilia of actual life" (1961, 18).

a geographical if not discursive mise-en-scène of fieldwork. Diana Forsythe addresses precisely this issue of outsider perception in her article "'It's Just a Matter of Common Sense': Ethnography as Invisible Work" (1999).[5] While Forsythe examines the use of ethnography by anthropologists and nonanthropologists in the design and evaluation of software and information processing systems, the perceptions of ethnographic practice she uncovers are precisely the same as those articulated in practice by archaeologists with whom I ostensibly shared a fieldsite. I can attest to at least two of the assumptions Forsythe documents in her own observations: "Since ethnography does not involve preformulated study designs, it involves no systematic method at all—'anything goes'" and "Doing fieldwork is just chatting with people and reporting what they say" (1999, 130).

For those embedded in the lexicon and accompanying ideology of "expert knowledge," of tried, tested, and true "research instruments" (i.e., those in the harder sciences), ethnography would seem a walk in the park of facility and transparency. Thus, I am sympathetic to the logic of their "native point of view"; yet I am equally riled (just as Forsythe seems quite exasperated) by the implication that ethnography represents a baseline, transparent approach to easily graspable phenomena and thus requires no training. If this logic were extended, what ethnography would entail is time and patience, a friendly and approachable disposition, and a willingness to put oneself "out there" and always be "on." These characteristics are set in the rhetoric of disposition—personal qualities that some people just have, rather than learned skills. While we would like to flatter ourselves into thinking that we are indeed *born* ethnographers, we know as well that there is quite a lot of work to *becoming* ethnographers.

And therein lies our concern: to consider the work of fieldwork in the pedagogy of apprentice research practice. While it is clear that "outsiders" perceive ethnography as neither specialized nor professionalized nor technical, perhaps we—especially by sticking with the phantasmatic image of the Traditional Fieldwork Model—have fallen into that very same trap. As part of a seemingly archaic discourse on methods, Freilich's "work-break game" brings the latent conservatism of the Traditional Fieldwork Model into bold relief. By playing it (perhaps without even knowing what it was!) ethnographers shoulder some responsibility for making our research practice appear to disappear from our

---

5. Forsythe's notion of ethnography as invisible work is related, I believe, to recent thinking about the organization of labor and the attendant new power relations under conditions of contemporary capitalism. Lazzarato (1996) and Hardt and Negri (2004) discuss immaterial labor in the context of intellectual activity. For them, immaterial labor is that which produces cultural-informational context or the intangible products (relationships, etc.) that precede the production of goods.

fieldwork engagements. There is, however, another option—refusal to play the work-break game. Not agreeing to conceal the work of fieldwork is one way in which the latent *experimental* nature of ethnographic practice, as this volume suggests, reveals itself in creative, productive, and highly "workable" moments in the apprentice field research experience.

Part 2

ON THE ETHICS OF BEING AN ANTHROPOLOGIST (NOW)

7

THE ETHICS OF FIELDWORK AS AN ETHICS OF CONNECTIVITY, OR THE GOOD ANTHROPOLOGIST (ISN'T WHAT SHE USED TO BE)

James D. Faubion

Only connect? I hesitate to join the legion who have appropriated Margaret Schlegel's passionate imperative from E. M. Forster's *Howard's End* (1921) even in the form of a question, but in the form of a question it invites the articulation of a point that captures the illocutionary force of all of the papers of this volume, whatever else their authors might intend. The point is not simply that anthropology is and has always been about making connections. Nor is it simply that the connections that anthropologists have made and continue to make are of diverse kinds and, within each kind, of diverse modes. More emphatically, the point is that only connecting is neither in fact nor in principle anthropologically adequate. Which connections the anthropologist makes—to the human subjects under investigation, to the scenes and sites of investigation, to subjects and scenes and sites already investigated, to analytical apparatuses, to anthropology as a discipline, to the world at large, and by no means least to herself—are also of critical moment to the best pursuit of any anthropological project and so to being a better anthropologist rather than a worse one. The point is further that the good anthropologist consequently is not and cannot be what she used to be. The point has been made before, but our contributors provide it with rich and novel substance, and it is under their inspiration that I proceed to develop it further in what follows.

Classical Connectivity

There has been no shortage of talk of "the ethics of fieldwork" in the past several decades. It continues to echo the radicalizations of the 1960s and the Vietnam War as a sort of background radiation, but its more constant pitch is now the work of the auditors of informed consent. Its norms of rectitude are contractarian at their broadest, legalistic in their more immediate ancestry. Its regulative situation appears to be that of the medical experiment or drug trial. As any number of anthropologists who have struggled to complete with even a semblance of authenticity the protocols of the Internal Review Boards of the colleges or universities who employ them are aware, the auditors tend to have little if any idea of what the situation of fieldwork is typically like. The subject they expect to sign on the dotted line is rarely the sort of subject that the anthropologist encounters in the field (and see Jennifer Hamilton's contribution to this volume). The dotted line itself is in fact often far more a hindrance to the process of conducting fieldwork than the mark of due diligence for the subject's welfare that it is supposed to be. For all of this, it now functions as a Categorical Imperative of anthropological fieldwork as it is obliged to be practiced, if not always as an actual practice—and all the more stringently, as Deepa Reddy observes in this volume, when one finds oneself coordinating one's efforts and collaborating with scientists and scientific institutions inclined to extract far more from their human subjects than "oral history" alone.

The anthropologist would probably not be considered very "good" in several senses of the term who embraced Margaret Schlegel's cause of the mystical fusion of passion and prose. Even so, the fieldworker is perhaps better who, as E. E. Evans-Pritchard suggested, has a certain aesthetic discernment, a sensitivity to pattern and coherence, to intentions and their expressions and disguises, to matters of heart as well as matters of mind (Evans-Pritchard 1951). Of course, a good dose of alienation from the ordinary course of social and cultural life is also useful. Bronislaw Malinowski's diaries alone are sufficient to establish that he who has a talent for fieldwork need not be someone who is naturally at ease in whatever human company he happens to find himself (Malinowski 1967). At the same time, the better fieldworker does well to have a considerable thickness of skin—if not an incapacity to recognize social disapproval then at least a generous gift of indifference to it. In ancient Greek, the *anthrôpologos* is someone fond of conversing about the personal affairs of others who in his less flattering incarnations might exhibit a curiosity bordering on or perhaps even passing into nosiness. Anyone with a knack for fieldwork is his characterological heir. If anthropologist and fieldworker remain at least as intimately entwined as they have ever been, the good anthropologist must not *ipso facto* be assumed to be a good person, much less a nice one.

With Michel Foucault's forays into the genealogy of the Western ethics of corporal pleasure and the care of the self, we have a protocol for approaching the ethics of anthropology neither merely as some ensemble of oughts and ought nots nor as the active exercise of some congenital endowment of temperament and penchant. We can approach it more broadly as consisting of the virtues and the exercises integral to the proper occupation of the position of a distinctive subject at once able and authorized to engage certain ends. The person who would become any such subject (and it is a matter not merely of being born but of becoming, as Lisa Breglia advises us, for the anthropologist as much as for the subject of any other kind) must be at least dimly aware of the ends at issue, but in any event must be trained or train herself in those competencies and virtues that would permit their pursuit in the first place. Foucault designates those capacities or particular dimensions of temperament or character or mind or being in the world that are the focus of such training as the "substance" of the ethics of that subject. Hence, for example, he designates the *aphrodisia* or "carnal pleasures" as the substance of the ancient Greek ethics of *sophrosunê* or "self-control" (Foucault 1985). The early Christian ascetic elite, who came to regard all that was fleshly as hopelessly corrupt, could not, in contrast, treat bodily pleasures as the substance of any possible ethical tempering or ethical development. They would instead turn their pedagogical attention to the only substance they thought powerful enough to enable them to put the carnal behind them—the soul or spirit (Foucault 1986; cf. Faubion 2001b).

Connectivity is as good a general candidate as I can find to advance for the ethical substance of the anthropologist qua fieldworker present and past. Its classical scope is fixed at the very foundation of anthropology as an academic discipline between two presiding ends: knowledge of other human social and cultural formations; and the reform of those social and cultural formations one would call one's own. Edward Burnett Tylor's conclusion to *Primitive Culture* is entirely exemplary:

> To impress men's minds with a doctrine of development, will lead them…often [to] move onward with clear view. It is a harsher, and at times even painful, office of ethnography to expose the remains of crude old culture which have passed into harmful superstition, and to mark these out for destruction. Yet this work, if less genial, is not less urgently needful for the good of mankind. Thus, active at once in aiding progress and in removing hindrance, the science of culture is essentially a reformer's science. (Tylor 1994, 410)

The reforms that Tylor chiefly has in mind have as their target the ritualism of Catholicism and its Anglican cousin. In *Primitive Culture*, Mary Douglas's *Natural Symbols* (1970) thus has its direct, if antithetical, ancestor. In between come a rather louder and more continuous stream of reformist Americans, none more seminal than Franz Boas and none louder than Margaret Mead. Emile Durkheim's

musings on "collective effervescence" for their part inspire the surrealist Jacobin-
ism of such irrationalist bad-boys as Georges Bataille, whose near-revolutionary
embrace of excess and transgression, sex and death will demand nothing less
imperious than Claude Lévi-Strauss's denunciation of the senselessness of sacrifice in *The Savage Mind* to tame (Durkheim 1995, 218–20; Lévi-Strauss 1966,
228; cf. Bataille 1989). From Tylor to Mead and Lévi-Strauss, national traditions
indeed vary, but the current of reformist reflexivity itself remains remarkably of
a piece. From one exercise to the next, it is a method of critique that resorts to the
Other in order to highlight the prejudices and the shortcomings—in short, the
less than perfect progress—of that great Same-That-Is-Not-One that is Western
civilization from the late nineteenth through the first two-thirds of the twentieth
century. It takes entirely for granted that the divide between self and other can be
securely and definitively drawn. Between the anthropologist and her informant,
connectivity might best consist in what Clifford Geertz distilled in introducing
the Balinese cockfight as a certain You're-O.K.-I'm-O.K. rapport (Geertz 1973b),
but anything more intimate remained beyond question and the rudimentary
admonition not to "go native" (and see again Breglia's contribution to this volume) quite enough to keep it that way.

The Problematization
of Classical Connectivity

The classical modes of connectivity, which continue (sometimes but not always
under the explicit banner of "public anthropology") to make the occasional academic and more frequent journalistic splash today, do not, however, come to the
forefront of the battles over disciplinary capital that constitute the sniper's war
that is today's anthropological fashion without undergoing a significant transformation. That transformation provides the rationale for George Marcus and
Michael Fischer's pronouncement that no anthropologist had ever practiced
"cultural critique" as they conceived it in 1986 as it does for the self-conscious
iconoclasm and vanguardism of many of the contributors that Marcus and James
Clifford publish in *Writing Culture* in the same year (cf. Marcus and Fischer 1986,
111; Clifford and Marcus 1986). I would, however, be remiss were I not to mention as an important precursor the volume drawn together by my fellow Reed
College alumnus Dell Hymes under the title *Reinventing Anthropology,* which
had its first incarnation in 1969 (cf. Hymes 1972). What the contributors to
the two latter volumes largely share is a sometimes more, sometimes less subtle
indignation at the collusion between anthropology and colonialist imperialism.
The reflexivity that the contributors to both exemplify is a reflexivity born in the

broader politics of consciousness-raising of which the young adults among the civil rights and anti-war activists of the period were such ardent champions. In *Writing Culture* and *Reinventing Anthropology* alike, the most sustained object of reflexive and reformist intention is, broadly speaking, anthropology itself, but more narrowly, none other than the prevailing ethics of anthropological connectivity.

Precisely this professional self-critique, this reflexive problematization of classical connectivity, is what distinguishes both volumes from any of their properly classical predecessors. Yet the critical scope of Hymes and his cohort is much more restricted than that of the group that Clifford and Marcus gathered at the precincts—quite distant from necessity, it might be added—of Santa Fe's School for American Research in 1984 to engage "the politics and poetics of ethnography." One might marvel at what can now only seem the naïve confidence in both the scientific integrity of anthropology and the fecundity of its role in a program of human liberation that Hymes and his cohort can still express. Their critical disapprobation is primarily reserved for the establishment politics and myopia of an anthropology already in the process of becoming past. The interlocutors at Santa Fe can take such disapprobation largely for granted. Their more immediate concern lies not with the dirty hands of ethnographers become spies or apologists for the imperialist centers from which they hailed. It lies rather with the distortions incidental and systematic wrought at every stage of the generation of what has passed as anthropological knowledge, from observation to participation, from translation to concept-formation, from the linearity of record-taking to the inescapable tropologies of textualization. At the School for American Research in 1984, it was not merely the bad behavior of anthropologists that was subjected to a cold critical eye. It was the disciplinary pretension ever to have produced anything that could count as genuine knowledge at all.

As critiques of the ethics of connectivity, both volumes nevertheless depart from very much the same charge. Both hold anthropological practice as they know it to have been guilty of a certain excess of distance from those who were or might be their "informants." None of the contributors to either volume was thinking for a moment to overturn the proscription against going native. Yet, as collective statements, both volumes take anthropology to task for an established aloofness of three sorts. One of these is a matter of the willful or simply conventional neglect of subjects—from inner-city minorities to corporate executives—who would enrich the anthropological corpus (and its reformist strategies) if only they could be brought into it. Another is a matter of the willful or unwitting disregard of the macro-structural and especially the politico-economic situation of its subjects actual and potential. The third, which is actually a more general version of the second, is a matter of the unwillingness or inability to meet the standards of familiarity and fluency with the natives' point or points of view of which the first chapter of *Argonauts of the Western Pacific* had long since become a disciplinary Leviticus.

During an interview that I conducted a few years ago in the course of seeking to fill an empty faculty position in the Rice department, a respondent confessed to me her relief that *Writing Culture* had not, after all, succeeded in destroying anthropology altogether, "as it had set out to do." If I rapidly erased her from the list of contenders, this was not primarily because I feared that she might fail of the sort of collegiality for which one might hope, but instead because she had revealed herself to be as poor a reader as so many others who have taken *Writing Culture* as a handbook for anthropological suicide. Were the joint upshot of the volume reducible to Clifford's satire of ethnographic authority there would be greater justification for treating it as such a handbook, though only marginally greater, since Clifford himself, then and now, has been as much admirer as critic of the discipline. Nor is the volume Clifford's alone; Paul Rabinow's essay on representations (not least among them representations of the end of all epistemic authority, ethnographic authority included) as social facts is a satire of the Cliffordian satire and a self-consciously classical counterweight to its modish hermeneutics of suspicion. Taken as a joint endeavor, *Writing Culture* does not destroy the possibility of ethnographic authority, but rather renders it with an almost cruel thoroughness an epistemological problem. If it has seemed to many readers not simply thorough but devastating in its problematization of such authority, this is because it was not forthcoming with a ready consensus on solutions and because every solution seemed to rest on an ethnographic method whose uncontroversially legitimate exercise would require the sort of unlimited finances and world enough and especially time that neither the Wenner-Gren Foundation nor any serious tenure committee could possibly countenance. In this respect, it was in fact a remarkably conservative volume, a reinscription of the Malinowskian orthodoxies of methodological thoroughness and relational intimacy precisely in order to call the bluff of the myriad compromises and shortcuts and ideological blindnesses of which fieldwork was actually made.

Reformation, Counter-reformation, and Counter-counter-reformation

Epistemologically preoccupied, *Writing Culture* nevertheless exhibits—in Talal Asad's exasperation with Evans-Pritchard, in Clifford's deflation of Geertz, but also in Asad's and Rabinow's and several other contributors' engagement with an "anthropology of the West"—the hallmarks of another vector of the disruption of the classic terms of anthropological connectivity whose broader sociological ecology should probably be traced back well before Vietnam to the end of the Second World War. It is an ecology for which such colonialist paroxysms as those of the Franco-Algerian War as well as that enduring trinity of human, all too human monstrosity—Hitler, Stalin, and The Bomb—remain iconic even today, as the Second World War is perhaps finally drawing to a close. Organizational theorists like to identify within it the transition from an industrial to a post-industrial or information society, but David Westbrook's remarkable *City of Gold* has almost convinced me that what they have really been seeing is the systematic institutionalization of the particular sort of reflexive constitutionalism that had as its aim the prevention of another Nazi Germany and as its means a slate of strategies intended to promote political and economic interdependency that coalesce in part into the Bretton Woods accords (Westbrook 2004). A great many of the activists of prevention and interdependency who belong to the "New Social Movements"—Anthony Giddens and company's "reflexive modernizers" (Beck, Giddens, and Lash 1994)—would no doubt be horrified to find themselves in less than complete disaccord with the guiding principles of what we are now calling "neo-liberalism," but in their ethics of vigilance as in their ontologies of intersystematicity and intersystematic overdetermination, they are in less than complete disaccord in fact, whatever their specific political predilections may be. The late Marxists are carriers of much the same current of what now passes under such terms as "internationalism" or "transnationalism," including the several existentialist Marxists who have a place in the Hymes volume. The hybridizing offspring (some Marx here, a dose of Weber there, even a Durkheimian undertone or two) of the late Frankfurt School join them there, as do the earliest and most haunted of the French poststructuralists.

Among poststructuralists, however, Pierre Bourdieu remains to his end the most unremitting classicist of them all. His foundational formula of anthropological connectivity is that of the strictly inverse correlation between the degree to which the investigator has vested interests in the practical arena into which he inquires and his ability to come to objective sociological terms with it (see Bourdieu 1992). Its realization depends on the establishment and maintenance of precisely the sort of great divide that informs the inquiry into Other Cultures from Malinowski through Geertz and against which the ecology of the aftermath of the Second World War would militate from its inception. Presuming that his own "reflexive" account of the putatively mutual exclusivity of the position of the (practicing) scientist and that of the (nonscientific) practitioner resolved the question of the substance of the good anthropologist (qua social scientist, of course) in its entirety, Bourdieu could once be overheard to dismiss the mandarinate of *Writing Culture* as a band of imitators who "thought they were Parisians, but were not." Perhaps a few of them would have liked to be Parisians, but not one of them in any event believed that Bourdieu's account, immensely tidy and complete in theory, amounted to anything more than a utopian fantasy of the actual situation of the fieldworker herself. Rabinow—here adopting a decidedly postclassical vantage—inaugurates the program of a more realist diagnostics of that situation in *Reflections on Fieldwork in Morocco* (1977). Jean-Paul Dumont soon follows with *The Headman and I* (1978). *Writing Culture* continues it and, in this respect at least, marks a moment that continues unabated into the anthropological present—here and now in this volume included. So Deepa Reddy and Nahal Naficy illustrate for us that "native" and "anthropologist" often find themselves to be identical but rivalrous twins. Christopher Kelty and troupe remind us that scientists often wear politically committed hats and Kim Fortun that anthropologists wear them as one among many inescapable stigmata of their guild. Naficy and Hamilton point out to us that such hats are nevertheless not always of one's own choosing and can sometimes fit very ill, indeed. For diverse reasons, Breglia, Reddy, and Hamilton register similar complaints about the scientific hat as well. Kristin Peterson and Jae Chung render the matter macro-structurally: it's all about embeddedness, and the anthropologist is no more capable of transcending it than any of her interlocutors, collaborators, epistemic partners, critics, rivals, or doubles are themselves.

The ethical problem of connectivity still before us is complex and is surely at once epistemological and ontological. It endures at once as the controversy—which frequently descends into campishness—over what actually counts as anthropological knowledge and as the controversy over what the situation—the placement and the relata—of the fieldworker is and should be. Symptomatic of its enduring lack of resolution is the ongoing proliferation of diagnoses and diagnostic terminologies of that situation—or rather, of those situations, for if anything at all is clear it is that anthropological situations are heterogeneous and plural. "Rapport" is much discredited—but not dead. One of very few anthropologists apparently not yet ready to throw up his hands at the problem, Marcus has been especially productive of alternatives. Hence, the situation of the postclassical fieldworker might be labeled "multi-sited" (Marcus 1995), "circumstantially activistic" (again Marcus 1995), "complicit" (Marcus 1997), or "collaborative" (Holmes and Marcus 2006). Marilyn Strathern has contemplated the diagnostic utility of a range of concepts emphasizing the open-endedness, the partial connectivity, the indefiniteness, even the artifice of the fieldworker's situation, of which the "cyborgic" is to her mind particularly apt (Strathern 1991). The anthropologists of Robert Borofsky's monographic series are out of bounds, Ruth Behar's have broken hearts (1986), and Rabinow's situation in the field appears to have evolved from one of constrained friendship (1977) to the rather more formal "adjacency" (2003). One of my most recent students, dissatisfied with every one of this scatter of possibilities, declared his own relation to his subjects to be "collegial—maybe" (Michael Powell, personal communication).

The upshot—which the Counter-counter-reformationist contributors to this volume, one and all, only make further patent—is not to choose one entry in such a variable and jointly inconsistent list and cling to it as if it alone, across all situational contexts, were the only appropriate successor to the classic posture of rapport and the only ratio of connectivity appropriate for the generation of "real" anthropological knowledge. The discipline in fact never imposed and was never able to impose so limited a construal of the proper substance of the fieldworker's connectivity, as the very different construal of that substance both within and between the traditions of British social anthropology and American cultural anthropology is enough to establish. The upshot—to which several of the contributors to other recent collections on the conduct of fieldwork in the contemporary world have also borne witness (see, e.g., Amit 2000)—is that the ontological categories that secured and sustained the analytical plausibility of the great divide between Self and Other from Malinowski through Bourdieu are effectively vacuous. We can no longer count cultures, one and then another, planetoid and of independent orbit. We can no longer treat societies as natural ensembles of a quasi-organic sort. We are left with processes and their intersections, dimensions of structure and causality whose articulations may differ radically in their historicities and temporalities, but whose shifts and constancies do not in any event permit of a secure and sustained distinction between Us and Them, home and field, what is and what is not potentially and properly of anthropological interest. Of the essays included here, those of Peterson and Chung are especially articulate in their revelation that the fieldworker today is caught in a field that is quite literally everywhere, that she is always already entangled in a matrix of multifarious ratios of connectivity from which there is no relief in sight except through the pretense of temporary retirement or disingenuous naiveté. Summarily put, the substance of anthropological connectivity is now perhaps more than it ever was not one but heterogeneously many things, a gamut of ratios defined not by their common content but by their standing between the still perilous Scylla of going native and the now phantasmatic Charybdis of declaring positively Other the native that one always already somewhat is anyway.

The Anthropological Triangle

Not a few of the recent anthropological inquiries into such relatively rationalized domains as finance or one or other of the natural sciences tend toward an epistemological naiveté and ontological freshness of face that may not always be inspired by but certainly have a mascot in Bruno Latour. Such inquiries are not of a single cloth, but do have fairly constant points of ontological orientation. One of these comes with the prioritization of production over reproduction, of difference over repetition. Another comes with the presumption that the basic tissue of the contemporary world is itself heterogeneous. The first of these orientations has frequent expression in the call to attend to the "emergent." The second has frequent expression as the pronouncement of the death or at least the outmodedness of "theory," at least in the singular. The former characterizes Paul Rabinow's recent trilogy of investigations of the domain of biotechnology (Rabinow 1999, 2003, 2005). The latter has characterized George Marcus's reflections on research design and procedure from his essay on fieldwork in and of the world system forward. Here as elsewhere, however, neither men nor their battles but the ecology they together inhabit has the greater influence on the prevailing tide.

In all too brief summary, I would suggest (echoing several of our contributors) that the increasing saliency of the emergent has much ecologically to do with the collapse of the Soviet geopolitical system and much to do with the expansion of a geopolitical Europe—and even more to do with globalization and with disorganized but culturally ever so thin capitalism and the double impulsion of both toward the deterritorialization of what remnants there might be of coherent cultural systems and toward the ever more normative individualization of the ever more normatively flexible citizens and subjects of a planet very much on the move. It has much accordingly to do with the ballooning of the suspicion that one has neither culture nor society to which to belong, and so with the increasing frequency with which anthropologists have been finding themselves summoned to act as secularized spiritual advisers to the human subjects of their research, which is often otherwise known as the blind leading the blind. The saliency of the emergent is linked to a disillusionment with grand theory. Both of these constitute a disenchanted response to the once enchanting esotericism of the epistemological and ontological maelstrom that various French and German and English poststructuralist intellectuals wrought. At the same time, both orientations stand in intimate symmetry to the current form and (dys)function of sociocultural anthropology itself. If the internationalization of the discipline—which with only a few exceptions began to transpire in earnest only in the 1970s and for which the appeal in the middle 1980s for a "repatriation" of anthropology as cultural critique was a further catalyst—is not complete, it is indisputably irreversible. We ourselves are heterogeneous. We know it. The question is what to make of it. No single theoretical edifice any longer appears to be even remotely the answer. This or that integrative concept of comparative relevance—or rather, an eclectic aggregate of many such concepts—seems likely to have to do. Sociocultural anthropology now is also a behemoth of sheer numerical but also organizational proportions that its founders could hardly have imagined it would ever be. We are a multitude. We know that, too. The question, once again, is what to make of it, what being we thus might claim. No single theoretical edifice—here, either—seems to afford a plausible answer.

Until revisiting the essays of this volume, I had been inclined to regard such an epistemico-ontological turn as a distinct and novel departure, a break not with reflexivity—though some of its champions have proposed to character-ize it as just that (Maurer 2005)—but a break instead with the phenomenalism (typically known as "constructionism"; cf. Faubion and Marcus 2007) that has dominated both social and cultural analysis since the early 1970s. The contribu-tions to this volume have inclined me to consider that the turn is instead the realization in clearer and less qualified form than we have previously seen of what is in fact simply one of the poles of the aporias of connectivity that I have already been visiting. Perhaps the blunt force of the geopolitical dynamics of the past two decades has finally shaken that pole free of the misplaced excrescences of positivism with which it might previously have been burdened. Or perhaps the same blunt force has emboldened those who were keeping their positivism largely to themselves to come out of their closets. Or, most likely, both alterna-tives are at play. In any case, what is at issue is a new wave of objectivism, whose objective meaning wants and needs more interpreting than the epistemologi-cal insouciance of such happy objectivists as Latour and his followers reflects. Such objectivism does not stand apart from the other dimensions of the working anthropologist's situation, and any of its particular formulations is always con-ditioned by the other dimensions of that situation.

Jointly, again, the chapters in this volume bring to light not just an oscil-lation between epistemologically or ontologically saturated endeavors of problem-formation and inquiry, but also a triangulation of the (field)working anthropologist's situation, each of whose three vectors imposes conditions on the two others and all of which impose a particular structure on the substance of connectivity from one case to the next. One of these is moral and affective and ranges from the coolest of professional acknowledgments—collegiality, maybe—to the most impassioned and intimate advocacy (or, if very rarely in fact, condemnation). Breglia and Reddy are masters of the understatement of this vector, even as they still make quite a statement. Hamilton and Peterson are less reserved. Naficy throws the curtain wide open. If for my part I somewhat neglect this vector here, I do so only because it has already been the object of a great deal of reflection and debate. My neglect notwithstanding, it unquestion-ably constitutes one of the lines of force of the anthropologist's encounter and involvement with her subjects, and just as unquestionably has an influence on the structure of anthropological attention throughout the course of fieldwork itself. Hence, it has an impact on both the production of the evidence that constitutes the basis of any diagnostic pronouncement and the selection and specification of the universe—the subjects and objects—under investigation. The evidential and perspectival vector of the anthropologist's labors has repercussions on the moral and affective vector in turn, if only because it defines the conditions of the assessment of possibility and plausibility on which all practical action depends. In defining such conditions, it must already engage the third vector, at least a hypothetical or provisional ontology of whose existence evidence is prima facie available—though of course, all our epistemological specters aside, most of us can and must go into the field with considerably more ontological confidence in the existence of such things as human beings than that. With whatever confidence, whether essentialist or anti-essentialist or simply agnostic, the ontology on which the anthropologist depends when entering and in involving herself in the field cannot itself but have a direct impact on the moral and probably also the affective relation she cultivates or sustains—or breaks off—with her subjects. Breglia's discussion of the "site" as a ready-made—but then again, a terrain or terrains in the making—is a fine evocation of all of these inter-implications.

So the circuit closes. The resolution of the triangulation of the anthropological situation is thus morally, epistemologically, and ontologically holistic. Alter one of its constitutive vectors and one is obliged to make adjustments to the two others. A fortiori, the same can and must be said of connectivity. Yet, the latter remains substantively too complex to permit of a single designation, and the terminological scatter it has inspired remains unresolved for two general reasons. The first of these is that anthropological connectivity cannot from one case to the next ever be fully abstracted from its (holistic) context. It remains resolutely particular. This is why, *stricto sensu,* there is not and cannot be a perfectly general method of anthropological inquiry. The second source of the complexity of connectivity is its instability or, better put, its inherent provisionality. The discipline's pedagogical lore is replete with advisories to just this end. The conventional wisdom that deems good fieldwork to consist of bringing about a change of the concepts, the presumptions, the theoretical affections with which the anthropologist enters the field is but one example. Such wisdom hardly amounts to a constant truth, much less a necessary one. Yet, it does appropriately underscore that fieldwork well executed is fieldwork pursued not as a quasi-philosophical elaboration of what is already—if perhaps obscurely—known, but instead as a post-philosophical exploration of the adequacy, even the very relevance, of what one has learned, or at least come to suspect, of the subjects and objects of one's proposed investigation. The complexity of connectivity on this front is only enhanced (or exacerbated, depending on one's attitude) by the holistic covalence of its parts.

The Telos of Connectivity (Now): Taking Measure

That anthropological connectivity resides logically within a moral-affective, epistemological, and ontological triangle does not itself imply anything at all about the manner, the Foucauldian mode, in which the anthropologist-in-relation is disposed toward the standards and possibilities—reformist and intellectual— of anthropological accomplishment, of the manner in which she pursues the transformation of the always irreducibly particular experiential stuff with which fieldwork leaves us into something for which she would claim a rightful place in the anthropological corpus. Nor does it imply anything determinate about that something—the presumptive telos of fieldwork, the purpose (if not neces- sarily the temporal end) of anthropological research. For the Old Believer, the Malinowskian or Radcliffe-Brownian manner of the inductive generalist might still suffice. If not that, the rather more Boasian manner of the counter-exemplary "case study" that undoes one or another Idol of the Tribe, in which one recent analyst perhaps over-reachingly sees a sort of deconstructionism (Bunzl 2003), provides a different path. The Evans-Pritchardian become Geertzian pursuit of translation, the classic hermeneutical mode of what was long ago known as the New and Higher Criticism, remains something of a third way.

Yet I discern no Old Believers among the contributors to this volume. If every one of them has undertaken field research that in many dimensions meets the exacting criteria of Malinowskian thoroughness, none is seeking to extract typo- logical wisdom—"theory"—from the tokens that fieldwork has brought her way. All are critics and several are critics indeed of one or another present-day Idol of someone's Tribe—from the nomadic NGOs to the very, very sedentary Econo- mists. Yet none resorts to and certainly none would rest merely with the vener- able, schoolish gesture of pointing out that "her people don't do it like that." If translation remains a real issue for most, it is for none the privileged mode of realizing the end—either as conclusion or as telos—of research. It is one means toward establishing commensurabilities in a world in which quite a lot of people speak—because they have little option but to speak—a bit at least of the same language already.

Commensurabilities, I would suggest, are key to the Foucauldian telos of our contributors as anthropologists. In their deployment of tropological lenses and conceptual frameworks through which to situate one or more of the dimensions or features of their "case" in relation to others, with which to establish the prox- imity of those dimensions or features to others concretely but also tropologically and conceptually elsewhere, our contributors offer us anthropology as a topology that refuses to abandon the particularity of its various cases even as it manages to pursue and indeed to grant pride of place to a topologically modulated enterprise of comparison. They are not alone in this mode of being an anthropologist, but the lingering echoes of failure in a few of their essays (Chung's, Hamilton's, Peterson's) indicate that they are not all yet fully aware that they are in fact executing a practice in and beyond the literal site of the field that has no need of an ethnographic totality or of any contribution to some generalist's gamut of human types in order to assert its anthropological credentials.

For our purposes, however crude they may be, it is enough to think of topology as the calculus of the systematicity of the relationships between or among particular phenomena. Phenomena so related are often designated as "singular instances" or "singularities" of the system to which they jointly belong. (Singularities are distinguished from mere "particularities" precisely because of the relations in which they stand to other particular phenomena, which are thus singularities as well: mere particularities are relationless.) In the uncommonly tidy universe of mathematics, systems usually permit of algorithmic characterization. In this our messy world, we should neither expect nor aspire to the same precision. We can nevertheless aspire—and the contributors to this volume are exemplary in aspiring—to effect distinctions between phenomena that do and those that do not express a specific causal or featural profile: between those that are and those that are not merely random, or between those that are and those that are not part of what diagnosticians in other human domains sometimes call a "cluster."

We can proceed, then, to two further tasks. One of these consists in distinguishing between which aspect or aspects of the phenomena we anticipate to have before us—or that actually are before us—we treat as a problem or topic of investigation and which aspect or aspects we relegate to the epistemological and ontological background, to the foil that we provisionally take for granted in investigating a foreground whose articulation is yet to be established. Kim Fortun offers us a touching and compelling treatment of this double issue of interchangeability and coherence in her analysis in this volume of the epistemology, ontology, and pedagogy of the resolution of figure and ground. Hence, another triad, which should not be understood as a series of steps to be taken one after another but, once again, as a triangulated process, each vector of which conditions the others in a closed but eminently adjustable circuit. What the matter is in any case are three modalities of the basic moments of the formation of any research project: the identification of a domain of inquiry; the articulation of a concrete or (beg pardon) operationalizable problem; and the establishment of ideational points of reference (with which, as we have already seen, moral and affective points of reference are bound to be intertwined). In terms more closely suited to those modalities in their own right, we might speak instead of the postulation of the commensurability of the domain of inquiry to another or to others; the articulation of the commensurability of one or more of the aspects of the phenomena within that domain as a question of investigation; and the stipulation of the conceptual metric or metrics provisionally taken for granted that place the domain of inquiry in conceptual proximity to other domains yet to be charted or already explored.

Such a twist might sound simple, but it is not. Beyond the internalization of nominalist caution and a cultivated sensitivity to both similarity and difference, it requires the institutionalization of a working—if always provisional and often less than complete—division of labor among those concepts that are central to the problem of research or the instances of which are themselves under investigation and those that constitute the background that serves research as a place of conceptual departure and return, a conceptual landscape of orientation. The former concepts function like hypotheticals or, more precisely, as potential metrics. The latter function as established metrics. The former do not need—and these days, have little ground—to be concepts of the ethnographic or sociographic totalities that the British tradition after James Frazer long insisted were the only appropriate objects of anthropological comparison. They do not need to be the products of Malinowskian sojourns of indefinitely long extent— which is not to say that they need no grounding in familiarity or acquaintance of the usual fieldworker's sort. Nor is the successful project—to which Chung and Hamilton were both able to rise, if only after exorcising a good many classic demons—necessarily the project that succeeds in the conversion of its potential into actual metrics. Nor is it even one that finds among its encounters in the field the materials to replace a potential metric malformed or misdirected with a metric more likely to be of heuristic and comparative service. As both Chung and Hamilton attest, such replacements may occur and may have to occur far away and long after the field's scenes of encounter have been played out. They may also be such that they effect a reassignation of conceptual functions in which one or more of the metrics previously relegated to the background comes to the fore or vice versa. This may add to what Marcus has deemed the unbearable slowness of being an anthropologist (Marcus 2003). It may sometimes feel like failure. It is in fact simply one of the outcomes possible in any enterprise that has left behind philosophical speculation or deductive exegesis for the riskier work of empirical investigation, empirical discovery, and diagnostic corroboration.

The anthropologist as conceptual measurer in this sense may be the provisioner of scales, but of scales that are not quite the same as those that Strathern puts forth in her foray into complexity theory, nor quite those that Anna Tsing has more recently considered in addressing the analytical shortcomings of the distinction between global and local (Strathern 1991; Tsing 2005, 57–58). The concept of scale used as a means of establishing the ontological or epistemological proximity between or among particular phenomena can certainly rest with establishing only partial connections between or among those phenomena. Yet the broader or more encompassing concept of scale does not necessarily or even regularly constitute a reduction of the complexity of a less broad or empirically more specific one. Nor by any means does a more encompassing concept of scale necessarily stand structurally in a fractal or other strictly recursive relationship to any more specific counterpart. Modernity, for example, frequently functions as a largely established metric not only in the work of most of our contributors but in an increasing number of monographs from an increasing number of anthropology departments in the United States, in Great Britain, even in France. None of the "alternative modernities" of which so many of these monographs provide the details is, however, a fractal variant, a smaller-scale or larger-scale structural replication, of the modernity of which it is an alternate version—else it would not be alternate. A recursive conception of scales as we have construed them variously in this volume—as registers of local, regional, national, transnational, international, and global scope as well as in the abstraction of figure from ground—are in fact far more appropriate to the "merographic" world of static and nested parts and wholes that Strathern deems in an only slightly later analysis (Strathern 1992) to have passed around 1960. Perhaps this is why she has not herself had much further use for it.

Tsing's scalar concepts derive for their part not from complexity theory, but primarily from what she identifies as "scale-making projects" that unfold or would unfold in territories of differing scope. The scale of finance capital is and would be global; that of "franchise cronyism" national; that of "frontier culture" regional; and so on (2005, 60). As they stand, these concepts are functionally ambiguous; they are at once collective constructions (and elements of still more elaborate collective constructions) to be parsed and analytical topoi to be deployed as quite literal placeholders. Tsing is quite explicit in recognizing in their duplicity the source of a self-ironization; she is compelled to treat the concepts accordingly as a bit of a joke. Whatever one might think of such self-imposed self-consciousness (and the infinite regress of the constructionism of constructionism of constructionism…with which it flirts), what distinguishes Tsing's concepts from those that function as topological metrics is first of all the straightforward fact that the former remain (quite literally) spatial. "Modernity"—to reiterate merely one example—is not, however, literally spatial, nor even spatializable. The proximity that, functioning as a topological metric, it establishes between, say, millenarianism in the middle of Texas (Faubion 2001a), pietism in urban Egypt (Mahmoud 2005), and devotionalism in a Mexican convent (Lester 2005) is a proximity that should in no sense be understood in literally spatial terms. Consider similarly the function of the "therapeutic economy" in Peterson's contribution to this volume; of "legal standing" in Hamilton's; of "the aggregate" in Chung's; of "feminism" or "ethnicity" in Reddy's; of "patrimony" and "heritage" in Breglia's. All of these concepts have spatial dimensions. All of them are nevertheless something more and something else besides spatio-temporal, and in some of their contexts of a temporality so abstract as to reduce the spatial to a zero degree.

Minima and Maxima of Anthropological Goodness (Now)

Our contributors' examples as well as the other examples that I have cited provide an approach to the troubled theme of the adequacy of field research quite distinct from those of any of the classic perspectives. The baseline of the project adequately executed is not and cannot any longer be the exhaustive description or salvaging of a complex totality that might subsequently be gleaned for typological generalizations or translated into the terms inherent to another totality of comparable order. Totalities of that sort are no longer part of the picture. The baseline is constituted instead precisely as the resolution of a problem—or in a more precise, topological idiom, the postulation, evaluation, and finally the provision of a metric that establishes a logical proximity between the phenomena that have been cast as a problem and are thus under investigation and phenomena that have already been investigated and for which metrics—at least one and perhaps several more—have been posed. One might venture to think of this as a standard of minimum "thickness," though I am far from confident that the classic notion of thickness of description is itself commensurate with the measure of adequacy as the provision of a metric. Better, I think, to rest with another terminology and a different formula: that the minima of adequacy follow from the question that guides research. The more complex the question, the greater its own number of dimensions, the more likely its resolution (which need not and rarely will be definitive, and which may be nothing more than the considered judgment that no resolution is possible) will require the provision of multiple metrics and, with them, that sine qua non of anthropological field research old and new, greater patience and greater time.

I am flagrantly begging the question of what constitutes a good rather than a bad question, which every pedagogue knows is an inescapably crucial element of any project. Any anthropologist's personal sense of what renders a problem worthy is in any case, qua anthropologist, dependent on the particular articulation of the triangulation of moral-affective, epistemological, and ontological commitments that define her situation. Of the three angles of that situation, the moral-affective angle is likely to have the most direct impact on her own sense of purpose and so on the purpose of the questions she poses. Though much more needs to be said than I am venturing here, the moral-affective angle of her situation is equally likely to have the most direct import for whom she imagines her readers—Ideal and Common—to be, whether fellow anthropologists, a more general academic audience, policymakers, activists, or her very subjects of investigation. The worthiness of a question is, however, neither merely personal nor merely imaginary. To be sure, it cannot be reduced to the simple numerical count of "stakeholders"—as the policymakers like to call them—for which its resolution matters or makes a difference. Yet, that a question "speaks to" others who have some stake in its resolution is not irrelevant or merely accidentally linked to its merits as a question. The worthiness, the significance of a question is always in some part due to its focus on unexplored or incompletely or inconsistently explored intellectual terrains, the terrains of Science. It is in some part always also due to its engagement beyond those terrains with the morally, ethically, politically, and economically windblown Ecumene—to which anthropology as a pedagogical discipline and the academy as a pedagogical institution are of course parties. A pedagogical rule of thumb seems in order: The clearer the anthropologist is about the angles of her situation and their tangents in both Science and the Ecumene, the more securely worthy the questions she poses and follows are likely to be.

Even with a worthy question as her guidepost, its resolution her minimal quest (and a little money in her pocket), however, the anthropologist today is not in general equipped to give any precise determination of the end—the conclusion—of fieldwork. This is not simply because, as we all know and as Breglia and Reddy remind us with particular vividness, once you've learned the craft of fieldwork, you can't stop doing it, even "on vacation." Two other factors carry more weight. The first is that the minima of the adequacy of anthropological (field) work do not constitute its maxima. The old truism that the best of questions only generate further questions is, for better or worse, still true. The second, which I have already raised briefly, if in slightly different terms, is that the parameters of even—or especially?—the worthiest of questions are not at all guaranteed to remain stable through the empirical course of their resolution, and what instability and mutation they exhibit make unstable and liable to mutation every one of their epistemological and ontological fortifications. That her questions are and must be acutely sensitive to the actual world, its actual slings and arrows and twists and turns, is the curse of the anthropologist's being neither philosopher nor grand theorist but just a plain inquirer instead. The blurring of the difference between field and home only adds to its irritations.

If anthropological (field)work today thus looms as the specter of a Sisyphean labor, endless and never redeemed, it does at least permit of functionally distinct divisions that give it a rather different look from fieldwork of the past. Neither the extended sojourn nor the serial return to the same or closely related physical sites yields a correct model of its physiognomy. Good anthropology will always take time. Yet I can see no reason for concluding that the time it takes must in every case be spent in its bulk in a physical fieldsite. I can see no reason, for example, to expect that the anthropologist who is already fluent in the language and the mores of the places to which she takes her question of investigation should need to spend as much time in those places as someone who has neither linguistic nor cultural fluency. On the other hand, not every worthy question demands for its resolution that its investigator have all the local colors of her sites under her belt. The ethical profile of the good anthropologist, in short, yields no methodological a priori concerning the appropriate duration of a project. Everything hinges on the terms and requirement of the question of research itself.

Given the marked inertia of granting agencies, the anthropological (field) project of the future—in that conventional understanding of a project that granting agencies impose—may well end up looking in fact much as it has looked for several decades: one roughly year-long, more or less continuous encampment at a primary physical site, a few satellite trips here and there, and probably a two- or three-month mop-up before the dissertation or monograph is complete. Yet, in a less conventional understanding of what constitutes an anthropological project, an understanding more in accord with the practices of our contributors, a seriality comes to light that is not merely that of the repeated return to the same physical site (classically, in order to develop an ever richer and deeper comprehension of the people inhabiting that site), but more frequently that of a concatenation of legs—some passed in what we still customarily expect a site to be, but others, no less integral a part of the project itself, passed at the library or in conversation with students and colleagues, legs in which the primary but still altogether integral activity is not that of encounter but instead that of the evaluation, articulation, thinking, and rethinking of what one has already encountered and what one is likely to encounter on the next go. The good anthropologist does go, and goes again, but as Marcus has been trying to convince us for years, the well-wrought question and the program of research that accompanies it by no means demand the occupation and reoccupation of the same site either physically or intellectually. Questions of modernity, these days, can take one just about anywhere and with considerable intellectual continuity from one leg of the journey to the next. In the more conventional understanding of the anthropological project, it might look of late as if many anthropologists radically change projects from the first to the next. In a less conventional understanding of the project, what we might be seeing is often an extension and elaboration of the parameters of the same question pursued, because it must be pursued, in other places than those of its previous pursuit. Perhaps anthropology thus does still amount for many practitioners to a life's work. If so, the good anthropologist will find her way through it. Judging from the work past and planned of the contributors to this volume, she has already done so quite a number of times.

Part 3

TEACHING FIELDWORK THAT IS NOT WHAT IT USED TO BE

8

FIGURING OUT ETHNOGRAPHY

Kim Fortun

When my daughters were very young, there was a game we often played. Each player put his or her hands into a cloth bag filled with wooden figures shaped like animals and also with flat wooden rectangles with cutouts that the various animal figures could fit within. The challenge was to match the figure of an elephant with the cutout space of an elephant, or the figure of a lion with the cutout space of a lion. The challenge, in other words, was to feel and figure out how figure and ground could be brought together. I loved this game from the outset, but only with time did I realize why its effect seemed so familiar. As I felt my own way around the bag of figures and cutouts, or talked my daughters through their wanderings (encouraging patience and creativity, attention to detail and extrapolation), I recognized how similar this is to the process of figuring out ethnographic projects. A process that also requires patience and detail, creativity and extrapolation. A process that is very much about the play of figure and ground. I've learned to enjoy this figuring out in my own work and in the work of graduate students with whom I've worked over the last decade or so in an interdisciplinary department of Science and Technology Studies (STS). In STS, it is not a given that dissertation research and writing will be ethnographic. Ethnography has to be defined, without much curricular support in my context, and often defended. I've had to be able to argue how, in the terminology of STS, ethnography is the "right tool for the job" (Clarke and Fujimura 1992). I've also felt the need to be quite overt and even programmatic in the teaching of what some would call "methods." I have thought about it as the need for purposeful research design.

Provocations to purposefully design ethnographic research have come from many directions. Through my own work on the Bhopal disaster (in which a U.S.-owned and -designed chemical plant blew up, in India) and through work in STS and the history of technology generally, I have learned of the fateful consequences of technical design (Fortun 2001; and, e.g., Perrow 1984). Different technical designs do different things and interact with their contexts in different ways. Some designs are inherently unsafe or (intentionally or not) exclude use by particular social groups. Some designs are more "appropriate" and sustainable than others.[1] Different ethnographic research designs also do different things, drawing out functional stability, for example, privileging what makes a particular system hold together and work, often discounting what destabilizes or queers the system. In some way, ethnographic research projects always build in time, sometimes by default and negation. Without purposeful temporalization, ethnographic subjects tend to be read as Other without reason, as unlikely to change and as indices of a particular context rather than as interpreters and makers of context themselves.[2]

I've come to appreciate, too, the dramatic import of literary form, which I also think of in terms of design. The structure of a discourse or text matters. Different things can be accomplished in a legal affidavit than in a press release. Comedy always ends differently than Tragedy. Form, in many ways, dictates content. I learned about this working as a political activist and ethnographer in Bhopal, where I did my Ph.D. fieldwork. The dictates of literary form were also drawn out by many theoretical currents of the mid-1980s, when I was in graduate school.[3] Arguments about the import of literary form synergized with what I learned about the significance of technical form, in turn attuning me to the significance of the forms through which we think about and carry out ethnographic research.

Most provocative, however, has been the unruly world of the late twentieth and early twenty-first century—a world that has not been easy to study within a traditional ethnographic frame. High awareness of dramatic change has

---

1. The concept of appropriate (or "intermediate") technology became popular in the 1970s through the work of E. F. Schumacher and others building on Gandhian critiques of mass production articulated during the Indian independence movement. Advocates argued that in order to be "appropriate," technology should be designed to fit into its local setting, synchronizing with available material resources, expertise, and labor-time. For a recent analysis that highlights the need for technology to match both users and needs in both complexity and scale, see Hazeltine and Bull's *Appropriate Technology: Tools, Choices, and Implications* (1999).

2. In *Advocacy After Bhopal*, I conceived of my informant groups as "enunciatory communities" rather than as "stakeholder communities" in an effort to avoid this problem.

3. *Writing Culture* (1986) and Hayden White's *Metahistory* (1973) made important impressions, for example, as did Michael Taussig's analysis of the different forms of discourse used by colonizers and colonized in *Shamanism, Colonialism, and the Wild Man* (1987).

characterized many sectors, offsetting informants' own sense of having durable cultural forms. People, ideas, artifacts, and information have circulated with unprecedented scope and speed. For many cultural analysts, focusing their studies on one particular locale or people just didn't make sense.

This has certainly been the case with my students in Science and Technology Studies. As topics, scientific and technological phenomena have always been difficult to pin down to one locale. Even in "lab studies," involving extended ethnographic engagement at one site of scientific production, the best work crosses scale, tracing out funding streams and what they enable and constrain, or tracing the way scientific interest colludes and collides with national interests (see, e.g., Traweek 1988, 1995, 1996, 2000). Studies of scientific practice can also center on research design—as an "object" of study—teasing out why and how scientists configure their studies as they do, how methodologies evolve, and how particular phenomena and problems fade in and out of view. Such studies reveal the temporal, organizational, and disciplinary specificities of science, highlighting the process of scientific work and the way scientists themselves read and strategize the contexts they work within (see, e.g., Fujimura 1987, 1992, 1997). Such studies also reinforce general understanding of the import of research design, whatever the field, and of the conundrums that predictably complicate all knowledge-making schemes.

The challenge of figuring out and fitting figure to ground, for example, is neither new nor unique to cultural anthropology. This challenge does, however, have particular intensity today. The capacity to see and move across scale—using a range of technical prosthetics and information resources—has turned oscillation between figure and ground into a routine even if always demanding move in many fields. Cultural anthropology can be said to be at the "vortex" of the challenge, in Marcus and Fischer's terms, because of its traditional mandate to provide both thick, particularistic description, and comparative perspective, and its contemporary compulsion to explicate both the global and the local, in motion (Marcus and Fischer 1986).

One result is increasing interest among cultural analysts in what can be thought of as open systems—systems that are continually being reconstituted through the interaction of many scales, variables, and forces.[4] Whether the system of concern is the global economy, an organization, or an individual subject, the task is in mapping an array of constitutive dynamics—including but not limited to dynamics at the local level. These kinds of project differ in important ways

---

4. I began working through the idea of ethnography of/as open systems in a review of the second edition of *Anthropology as Cultural Critique* (Fortun 2003). An essay in the *India Review* elaborates on the idea (Fortun 2006).

from traditional anthropological projects while preserving in-depth engagements with real-world situations as a defining methodology. They are often based on complex research designs, often involving ethnography at multiple sites, engagement with multiple scholarly literatures and disciplines, and fluency in many languages, technical as well as natural. At their best, these projects result in dense and complicated accounts of how the contemporary world works, which have relevance both to scholarly debates and to practical efforts to respond to social problems. An open system analysis conjures and temporalizes its "object," both synchronically and diachronically, recognizing diverse forces of change and diverse ways change happens. Identifying pressure points where a given system is subject to change is critical to both description and transformation of an open system.

Talk of open systems and complexity is of course high fashion today. Environmental and computer scientists—informants in my own research—rely on it, as do other kinds of scientists, military strategists, and financial analysts.[5] Nature, the stock market, and organizations of all kinds—among other things—are all captured by the complexity heuristic. I'm game to think in terms of open systems well aware of this discursive context, imagining it as an opportunity to play into and with this context, experimenting with what is becoming hegemonic, creating a shared language for collaboration with different kinds of people. Such an approach makes ethnography itself an open system.

In what follows, I trace the development of my understanding of and my pedagogy to support open systems analysis. I briefly discuss my own research, but primarily focus on how and why I have come to teach ethnographic research design in the way I do, in a course titled "Advanced Qualitative Methods" in particular. In this course, students do a series of short, highly structured "memos" in which they articulate different ways of thinking about their dissertation projects, mapping out possible informants, different data resources, and different ways of configuring figure and ground, among other things. The promise and problems of structure are in play on many levels.

As I will explain, the research memos that I assign are intended to give students a structured place to play with what can be overwhelming ideas. This approach builds on Winnicott's ideas about how play becomes possible, and becomes a "potential space" that opens up without determining what goes on in the "real world" (i.e., outside of play or the therapeutic session [1971a, 1971b]).

---

5. See, for example, a Rensselaer Polytechnic Institute STS dissertation recently completed by Sean Lawson, which examines uptake of concepts from nonlinear science in the U.S. military (Lawson 2007).

In other words, research design is conceived as preparatory without being deterministic. This is particularly important in ethnography since openness to what one encounters "in the field" (however "the field" is defined) is part of what makes ethnography a distinctive approach. Structure, at the level of method, is used to facilitate play.

Structure is also at the center empirically. A critical intent of my teaching is to help students draw out the many structures—social, discursive, technical, etc.—that enable and constrain what their informants say and do. "People" thus remain at the center of ethnography, as in traditional ethnographic projects, but conceived of as nodes and indices of larger systems.

Ethnography of open systems positions people within larger systems, accounting for systematicity at every scale and across scales. It involves accounts of systems within systems. Accounting for how relevant systems function is one goal, but another is to account for how systems dysfunction and disseminate. Structure, in other words, is accounted for as both over- and underdetermining.

Poststructural theories of structure are thus also at the center of things, directing attention to the funny ways structure functions and fails (Derrida 1976, 1978). Figuring out how to extrapolate insight from poststructuralism into empirical projects is part of the game. The implications are complex, and—in my view—politically charged. Play can be a serious matter.

From Bhopal to "Advanced Qualitative Methods"

Think 1989. The Soviets leaving Afghanistan. Joyous Germans dancing on top of a fallen Berlin Wall. Ayatollah Khomeini sentencing Salman Rushdie to death for writing *The Satanic Verses*. Trade agreements promising "harmonization" are making the rounds, though "globalization" is not yet in the vernacular. Time Inc. and Warner Communications Inc. announce a deal to merge into the world's largest media and entertainment conglomerate. Union Carbide agrees to pay $470 million to the government of India in a court-ordered settlement of the 1984 Bhopal gas leak disaster. The government of India claims that the Bhopal decision demonstrates India's openness to foreign investors.

Foucault is already dead and Salvador Dali dies. Poststructural and experimental sensibilities intensify and are institutionalized in the U.S. academy, nonetheless. Theory is hot throughout the humanities, but speaking of methods is in poor taste. "Methods" are the tools of positivism and Science. They are understood as inevitably reductive, and passé. I left the United States for fieldwork in India, with *Of Grammatology* (Derrida 1976) and Gayatri Spivak's *In Other Worlds* (1987) in my backpack.[6] With time, "Bhopal"—a place, an event, and a politically charged symbol—became my field site. My goal in writing about Bhopal was not to account for a stable, bounded culture that had been disrupted by disaster. Instead, I focused on how people's identities, positions, and claims emerged in the aftermath of the gas leak, shaped by myriad forces and inter-actions. The ways human rights and environmental justice discourses touched down in Bhopal were part of the story, as were ways survivor testimonies cir-culated outside Bhopal, among activists in India, in plant communities in the United States, at meetings of Union Carbide shareholders. Action and inaction by the government of India were part of the story, as were action and inaction by U.S. courts. What people said about Bhopal was of critical interest, as were the forms—literary and technical—of delivery. I also was interested in what could not be said, particularly in available legal venues and discourses. Pieces of commu-nication became "evidence" of how and why different "stakeholders" understood Union Carbide's gas leak and its aftermath so differently. An anarchist tract from Ireland, for example, helped me understand and describe middle-class Indian activists in Bhopal. Boxes and boxes of Union Carbide documents, stored in the already cramped home of former plant worker T. R. Chouhan, helped me posi-tion him, drawing out his sense of betrayal by the company, and by the govern-ment of India. A pamphlet celebrating the fiftieth anniversary of Union Carbide India Limited helped me understand and show the way foreign companies played into nationalist goals. Glossy brochures advertising the chemical industry's post-Bhopal commitment to "Responsible Care" helped me show how "Bhopal" has brought about a new era of environmentalism, synchronized with neo-liberal ideals. Figuring out what could be "data" was a key challenge, as was figuring out what my study was really about. Figure and ground continually oscillated.

It took me years to turn my research on the Bhopal disaster into a book, in part because it seemed imperative to include material collected in the United States in my account—as a critical response to industry claims that "it [a Bhopal-like

---

6. In *Anthropology as Cultural Critique*, Marcus and Fischer describe the 1980s as a time when con-ventional ways of thinking about the world needed to be—and indeed were—intensely questioned and challenged. Across academic disciplines, there was a sense that many of the concepts that had oriented empirical work and social theory since the nineteenth century—the social actor, class, the state, even culture—were out of date, if not obsolete. Technological advance, economic globalization, and the reordering of social relations at all scales had created a reality that was difficult to encompass within these categories, and all but impossible to encapsulate within general and historically com-prehensive theories. This provoked what Marcus and Fischer refer to as a "crisis of representation," which marked a generalized lack of confidence in the adequacy of established ways of describing social reality. I left for the field, as a student of Marcus's and Fischer's, acutely attuned to this crisis of representation. Bhopal was an intensely charged site for working through its implications.

disaster] can't happen here [in the United States]." I also struggled hard with text design, painfully aware that even well intentioned ways of representing disaster easily played into the workings of disaster.

Meanwhile, I had begun a job as an assistant professor in a department of Science and Technology Studies. The first graduate course that I taught (in 1996) was called "Cultural Analysis" and fulfilled a methods requirement. Through a few previous years of work with graduate students, I already sensed the need to support research design pedagogically. Eventually, "Cultural Analysis" iterated into a required methods course called "Advanced Qualitative Methods."

In its initial form, the course included a fair amount of reading (about methods, but also theoretical and ethnographic texts). It quickly became clear that there was more than enough to do in the course of a semester just working out students' projects. We do this through a series of about thirty "memos," with a couple due each week. The first memo is simply a "laundry list" of topics, questions, people, and data resources that a student is interested in pursuing. I encourage students to make the list long and inclusive, so that they have lots of options to consider in putting their project together. In the process, I also try to make clear that having ideas, or even a field site, is not the same thing as having a project. I also encourage them to keep this memo (and most others) going throughout their research, as a way to keep track of what gets pushed in and out of a project as it develops. A project, I insist, always has a provisional starting point, a constructed and ever moving center, and margins. Projects, like other meaning-making processes, work in part because they exclude. Signal becomes signal, through often painful designations of what will, for the moment, count as noise.

As students are working on their research "laundry list," we are reading a few ethnographies—using a template that I titled "Questioning a Text" to direct our attention. The goal is to help students read as practicing ethnographers.

QUESTIONING A TEXT: What is the text "about"—empirically and conceptually? What modes of inquiry were used to produce it? How is the text structured and performed? How can it circulate?

What is the text about—empirically?
- What phenomenon is drawn out in the text? A social process; a cultural and political-economic shift; a cultural "infrastructure"; an emergent assemblage of science-culture-technology-economics?
- Where is this phenomenon located—in a neighborhood, in a country, in "Western Culture," in a globalizing economy?

(Continued)

- What historical trajectory is the phenomenon situated within? What, in the chronology provided or implied, is emphasized—the role of political or economic forces, the role of certain individuals or social groups? What does the chronology leave out or discount?
- What scale(s) are focused on—nano (i.e., the level of language), micro, meso, macro? What empirical material is developed at each scale?
- Who are the players in the text and what are their relations? Does the text trace how these relations have changed across time—because of new technologies, for example?
- What is the temporal frame in which players play? In the wake of a particular policy, disaster or other significant "event?" In the general climate of the Reagan era, or of "after-the-Wall" globalization?
- What cultures and social structures are in play in the text?
- What kinds of practices are described in the text? Are players shown to be embedded in structural contradictions or double binds?
- How are science and technology implicated in the phenomenon described?
- What structural conditions—technological, legal and legislative, political, cultural—are highlighted, and how are they shown to have shaped the phenomenon described in this text?
- How—at different scales, in different ways—is power shown to operate? Is there evidence of power operating through language, "discipline," social hierarchies, bureaucratic function, economics, etc.?
- Does the text provide comparative or systems level perspectives? In other words, is the particular phenomenon described in this text situated in relation to similar phenomena in other settings? Is this particular phenomenon situated within global structures and processes?

What is the text about—conceptually?
- Is the goal to verify, challenge, or extend prior theoretical claims?
- What is the main conceptual argument or theoretical claim of the text? Is it performed, rendered explicit, or both?
- What ancillary concepts are developed to articulate the conceptual argument?
- How is empirical material used to support or build the conceptual argument?
- How robust is the main conceptual argument of the text? On what grounds could it be challenged?

(Continued)

- How could the empirical material provided support conceptual arguments *other than those* built in the text?

Modes of inquiry?
- What theoretical edifice provides the (perhaps haunting—i.e., non-explicit) backdrop to the text?
- What assumptions appear to have shaped the inquiry? Does the author assume that individuals are rational actors, for example, or assume that the unconscious is a force to be dealt with? Does the author assume that the "goal" of society is (functional) stability? Does the author assume that what is most interesting occurs with regularity, or is she interested in the incidental and deviant?
- What kinds of data (ethnographic, experimental, statistical, etc.) are used in the text, and how were they obtained?
- If interviews were conducted, what kinds of questions were asked? What does the author seem to have learned from the interviews?
- How were the data analyzed? If this is not explicit, what can be inferred?
- How are people, objects, or ideas aggregated into groups or categories?
- What additional data would strengthen the text?

Structure and performance?
- What is in the introduction? Does the introduction turn around unanswered questions—in other words, are we told how this text embodies a *research* project?
- Where is theory in the text? Is the theoretical backdrop to the text explained, or assumed to be understood?
- What is the structure of the discourse in the text? What binaries recur in the text, or are conspicuously avoided?
- How is the historical trajectory delineated? Is there explicit chronological development?
- How is the temporal context provided or evoked in the text?
- How does the text specify the cultures and social structures in play in the text?
- How are informant perspectives dealt with and integrated?
- How does the text draw out the implications of science and technology? At what level of detail are scientific and technological practices described?

(Continued)

- How does the text provide in-depth detail—hopefully without losing readers?
- What is the layout of the text? How does it move, from first page to last? Does it ask for other ways of reading? Does the layout perform an argument?
- What kinds of visuals are used, and to what effect?
- What kind of material and analysis are in the footnotes?
- How is the criticism of the text performed? If through overt argumentation, who is the "opposition"?
- How does the text situate itself? In other words, how is reflexivity addressed, or not?

Circulation?
- Who is the text written for? How are arguments and evidence in the text shaped to address particular audiences?
- What audiences can you imagine for the text, given its empirical and conceptual scope?
- What new knowledge does this text put into circulation? What does this text have to say that otherwise is *not obvious*?
- How generalizable is the main argument? How does this text lay the groundwork for further research?
- What kind of "action" is suggested by the main argument of the text?

I ask them to read for what a text is "about" empirically, for example. A social process? A cultural and political-economic shift? An emerging cultural assemblage? I also ask them to draw out the historical trajectory that the text mobilizes, and to consider the different scales of analysis and whether a particular scale operates something like a center of gravity. Next, I ask what the text is "about" conceptually and how empirical material is used to build a conceptual argument. Modes of inquiry are then queried, helping students imagine the kinds of real-time engagements and questions that produced the "data" presented. Critical as well is getting students to think through implicit and explicit categorization schemes, attentive to the political implications of the ways social groups are grouped, for example. Then there is a section called "structure and performance" through which I try to get students to consider how the text is organized and operates and how it is situated in ecologies of other texts. Consideration of how images and footnotes are put to work is important, for example, as is consideration of how the text moves, from first page to last, possibly performing as well as overtly articulating an argument. Last is a section that considers circulation: whom the text appears to be written for; what other audiences are imaginable. Reception of ethnographic work, I argue, is hardly straightforward. A good text to bring in here, because of the many levels on which it works, is Paul Berliner's *Thinking in Jazz: The Infinite Art of Improvisation* (1994). The key argument of the book is that the play of improvisation requires extraordinary discipline and structured preparation.

Early on in the class, I also ask students to begin peopling their projects, by filling in three templates that I sometimes think of as the Foucault 101 templates. The first template asks students to run a list of types of people in their "site," or search space. Most often, the list is easily long and differentiated—peopled with cryptographers (today, a particular type of computer scientist), lawyers, notaries, and immigrants in France, for example, in a project about the development in the late 1990s of electronic forms of authentication in governance (Blanchette 2002). Most students that I work with simply don't think about their projects as centered on a particular social group, at least at the outset. With time, a particular social group may come to center their accounts, but this center emerges as the project develops rather than serving as a starting point. Even in those cases when a particular social group is a starting point, differentiation within, early on, is critical. If a project is about physicists amid new information infrastructure, for example, it is important to tease out how topical, national, generational, and gender differences among physicists matter. Beginning to tease out the differences that make a difference early on can orient without determining where a project goes, preparing a researcher to look out for the differences already identified as likely to be significant while having an analytic frame in place that makes it easy to add to the list. This memo, too, can be maintained throughout a project.

In addition to the list of types of relevant people, this memo also asks for a snapshot of the force fields that these people work within. The list of social groups runs down the center of the page. A column to the left lists forces—economic, political, discursive, technical, etc.—that enable people in that group to say what they say, and do what they do. A column on the right list forces that constrain or corrode what each group is able to say and do. In a page, one is able to see the swirl of people and forces that are the "site" of ethnographic study.

The next, related memo zooms into a particular group and maps many different forces that compel them to say and do what they do and don't do. I encourage students to be as historically specific as possible, recognizing that groups don't cohere naturally or automatically, but in specific ways in specific times and places. I often talk through work in critical race theory that teases out the political import of the ways groups are conceived. Anthropological studies of the making of ethnicity, sometimes quite intentionally, are also illustrative. The challenge, as

Table 8.1 Situating Subjects

CATALYSTS	STATEMENTS	CORROSIONS
_____	_____	_____
_____	_____	_____
_____	_____	_____
_____	_____	_____
_____	_____	_____
_____	_____	_____
_____		_____
	SPEAKING	
	SUBJECT	
_____		_____
_____	_____	_____
_____	_____	_____
_____	_____	_____
_____	_____	_____

I learned in my work in Bhopal, is not to identify obvious "stakeholders" in the issues at hand, but to figure out how particular "enunciatory communities" are structured (Fortun 2001).

With this memo, I also share my sense of the critical value of thinking in terms of double binds, as forces that can turn otherwise different people into groups, in particular.[7] Double binds, I explain, don't determine what people do. They set up search spaces that people must wander within. Ethnographic observation of these wanderings (and processes of figuring out workable even if imperfect solutions) often yields material that can operate as cultural critique.

The last of this set of memos (see Table 8.1) zooms in even further, centering on one particular individual, mapping—in brief—"subject constitution." Often, students can't fill in this memo at the research design stage. They don't yet know particular informants in sufficient depth. But the analytic frame is in place, to be filled in and played with later. With this memo, I encourage students to think about the funny way "culture" operates. Culture is out there, so to speak, but it settles into different people in different ways. Each person is a tangle of different cultural impulses. Each is constituted and operates at a specific nexus of cross-cutting forces.

---

7. The double-bind concept as articulated by Gregory Bateson was very enabling in my analysis of *Advocacy After Bhopal*. On the double bind, see the collection of essays edited by Sluzki and Ransom (1976), and particularly the seminal essay "Toward a Theory of Schizophrenia" (Bateson, Jackson, Haley, and Weakland 1956).

People, conceived in this way, are very subject to change because they operate in always moving currents. The force fields they are in continually move, and compel them to move. The need for active sense-making, often without authoritative models, is incessant. There is a lot of figuring out as they go. What they don't know, and how they deal with what they don't know, are as interesting as what they know. How their statements cohere and confirm each other is interesting, as is the way their statements disseminate and contradict each other. Like the previous memo, centered on social groups, this memo has a center column where various statements are run in sequence so that confirmations and coherences are easy to see.

In yet another memo, I ask students to map the binary oppositions that structure the discursive space that their various informants work within, with a center column that lists terms their informants use that point to and work around the ways these binaries fail to describe the everyday realities with which they deal. It is a way to draw out moments of cultural criticism in the discourse of informants. The same memo structure can be used to map the binaries that structure the discursive spaces the ethnographer works within—in science studies, for example, or in particular area studies. The center column provides space for the development of new terms for understanding the realities the ethnographer aims to describe. I think of this memo as *Anthropology as Cultural Critique* by worksheet.

I also have students write abstracts for various essays they could write with their dissertation material, each with its own focus, argument or narrative, choice of material, and audience, and also for the book-to-be as a whole. The abstracts for essay-length articulations of their material are meant to keep students thinking about their projects in different ways. When timing allows, I have students figure out, together, how their various essays could become conference panels. This exercise helps them imagine different conversations that their work can become part of, an exercise like but less rigid than one that asks them to specify the "literature" they will draw on and contribute to. I've come to value the latter exercise, though I don't think it should be assumed that bounded literatures are out there waiting to be built on. Indeed, a critical part of research design is figuring out how diverse streams of thinking can be brought together in a way relevant to the project at hand. Researchers often have to constitute the literatures they will draw on and contribute to, just as they have to constitute the social groups they will attend to.

The abstract of the book-to-be as a whole is particularly hard, especially for students who are at their best contextualizing and complicating their topic. The exercise is very reductive, on purpose. There are four sentences. The first begins with the phrase "The aim of this study...." The second sentence is the methods sentence. It should say something like, "Data collected through participant

observation, interviews, and context mapping were analyzed to understand con-
tinuities and changes in the way people conceive of X." The third sentence begins
with the phrase, "Primary findings of this study are...." The fourth and final
sentence is about the implications—theoretical and practical/political—of these
findings. The point is to force a figuring out of figure and of ground.

A student who undertook this exercise recently started referring to it as the
"disciplined abstract." He rewrote his about ten times, sending me iterations by
e-mail with a recurrent message: "this is closer." The exercise worked very well
for him, even though it did not come easily. It helped that he knew a lot about
gaming and was invested in gaming as a practice. His dissertation was titled "The
Work/Play of the Interactive New Economy: Video Game Development in the
United States and India" (O'Donnell 2007).

In one particularly memorable semester, there were twenty-two students in
this class. I felt as if I were part of an enormous circus, with each project having at
least three rings, with different kinds of things going on in each. It was a bit overwhelming, but also exciting and fun. The play of it was, and always is, crucial.

Research design always, inevitably, is an anxious endeavor. Joking along the
way, about the process, about oneself, about the world in which research happens
and, one hopes, makes a difference, is important. Joking, as Freud has taught us,
is a way to approach what we would otherwise avoid. The condensations that
happen in jokes, and in dreams, are not unlike the condensations that research
memos are after. Brevity, Freud promises, can have punch.[8]

For research design to work, without becoming formulaic, students must
engage with it as play (or perhaps calisthenics). One moves through a research
design process to be ready, quick on one's feet, attuned to what many would
discount as noise. The task in teaching research design is to stage it as what Winnicott has described as "potential space"—a place where play can happen, opening
up without determining future possibilities. The therapist in Winnicott's account
provides the enabling frame.

It takes play on the part of the teacher, too. Ethnographic eyes and ears, in my
experience, have been as vital in the classroom as in "the field." An important way
that I can help my students is by listening to them very closely, attentive to what
drives and concerns them, to slips and to what they cannot yet find words for. At
the outset, some find my quite incessant questioning stressful. I try to pull them
into the game.

Winnicott explains that "psychotherapy takes place in the overlap of two areas
of playing, that of the patient and that of the therapist. Psychotherapy has to do

---

8. Playing off Shakespeare's *Hamlet* in "Jokes and Their Relation to the Subconscious," Freud
reminds us that "brevity is the soul of wit" (1963).

with two people playing together. The corollary of this is that where playing is not possible then the work done by the therapist is directed towards bringing the patient from a state of not being able to play into a state of being able to play" (1968). I think of my work as a teacher of ethnographic research design in similar terms.

Constituting Ethnographic Subjects

> The concept of centered structure is in fact the concept of freeplay based on a fundamental ground, a freeplay that is constituted upon a fundamental immobility and a reassuring certitude, which is itself beyond the reach of the freeplay. With this certitude anxiety can be mastered, for anxiety is invariably the result of a certain mode of being implicated in the game, of being caught by the game.
>
> —Jacques Derrida, "Structure, Sign and Play," *Writing and Difference*

At the end of some session or another, I send students away with yet another game. Figure out, I tell them, if you are obsessive-compulsive or paranoid, and—thinking in terms of Roman Jakobson—whether you have a combination disorder, or a selection disorder.

If you are an obsessive-compulsive, you will tend to focus so intently on the object of your concern that context falls away. Your desire is to name, specify, and control your object. You want figure. Its ground is an annoyance. If you are paranoid, context is your focus, and obsession. All is signal. Only begrudgingly will you admit that something is noise, outside the scope of your project. Figure is hard to come by. Its ground has captured your attention.[9] Evelyn Fox Keller

---

9. STS students are exposed to this distinction in a seminal (*sic*) essay by Evelyn Fox Keller, "Dynamic Objectivity: Love, Power, and Knowledge." Keller, drawing on Shapiro's *Autonomy and Rigid Character* (1981) and *Neurotic Styles* (1965) explains: "The central concern of the obsessive-compulsive is control, not so much of others as of oneself....Under this harsh regime, attention is subject to the same kind of control as is the rest of behavior, leading to a focus so intensely sharp and restricted that it precludes peripheral vision, the fleeting impression, the hunch, the over-all feeling of an object....And what does not fit is not acknowledged: The rigid or dogmatic compulsive person simply ignores the unusual; he narrowly follows his own line of thought and goes right by anything out of the way. The cognitive style of the paranoid, although similar in some ways, is ultimately quite different. Grounded in the fear of being controlled by others rather than in apprehension about the loss of self-control, in the fear of giving in to others rather than to one's own unwelcome impulses, the attention of the paranoid is rigid, but it is not narrowly focused. Rather than ignore what does not fit, he or she must be alert to every possible clue. Nothing—no detail, however minor—eluded scrutiny. Everything *must* fit. The paranoid delusion suffers not from lack of logic but from unreality. Indeed, its distortion derives, at least in part, from the very effort to make all the clues fit into

describes how natural scientists inhabit these tendencies. Ethnographers, I insist, do as well.

In Roman Jakobson's terms, writing of "two aspects of language and two types of aphasic disturbances," there is selection disorder, and combination disorder. The person with a selection disorder has trouble articulating the frame in which something occurs. Metanarrative escapes her, though she easily finds focus. The object of her research is taken to represent the quality and reality of the whole. She is likely to be something of a realist and materialist.

The person with a combination and contexture disorder has trouble identifying a focus. Things don't add up. She knows where her object of concern is, in a very expansive sense, but not what it is. I imagine her circulating round and round her object of concern, gaining increasing understanding of the system in which it operates, but forever hesitant to name the object itself.[10] Her thinking is far-reaching, but sometimes difficult to pin down.

All of us, I insist, are beset by these disorders, in one way or another. We must learn to play within these limits.

This kind of recognition of one's own tendencies and dispositions is, in my view, critical to ethnography and needs to be cultivated pedagogically. Critical ethnography—particularly conceived as in/of open systems—requires intense attunement to what is being considered in the frame and what is not, to subtle slides between figure and ground, and to the many forces that shape what a particular study comes to be about. Access to visas and fieldsites, nondisclosure agreements, and gender dynamics are all constitutive, of course, as are the genre conventions of the anthropological dissertation and monograph. Thought and writing "disorders" like those described by Keller and Jakobson are also critical. What is often termed "reflexivity" requires attention to all these things. I prefer to think in term of recursivity rather than reflexivity, highlighting how ethnographic subjects—both researchers and their objects of concerns—are constituted through repetition and relationality. Indeed, as I mentioned before,

---

a single interpretation. Once accomplished, the logic is such as to leave no room for an alternative interpretation; the pieces are locked into place by the closeness of their fit. So convincing is the result that 'nothing but' that interpretation can be imagined" (1985: 121–22).

10. Jakobson contrasts a "logic of recognition," which is a logic of semblance and metaphor, and a "logic of touch," which is a logic of contiguity and metonym. The development of a discourse may take place in two ways: one topic may lead to another through similarity (metaphor), or one topic may lead to another through contiguity (metonym). Jakobson further discusses how either metaphor or metonymy dominates in various kinds of expression, both verbal and pictorial. Crudely, poetry moves through metaphor while prose moves through metonym. Metaphor is associated with romanticism and symbolism, metonym with realism and rationalism. The Cubists were metonymically oriented. The surrealists were metaphorical. Jakobson complicates these extrapolations, noting that over-attachment with a simple binary scheme would demonstrate a "continuity disorder" (Jakobson 1956).

I have a memo for this, too, in which students map the many determinants of their own interests and research trajectory.

Ethnography—even of open systems—is not about everything. There are always margins and disavowals. Research design is a key space for working this through and for learning to be caught by and implicated in the ethnographic game. Certitude about what one is doing should not be the goal. Anxiety should be played rather than mastered. Practices and pedagogy of ethnography have to cultivate playfulness—and understanding that what at times feels like free play is a structured effect. A patience for and sensibility for what many would term "method" is thus critical.

Structure must be understood as both ethnographic object and context, as itself the ground on which the figure and ground of ethnographic studies are figured out. Thinking in terms of structure, sign, and play needs to become second nature, so to speak.[11]

---

11. Derrida's essay "Structure, Sign and Play" describes how the organizing principle of any structure allows free play within the structure, while closing off other kinds of play. The center of the structure thus enables and constrains, creating both sense and non-sense, designating what is signal and noise (1978). Derrida describes how noise becomes noise, and the historical condition of its production. He also suggests the promise of noise—the way it can intercede in signal, displacing what makes most sense, allowing something new to emerge. The promise of ethnology, according to Derrida, lies in its potential to intercede in this way. At the same time, however, ethnology itself is delimited. The organizing principles that ethnology has the potential to upend give structure to ethnology itself.

9

COLLABORATION, COORDINATION, AND COMPOSITION

Fieldwork after the Internet

Christopher Kelty (with contributions from Hannah Landecker, Ebru Kayaalp, Anthony Potoczniak, Tish Stringer, Nahal Naficy, Ala Alazzeh, Lina Dib, and Michael G. Powell)

The essays in this volume are all in dialogue with the debates and controversies for which *Writing Culture* and *Anthropology as Cultural Critique* are emblematic. For a generation of anthropologists, and those with landed immigrant status in the discipline, like myself, these debates center around *writing* as a key component of the epistemological and practical challenges of anthropology. Doubly so do these issues present themselves for a generation dealing with the upheavals and transformative promises presented by the Internet, which crisscrosses the topological triangle of ontological, epistemological, and affective issues outlined by James Faubion in his essay. As someone trained to think anthropologically about these issues—but not exclusively anthropologically—I naturally tend in exploring them toward questions of what difference the Internet makes for fieldwork (now). A 2002 article in *Current Anthropology* by Johannes Fabian serves as a starting point: it proposes that the Internet turns the old art of commentary on texts into a new genre of writing about ethnographic research. Fabian reported on his experience with the creation of a "virtual archive" of popular Swahili texts, which he translated and on which he wrote commentary.[1]

All authors are members of the Rice University Department of Anthropology. This article was written by Kelty, but the material for the projects, including interviews, commentaries, and additional papers, was created by all participants. Additional commentary and material were provided by Geoffrey Bowker, Gabriella Coleman, and Michael M. J. Fischer. Research was funded by an Innovation Grant from the Computer and Information Technology Institute of Rice University (CITI) and the Center for Biological and Environmental Nanotechnology.

1. See Fabian 2002; the website he created with Vincent de Rooij is, quite despite the label "virtual," still at http://www.pscw.uva.nl/lpca/.

Fabian's experiment poses several questions, which this chapter explores: Does it prove the need for a new kind of anthropology, or reveal new modes of fieldwork? Does it ramify existing problems long plaguing research and writing in the discipline? Is commentary really a newly transformative genre, or is it just glorified blogging? How can we tease apart millennial promises of Internet-inspired radical transformation from the clearly felt, but dimly perceived, material changes in how we research, write, disseminate, and receive our work, specifically in terms of the practice of fieldwork?

This chapter confronts these questions by reflecting on a series of experiments in fieldwork and writing conducted in 2003–2005 at Rice University. The project is similar to Fabian's in that the practical component is "merely" a compilation of interviews, primary sources, and commentary conducted around the theme "Ethics and Politics of Science and Technology."[2] The project focuses on two areas: computer science and nanotechnology. Both are areas of vibrant research at Rice University (where our research was conducted) as well as "emergent" or "strategic" (van Lente and Rip 1998) sciences that are organized in response to broad ethical, political, and cultural demands. The material of the project is thus a substantial collection of interviews with scientists, commentary on these interviews by faculty and graduate students, and conceptual articulation of ongoing and new research problems related to existing and past research. The project is open-ended in two senses: first, it was not intended to reach its apotheosis in published articles or books, but to go on living in diverse print and electronic forms as long as there were (or are) graduate students or faculty interested in using or expanding the materials or addressing the problems; and second, it is open to participation by anyone wishing to make use of the existing materials, provided they contribute their work back to the project.

In reflecting on this experiment, this chapter touches three issues: 1) it responds to some of the issues raised by Fabian concerning the status of ethnographic materials and data, and of commentary as a "genre" of ethnographic writing after the Internet; 2) it distinguishes conceptually the practices of coordination and collaboration as they relate to ethnographic fieldwork after the Internet; and 3) it reports briefly on the outcome of the Ethics and Politics of Science and Technology projects (as they stood in 2005, when this article was written) and how they exemplify the first two issues.

The practice of "commentary" and the more general concept of "composition" are intended to augment or extend the familiar critiques around anthropological writing (such as those raised in *Writing Culture* [Clifford and Marcus 1986])

---

2. Project Website: http://kelty.org/epit and http://kelty.org/epnano.

by including the Internet and new media and the challenges and opportunities they pose. From the perspective of digital media, the concept and the practice of "writing" neither exhaust the challenges of conceptual innovation and anthropological analysis, nor are they sufficient to describe the range of practices in which anthropologists increasingly engage, from fieldnote writing to blogging, from book-lending to social book-marking, from letter-writing to listening and observing, from qualitative data analysis to collaborative interviewing, from draft articles circulated among informants and colleagues to public wikis. All of these activities involve writing of some kind, but the term hardly captures the complexity of the activities of organization and conceptual innovation that thereby result—much less the multiple ways the Internet and digital media impinge on them or pose new opportunities. At a pragmatic level, this profusion has affected every discipline, changing the micro-practices of everything from bibliographies to photography to the ease with which sophisticated software can transform "raw" material.

Despite all this, the only lasting marker of success in research in social and cultural anthropology remains the article or book—and in the last twenty years particularly, books that display the virtuosity and innovative genius of individual researchers, and not the expansion and consolidation of concepts and problems specific to communities of researchers, much less disciplines (Collier and Lakoff 2006).

"Composition" therefore is intended to be a somewhat broader concept that captures this diversity.[3] We say "composition" here because it is more inclusive than "writing" (paintings, musical works, and software all need to be composed, as poetry and novels do). Writing implies the textual and narrative organization of language—still a difficult enough problem of composition, and still the gold standard; but it leaves out the composition of images and sounds, or especially how other kinds of objects are composed as part of an ethnographic project: documents, statistics, forms, legal documents, unpublished works, audio transcripts, blog-entries, and so on. The Internet neither solves this problem nor simplifies it—if anything it makes it more difficult at the same time that it provides the possibility of solving it. Fabian put it well: "no more than other 'media' does the Internet guarantee its own communicative or informative success. It does not preempt the labors of ethnographic representation; it only changes

---

3. Gregory Crane, creator of the Perseus Archive of Greek and Roman texts, articulated the concept of composition in an article in Current Anthropology from 1991 (Crane 1991). He distinguishes between "writing (a particular historically contingent task) and composing (what authors do, no matter what the medium or technology)" (293). Such a notion of composition as an activity distinct from writing is also explored in detail in the work of Mary Carruthers (2000, 2008).

some conditions, and it was to the latter that I wanted to direct our attention" (Fabian 2002, 785).

Similarly, the challenge of dealing with huge volumes of information—not only as a consumer of information, but as a producer as well—means experimenting with new modes of composition that can give specialist and generalist colleagues alike quick synoptic overviews of research materials and problems and trajectories without sacrificing the scholarly detail and individual virtuosity that has come to be valued in the discipline. It is in some ways an attempt to have our cake and eat it too: composition is a practice that crosses between writing understood as an artful craft and research understood as conceptual innovation (or more specifically, fieldwork understood as an epistemological encounter and a platform for shared conceptual work). The article and the book are, and will continue to be, the primary locus and container of concepts and ideas—but they will have been transformed by the array of new media and new technologies, each of which will have effects on the kinds of research and writing that are now possible. That is to say, somewhat awkwardly, that the book of the era of the Internet will look and act differently from the book of the era of the book.

Alongside the problem of composition, our research project also demonstrates the need to distinguish carefully and clearly between collaboration and coordination in anthropological work. Traditionally, collaboration has had two meanings in anthropology: collaboration among researchers, and collaboration between researchers and research subjects (on the latter see Lassiter 2005a). Both forms of collaboration are active here, but we distinguish between coordination and collaboration in the following way: coordination is the media-specific material and technical choices that allow a group of people to work together on similar topics, in the same places, in structured time frames, and with the same group of subjects. Collaboration is the conceptual and theoretical work that results, if it results. Coordination does not imply collaboration, but collaboration entails coordination.

By this definition it is possible to imagine both axes of collaboration—among researchers and between researchers and subjects—starting from different forms of coordination. Coordination between anthropologists takes different forms and happens at different time-scales than does coordination between researchers and their sites and subjects. While we would never suggest that anthropologists have not coordinated research among themselves, or with informants, or achieved collaboration in both cases, we would suggest that there has been little reflection on the media-specific differences of coordination that make a difference in attempting to foment collaboration of either form. Or to put it in terms of "connectivity," there are scales and metrics of connection between researchers and between informants that can help elaborate which kinds of coordination might yield conceptual innovation (which I associate with collaboration) and which do not.

For instance, the management of power relations between anthropologist and informant (both "up" and "down") demands specific, material strategies and tactics of coordination. A researcher must design ways of interacting, observing, or participating, must lure informants into conversation somehow, must find ways to register (record, remember) a conversation, devise means of (co-)interpreting a conversation, transform it into an accessible written form, and disseminate it (these last two forms of coordination have been traditionally structured almost exclusively by the academic publishing industry), as well as managing the affective or emotional tensions of interaction, friendship, suspicion, and the like. In each given case these activities will be organized differently depending on the vagaries of the situation. Only in some cases will such coordination come to be, in hindsight, seen as collaboration; as for example when researcher and informant end up working together in the field, or writing together (e.g., Fischer and Abedi 1990); or when researchers literally work for an informant (in a corporation, for instance) or when researchers, in extreme cases of "going native," cease to make such distinctions.

By the same token, the most elaborate and hierarchical forms of coordination in science do not necessarily imply collaboration—they often serve only to break up a problem into identifiable, exclusive chunks that will then be addressed by individuals (perhaps with some recursion through which collaboration again becomes possible within the chunks) who are in turn not expected to exercise virtuosity or genius except at the level of such general systematic planning and coordination. Classic forms of anthropological collaborations such as the New Nations project might be seen as a kind of middle ground—and, in some narratives of the project, produced irresolvable tensions as a result.

Given this distinction between coordination and collaboration, it is also clear that there is far less coordination between anthropologists (who are trained and evaluated in highly individualized frameworks) than there is coordination between researcher and research subjects (which is after all the one form of coordination that requires utmost attention in all cases of ethnographic research). Graduate students and faculty may keep in touch with colleagues who are in the field, but are very rarely invited to participate in the research in structured ways (though compare the account of "improvising theory" in Cerwonka and Malkki 2007). Traditionally, it is the disciplines and subdisciplines themselves that have served this coordinating function between academics' projects (and hence also as the platform for collaboration) by keeping track of current problems and research directions, by disciplining scholars into forms of research that respond to these problems and by adapting problems to new and emergent phenomena.

In the age of inter-, trans-, multi-, and anti-disciplinary critique and innovation, however, the question is raised anew: If not by discipline, then how does one identify a significant problem, how does one become satisfied with the appropriate methods of research to pursue such problems, indeed, how does one determine to whom one is speaking about these problems and for what purpose, in the absence of strong disciplinary signals?

Befitting the role of ethnography as epistemological encounter, my understanding of these issues emerges from my own fieldwork experience among Free and Open Source software developers and advocates—an example and a template that I will return to throughout this article for what it can tell us about coordination and collaboration in anthropology. From this perspective, Free and Open Source software projects provide not just field sites, but exemplary cases of a response to a reorientation of knowledge and power that is also facing anthropology and other disciplines (Kelty 2008b). The response of Free and Open Source software is a template from which to imagine the more precise kinds of changes necessary in anthropology and a foil against which to judge proposals for new forms of writing or research.

The distinction between coordination and collaboration also has a strategic purpose in the "Ethics and Politics of Science and Technology" projects which are reported on herein: the intentional and sustained attempt to innovate forms of collaboration (based on practices of coordination) that do not sacrifice the eminently practical need for individual projects to develop, progress, and be evaluated as such. We seek to create coordinated projects that fertilize multiple individual, idiosyncratic interests, allow them to develop in parallel, and reap the benefit of continuous, partial collaborations. The "collaboration" emerges not from a top-down concern with answering a set of discipline-defined research questions, but through the problem-seeking activities of the individual researchers, conducted alongside one another, coordinated both through technical means and through structured engagement.

The Ethics and Politics of Science and Technology

Starting in 2003, we began two related experiments in ethnographic research on the general theme of ethics and politics of science and technology—one on computer science called EPIT (Ethics and Politics of Information Technology) and one on nanotechnology called EPNANO (Ethics and Politics of Nanotechnology). Both experiments were conducted primarily at Rice University, the substantive topic areas reflecting two of the more vibrant research areas at this small university, and each involved one or two faculty and around four graduate students. The methodology of the two projects, along with some of the preliminary results and conceptual work, is described herein.

EPIT, the initial project, was funded by the Computer and Information Technology Institute (CITI) at Rice University—an institute devoted to brokering relationships across the schools and disciplines and, through funding, lectures, lunches, and other activities, to encouraging individuals to seek out and form collaborations with people in faraway disciplines. CITI is one of four such institutes at Rice (the others are in Biology, Environmental Science, and Nanotechnology) whose aims are to foster interdisciplinarity and enhance communication of research results across departmental and disciplinary borders. CITI's institutional mandate is to see research that would not otherwise be funded, or necessarily even performed, seeded on their dime and then, if possible, leveraged into larger funding sources. They were therefore successful in convincing members of the anthropology and philosophy departments (albeit scholars trained in science studies and philosophy of science) to develop a project that loosely asked the question: What kinds of ethical or political issues currently face working engineers and computer scientists and how can we collaborate to address them?

From the perspective of the anthropologists and the philosopher involved, the project was not conceived of as beginning with philosophical definitions of ethics; instead, we sought only to investigate, ethnographically, the projects and practices of particular computer sciences, in the hope that our dialogue with and observations of particular computer scientists would bring out several "ethical" issues to be refined over the course of the project. On the one hand, such a goal is trivial: nearly any practice worthy of the name can be understood in terms of its ethical dimensions. On the other hand, we sought to discover not only what the scientists themselves considered ethical problems, or what "normal" practices they engaged in, but especially the problems that confronted them for which they had no name—emergent, unusual, or contingent issues for which their training did not prepare them.[4] More often than not, they referred to these issues (issues that were not part of everyday practice) as ethical. The choice of scientists and research areas was therefore strategic.[5]

---

4. On this subject, we are guided by a number of recent attempts to theorize the modern transformation of the ethical: Fischer 2003; Rabinow 2003; Faubion 2001b; Lakoff and Collier 2004.

5. Indeed, the ability to make such a strategic choice depended largely on the extensive topical knowledge of one of the research group members (Kelty), who had already conducted significant research in this area and was therefore attuned to which research areas might be most salient for our questions; a second project on nanotechnology has therefore proven somewhat more challenging in that there are no experts among us, making the choice of subjects a slightly less principled one.

The second project, EPNANO, was funded by the Center for Biological and Environmental Nanotechnology (CBEN), an NSF-funded center devoted to exploring the "wet-dry" interface between natural and human systems, and emerging nanomaterials and particles. All of the NSF centers funded through the National Nanotechnology Initiative (NNI) also have educational/outreach programs and social and ethical impact programs as part of their purview. In the case of CBEN, the researchers are funded through the latter program and are expected to contribute research to the center.

The nanotechnology project was also conceived as a way to discover, through ethnographic research, the emerging issues being labeled ethical or political; the demand for such research has been extremely high in the last four years, and the availability of funding for social science research on nanotechnology stands to transform the kinds of topics and issues that science studies, policy studies, technology assessment, science ethics, and other associated fields might pay attention to. In 2005, three NSF Centers for Nanotechnology and Society were funded to pursue this research (see, e.g., Guston and Sarewitz 2002). Whereas computer science has a sense of its history, the tools it has developed, and its concepts and problems, nanotechnology represents a much earlier stage of the constitution of research fields and projects, and a large part of our research has been the investigation of who participates in it and how they conceive of its novelty and historical emergence.

Method

In both experiments, the research protocols have been similar. The research has been primarily participant observation and interview-based, with graduate students and faculty pursuing leads to hang out in labs, attend meetings, or conduct associated research and reading. A significant component of the "coordination" is the coordination around the various formal interviews; it usually follows the same protocol. The research group meets to read and discuss materials that have been provided by the interviewee—usually impenetrable and obscure research publications, of which we can normally parse only the first sentence. Of the abstract.[6] The research group delves into these areas and develops a loose set of

---

6. One of the small satisfying successes of this project was the fact that anthropology graduate students—most of whom were avowedly uninterested in computer science—went from being intimidated and bewildered by the research articles to being comfortable with and unthreatened by the language in the space of six months. They only really came to believe the abstract assertion that there is a difference between knowing a lot of science and knowing the meaning of science via the practical experience of exploring and discussing the works with practitioners. This, if anything, is confirmation

questions together based on discussions and reading. A subset of the group con-
ducts an interview and transcribes it. The transcription is sent to the interviewee
for comment, and the research group meets again to determine which, if any, of
our questions were answered, which need further clarification, and what direction to head in for a second set of questions and interviews. The development of
question areas and the response to the interview are guided not by a predefined
set of research questions, but primarily by the research interests of the participants, many of whom are graduate students whose dissertation projects have
nothing to do with computers, nanotechnology, or ethics. As a result the range of
questions can be quite surprising and the kinds of connections startling to the
interviewees.

Over the course of the two experiments, the process has been given a more
formal or abstract description consisting of more or less explicit stages: problem,
inquiry, and analysis.[7] The process is intended to be circular: problems are identified in such a way that inquiries about those problems make sense (ranging from
questions to ask in interview, to archival questions to follow up on, to observational questions to pursue in a lab); inquiries are meant to yield some kind of
raw data: interview transcripts, descriptions, papers or documents, and the like;
inquiries serve as the basis for analysis (writings and discussion of various sorts);
and analyses are intended to refine problems for the next round. The circular
process itself is the basis for experiments in "composition"—experiments that
aim to fix this process in multiple media: as an accessible and navigable website
(navigable to both researchers and potential readers); as a glossary of concepts
that emerge from the problem-inquiry-analysis circle; and as papers, articles, and
other standard scholarly forms. Coordination between researchers takes place in
all three stages. Coordination between researchers and subjects takes place primarily in the inquiry stage, but overflows into the others to the extent that interviewees are interested in reading or contributing to the material.

As researchers read and reread transcripts, make annotations, and attempt to
think through their own research questions and interests, a heterogeneous body
of objects begins to develop—results of inquiry and analysis. Often the objects
take very conventional forms: audio and video files of the interviews, transcripts,
reading notes, face-to-face research meetings, shared ideas and annotations on

---

of what one participant asserted concerning the project: "interviewing is not ethnography." The relatively long-term immersion in the material and the interaction with both subjects and colleagues
concerning it were essential, if ephemeral, aspects of the project, and confirmed our assertions (when
questioned by computer scientists) that there was no "algorithm" for ethnographic research.

7. These three terms first emerged from discussion with Andrew Lakoff and Steve Collier in
comparing research processes with that evolved in the Anthropology of the Contemporary Research
Collaboratory (ARC): http://anthropos-lab.net/.

the transcripts, related news stories, and events and analytical writings in various stages. These objects can take form through classic ethnographic techniques, such as literally cutting up transcripts and putting them in coded piles, as well as with digital tools, such as wikis, content management systems, and online editors of various kinds for collaborative mark-up of transcripts. No single tool is intended to become the de facto tool of inquiry or analysis, though we do have a commitment to tools that are freely licensed (Free Software/Open Source) in order to ensure legal and technical archivability. Tools that allow multiple users to edit the same texts at the same time and record both the commentary and who made the commentary are particularly sought after.[8] The interviews themselves tend to be open-ended, though we are careful to give the interviewees a chance to read and discuss the transcripts prior to the second interview.

Once a suitable body of transcripts, articles, notes, and observations have been shared and read by everyone, the next step is defining constraints and goals for short commentaries or analyses. It is here that the problem of composition is explicitly broached: the problem of making commentary fit into a synoptic genre; that is, to make it more than a proliferation of details and notes. At the same time that participants are asked to think about their own detailed interests, they are asked to think about making those interests respond to a core set of concepts that would allow a new reader to understand and navigate the material we produce. Practically speaking, commentaries have taken the form of assignments (we call them "missions" which participants can experience either in deference to anthropology's past or with a James Bond–style enthusiasm), usually to produce less than 2,000 words focused on responding to a particular concept or problem. These assignments might ask all participants to write something about a particularly rich passage or two in a transcript; or to undertake etymological, rhetorical, or linguistic analyses; or to analyze transcripts with respect to a particular concept ("trust," "scale," "security," "membrane," etc.); or to pose or answer a question in relation to a given article or book. The goal of such assignments is not artificially to restrict the work of participants, but instead to promote a kind of contrastive approach. The value in such assignments lies not in their ability to encourage virtuosity, but instead in their ability to instantly provide a kind of

---

8. The array of tools for this kind of collaborative writing have mushroomed in the period 2005–07, in part because of innovation around wikis, but wikis tend not to record the identity of the contributor in an obvious way; blogs and content management systems are almost always structured around a text followed by a string of threaded comments, making it hard to insert comments as annotations to a text. In part online collaborative word processing has been driven by Google's challenges to Microsoft. Writely.com (now "Google Docs") was the first successful example, though not quite easy to use and not Free or Open Source. Other such tools are likely to proliferate. Tools for annotating and sharing video and audio are even rarer, as are Free/Open Source qualitative data analysis tools; the TAMS analyzer (Weinstein 2006) is one important step in this direction.

Rashomon-like perspective on a given phenomenon. Often the assignments are developed through discussion and argument—but the writing of them is generally conducted in private. The key to reading such documents is to know how they all respond to a central mission. It has always been a goal to make these texts link to one another, to the mission, and to the details in the transcripts that they are referencing, although it hasn't necessarily worked in practice (for both technical and methodological reasons).

The objects produced by the research process proliferate quickly: notes, questions, transcripts, highlighted transcripts, annotated and condensed transcripts, lists of keywords, sets of annotations, commentaries on the transcripts and annotations, structured assignments, commentaries that responded to a structured set of questions, commentaries that emerged according to the interests of individual researchers, definitions and conceptual glossaries, conference papers and articles, reviews and blogs, and so on. Such a heterogeneous set of documents is a familiar body of work for most social scientists, and often the work of synthesizing this into a single coherent article or book is what is most highly valued. While this project does not shy away from that challenge, it nonetheless highlights two different challenges: 1) making visible the process and materials that constitute that work, documenting in some form the work of conceptualization that goes into the valued articles, books, and concepts developed by anthropologists; and 2) maintaining an openness to new directions that would otherwise be closed off by the demands of individualized article and book production. Indeed, the very challenge of imagining what that kind of openness looks like has not been an explicit concern of social scientists: What technical, social, and practical constraints are necessary to keep such a project "alive"? And, if a project is not to reach its apotheosis in a book or article, what might be the signal that such a project is in fact complete? In the case of the first project (EPIT), while the interviews and annotations done by the initial group have come to a standstill after a successful workshop that included three outside researchers, work on the development of ideas and articles related to this initial project continues for one faculty member (Kelty) and at least one graduate student (Kayaalp).

In many ways this research process was absolutely conventional: it involved only interview, observation, transcription, and analysis followed by a workshop and discussion. It was therefore indistinguishable from most work in cultural anthropology—which was good news for the graduate students, whose self-definition as professional researchers is at stake. However, there are two aspects of this process that we consider to be novel and that were raised as questions throughout the project. The first was the question of commentary: What form could it take that would make it stand out as more than a footnote or a response? Should we aim at producing some kind of "case study"? Should we turn to the figure of the Talmud (this seemed to give too much credit to both the interviews and the commentaries)? How should we organize (hierarchize?) the commentaries? Do we do so at the outset, or wait until they are written? How do we give them structure, but keep them open-ended? Do the available software tools liberate us to think about composition, or straitjacket us into particular modes of presentation?

The second was the need to clarify the meaning of collaboration. Many students who participated in these experiments were fundamentally frustrated by my perceived failure to say why we were doing this research: What were or are the goals, what did I (Kelty) want to find out? From one perspective collaborative research is appealing (especially paid collaborative research) precisely because it gives students defined research tasks, for which they are not responsible in any profound intellectual sense, but through which they might learn "how research is done." By contrast, my injunction that they generate their own questions and follow their own interests and leads was always met with approval, but confusion: How then is it "collaborative"? What makes it different from the individual research projects they are asked to pursue as graduate students? It is through this tension that the distinction between coordination and collaboration was developed.

In this respect, my own work on Free Software provided a useful foil and template for understanding our goals (Kelty 2008b). One of the most well known claims about Free Software is that it involves the collaboration of hundreds if not thousands of volunteers who work together on the creation of highly complex software projects, like the Linux operating system kernel. Common wisdom suggests that this mode of collaboration (or "peer production," to use Yochai Benkler's term) is somewhat anarchic and free-wheeling—a bazaar, not a cathedral (Benkler 2006; Raymond 2001). Further research has revealed that it is not anarchic at all, but that it does proceed in ways strikingly different from those in which a conventional software company might proceed. Although it is driven by volunteerism and individuals are free to work or not work on whatever they choose, it is nonetheless extremely highly coordinated.

The Linux project, for instance, consists of a leader (Linus Torvalds) with a hierarchy of lieutenants, each responsible for different parts of the kernel; a mailing list on which all participants are free to communicate (the Linux Kernel Mailing List, or LKML); and a source code management system that keeps track of who writes what and when and allows for a certain degree of automatic management of asynchronous, distributed contributions from participants around the world. There are, however, no goals and no planning. The project privileges a particular form of adaptability at all cost—whatever someone creates, it can be incorporated so long as it passes a series of tests having to do with a largely unarticulated, but learned, intuition about technical elegance, functionality, and the structure of the kernel itself. Torvalds and lieutenants facilitate this kind of contribution, but do not direct it. As a result, the Linux kernel does a great many things, some of them relevant only to very obscure architectures or uses, some of them useful to every user—but it was never designed to do any of them.

Of course one should ask: How do people know what to do? In some ways, this is the role of pedagogy: the construction of a disciplinary structure within which it makes sense to pursue one kind of problem rather than another. Linux makes sense because generations of students have been taught what an operating system is and should look like by studying UNIX (in the 1980s and 1990s) and Linux (today). The coordination of contributions to Linux is largely routine and invisible. People learn what to do and how to do it, and they simply do so. What emerges, sometimes, but not always, are forms of collaboration: co-work, co-labor, co-thinking about how to identify problems and functions, and how to solve them. Much of this work takes place on the LKML, simply as a kind of question-and-answer discussion, often with flame-wars around controversial topics. As people settle into these collaborations, coordination sets the stage: the structure of lieutenants, the mailing list, and the Source Code Management (SCM) tool sets the constraints around how that collaboration will unfold, and more important, keeps track of it and manages it as an experiment. The success of a collaboration is in the outcome, not in the justification or planning—higher risk, higher reward, less bureaucracy and planning mentality.

As a result of this particular kind of coordination, the Linux kernel emerges as a collaborative project only in a weak sense: it is an architecture that allows multiple kinds of individual contributions to be included, and privileges this "adaptability" above any other design criteria.

The EPIT and EPNANO projects share some of this commitment to adaptability—even though there are significant differences (far fewer participants, a completely different domain of knowledge). The reason the commitment to adaptability is privileged is because one of the core conceptual claims of ethnographic fieldwork, especially in the tradition referenced here, is that ethnography is an epistemological encounter, one that might require, as George Marcus put it somewhere: "a theorem [!] of planned incompleteness, but not sloppiness or indeterminacy." Adaptability in the Linux kernel is a precise form of planned incompleteness—a way of insisting on openness to new questions and directions (and this takes legal, technical, and social forms). Ethnographic fieldwork shares this commitment over against a commitment to research design that sets questions in advance and for which fieldwork is mere data-gathering. The EPIT and EPNANO projects are ways of making visible that activity through coordination.

In the EPIT/EPNANO case, the initial gambit is that "sites" or the areas of study (computer science and engineering or nanotechnology) are capacious enough to allow for a wide array of directions to pursue, each in his/her own way, upon a shared platform that is coordinated fieldwork. Coordination is achieved through the technologies (shared content management systems, e-mail, collaborative tools for editing), but more importantly through setting up "missions" with defined time-frames and limits, and identifying projects (like clarifying concepts or collecting data) that people can pursue on their own.

If, in the case of Linux, contributors know what an operating system looks like, then the relevant comparison in anthropology is that researchers know what an anthropological research question is and how to research it. But fieldwork is precisely the tool by which such research questions become fully formed, or, at least, by which they transform from an initial speculative proposal into a practice of forming concepts in specifiable contexts. If Linux were a conventional engineering project that proceeded through strong design management, it would seek merely to adapt the idea of "operating system" to changing conditions. Similarly, a strong disciplinary focus merely adapts traditional anthropological questions (anthropology of exchange, African political institutions, kinship studies, linguistics) to changing conditions (kinship studies confronts reproductive technologies; anthropology of exchange confronts the new economy, etc.).

But Linux does not proceed by strong design criteria; it proceeds only with respect to what contributors produce and what the leaders accept as "working"— a nontrivial problem that entails a fantastically refined engineering knowledge and aesthetic sensibility and is analogous to the problem of "composition" raised here. Contributors to Linux "compose" new ideas and forms out of the existing platform without regard for, or against, the historical plans, meanings, and functions of "operating system."

In our case, fieldwork as a coordination platform is intended to open up the same possibility: that fieldwork can pursue multiple different significant problems based on the intuitions of the fieldworkers and the coordination constraints of the project. Composition thus is analogous to coming up with a protocol for making all of these partially restricted contributions of multiple participants "work" together—a nontrivial problem that entails a somewhat less fantastically refined, but nonetheless deep sense of scholarly pursuits generally, anthropological problems in particular, and an aesthetic sense of form in new media.

Such an experiment, if successful, amounts to a strongly, perhaps radically "conventionalist" approach: research problems and approaches do not refer back to disciplinary questions or to "theory" as a guiding hand but directly to the practice and outcome of fieldwork itself—an immanent theory and critique.

And such a practice opens one up to going beyond going native, and into the domain of finding friends and mentors in the field, not only in the discipline.

Substance

Given the methodological orientation, the broad theme of our experiments is focused on forms of immanent critique, especially novel questions and answers about ethics and politics of science and technology. The EPIT project revealed three areas of such interest: norms of practice in computer security, the "immanent critique" of electronic voting machines, and the status of "trust" and "risk" among computer scientists. The EPNANO project by contrast has uncovered a number of different issues which, at the time of this writing, were still in the process of formulation (and later developed into a concern with nanotechnology and responsibility [Kelty and McCarthy n.d.]).

EPIT

While numerous anthropological projects have been completed or are under way that study hackers, geeks, and Internet-based social movements, there is relatively little recent work on academic computer scientists (notable and formidable exceptions are Star 1995; Bowker 1997; Bowker 2001; Forsythe 2001). Academic computer scientists represent a crucial point of comparison, especially for recent work on Free Software/Open Source and hacker ethics and politics (Coleman 2004). Several EPIT project participants were fascinated with the discourse around bugs, security, and the norms concerning "good and bad bug hunting." Security researcher Dan Wallach explained in detail the mechanisms whereby one hunts for and finds bugs in software—much the way a hacker (or cracker) would search for vulnerabilities that might be exploited for good (or evil) purposes. Wallach (like other academic security researchers) is concerned with building a career out of this activity, and two salient points emerged from the discussion.

The first was that Wallach talked of his "research pipeline": "Find a bug, write a paper about why the bug was there, fix the bug, write a paper about how you fixed the bug, repeat."[9] His list of publications bears this out, numbering more than forty by his early thirties. Wallach's narration of the norms of bug hunting was the explicit focus of one researcher (Potoczniak) as well as a topic of frequent discussion. On the one hand, they revealed much about the very fragile

---

9. Dan Wallach/transcript #1 available through the EPIT website.

line between legitimate and illegitimate types of research in the computer security research community and even to some extent how cultural background can
play into the construction of these lines.

The lines between legitimate and illegitimate research were also central in
interviews with Peter Druschel, whose work on peer-to-peer systems raised difficult questions about how to legally pursue research that can result directly
in more efficient and robust file-sharing programs (Kelty 2008b). Druschel
was also a point of contact for comparison with studies of hackers and Open
Source programmers, and our work suggests that there is still a significant difference between the vocation of the scientist and that of the tinkerer or bricoleur—
one that has less to do with savage or civilized minds than with the bureaucratic,
deliberate, and methodical practice of contributing to science in a structured
and cumulative form. By contrast, hackers and tinkerers engage in fast and furi-
ous creation of often mind-bogglingly clever or elegant code, which is nonetheless inscrutable or difficult to use on account of its idiosyncratic creation by
hackers or Free and Open Source projects with ad hoc management and little
concern for replicability or archivability of results. They have "users" who need
to be satisfied—computer scientists usually do not.

A key point of entry for researchers into the arcane interests of computer
security researchers was the surprising use by Dan Wallach of the concept of a
"gift economy" to explain the practice of finding and revealing security flaws in
corporate software. It was surprising simply because it's always surprising to see
concepts from anthropology circulating in a foreign place, but, more important
for anyone who has had the pleasure of associating with geeks, hackers, or Free/
Open Source software aficionados, they know that the concept of "gift economy"
circulates quite widely (first used by Rheingold 1993, then in Ghosh 1998 and
Raymond 2001) as a folk explanation of reputation and value creation. So it was
doubly surprising to see it used by Wallach (who admitted that he probably knew
about it only because of Raymond) to refer in this case to the specific activity of
"giving" a security flaw to a corporation (rather than "giving" it to the world—
i.e., making it public), in return for which he was "given" a $17,000 computer.[10]

This exchange was deeply formative for Wallach, and he often uses it to
explain to his own students the proper "ethical" practice of finding, reporting,
revealing, and expecting payment (or not) for security flaws. At the time of this
event, Wallach was a graduate student and the Internet was just emerging as an
everyday object; he was thus one of the first people in the history of the discipline to perform this kind of action and one of the first to call it research. Prior

---

10. This story is in Dan Wallach/transcript #1.

to this point, security flaws were simply problems a company might or might not choose to deal with—Wallach and a handful of others introduced a way for them to become an issue of public safety or commercial accountability. Wallach further illustrated the security flaw gift economy through his explanation of Netscape's early "bugs bounty" program—in which Netscape paid $1,000 for security flaws (beginning in roughly 1996). According to Wallach, this system was very soon abused, providing as it did an incentive for people to find as many bugs as possible and then demand payment for them. Wallach refers to this explicitly as "blackmail" and differentiates it from the ethical incentives that he had (very rapidly) evolved to make security research into more of a cat-and-mouse game between researchers and corporations, as opposed to what he saw as a kind of protection racket.

A second area of intense interest for the EPIT project—primarily because of the high-profile aspect of the research—was Dan Wallach's involvement in the nationwide (and eventually global) controversy over touch-screen electronic voting machines (EVMs). Wallach was a co-author on the report that analyzed the Diebold electronic voting machines and found them vulnerable to various kinds of attacks (Kohno et al. 2004). As was clear from discussions with both Wallach and Moshe Vardi, CS researchers are reluctant to grant absolute security status to any software system—it is therefore not at all surprising that the EVMs contained security flaws that could be exploited to rig an election or change the results. This was not, however, the core of the controversy.

The EVMs made by all of the major manufacturers by 2003 (helped along by the Help America Vote Act, which disbursed large amounts of funding to local election officials around the country, who in turn signed contracts with EVM companies) were touch-screen-only machines. None of them possessed any mechanism that would allow 1) a voter to verify in some tangible way (i.e., other than on-screen) that the machine was recording a vote correctly or 2) an independent recount of the votes based on something other than the potentially compromised software itself (i.e., a paper ballot). The research that Wallach and friends conducted, therefore, was not necessarily directly connected to the main problem—that is, though they proved the existence of flaws in the machine they were not asking Diebold to make the machine one hundred percent secure. They were instead asking them to provide an independent verification of the vote, when the machine is broken or compromised. In some ways, it could be simply stated as a core engineering principle: make the function of the machine robust. The call went out, both from Avi Rubin of Johns Hopkins and from a well-known CS researcher from Stanford, David Dill, for a "voter-verifiable paper trail."[11]

---

11. Two sites with more information on the controversy are http://www.verifiedvoting.org and http://www.voterverifiable.com.

Through protest, public speaking, activism, and organizing, these CS researchers, along with other activists and organizations (such as the Electronic Frontier Foundation), were successful in convincing several states retroactively to require EVM makers to include a vote-verifiable paper trail on the machines they sell.

The problem of verification in this case includes a palimpsest of transparency issues—adding up, as one might suspect, to a pretty opaque problem. In the first place, Wallach and friends never actually had access to a real Diebold voting machine for their study. They had only a collection of source code that had somehow or other been "liberated" from Diebold's webservers (according to Wallach, activist Beverly Kaufmann claims to have "found" the code lying open for anyone to see on a webserver based perhaps in New Zealand).[12] Wallach and friends' article (Kohno et al. 2004) was therefore based not on the "official" Diebold machine, but on the only code they could obtain. Of course, from Wallach's perspective, there was no other choice: in order to inspect any of the corporate machines, Wallach would have had to sign a nondisclosure agreement that would effectively stifle his ability to publish the results of any research. So they decided to base their research on the liberated code, risking violation of trade-secret law, which, as Wallach likes to point out, not without some glee, is a felony offense in Texas.[13]

A second layer of opacity comes at the level of certification. Because of the trade-secret status of the software code owned by the corporations, certification by the U.S. government happens in secret and, according to Wallach, both the certification process and the certification itself are classified, unavailable for review by anyone. Wallach is justifiably appalled by this state of affairs—but ever the scientist, he offers an explanation in the form of "regulatory capture": that government bodies set up to regulate the process and mechanics of national elections in the United States are effectively controlled by the corporate interests creating the machines. While this response may sound cynical, it is actually a kind of analytic device that allows Wallach to pinpoint where the weaknesses are in the system—that is, they are not only in the code, but in the democracy itself.

A third layer of opacity concerns what happens in the voting booth. The controversy concerns the fact that many voters and many voter organizations are appalled at the activism of CS researchers, because they see it as a big step backwards. For these organizations, EVMs represent huge strides in achieving equality and access at the voting station: blind voters can vote alone with an audible ballot, elderly voters can increase the font size or fix a miscast vote, and voters with motor disabilities are better accommodated by the machines. In addition, election officials see great benefits in eliminating paper: they see the machines,

---

12. This story is recounted in Dan Wallach/transcript #2.
13. Ibid.

and rightly so, as potentially more accurate, and certainly much faster at counting votes, than any other system.

CS professors, however sympathetic (or not) they may be toward such concerns, are pointing to something else: the superimposition of particular technical structures onto long-standing democratic structures. They decry the potential for the effective relegislation of democratic election policy. CS researchers, possibly for the first time in history, find themselves arguing that we should trust technology less and use more paper. They can see clearly that it is not the technology that is at issue, but the structure of democracy and the protocol by which elections are carried out, recorded, verified, and ultimately legitimated.

The implication of this experience, for our research group, is that deep within computer science, there is an immanent critique of government and one which CS researchers find themselves reluctantly and somewhat awkwardly trying to articulate in the only language they know—that of science. Part of the goal of this project, then, has been the attempt to articulate, through dialogue and commentary, the nature and meaning of this immanent critique. Of course, given the very high-profile nature of this issue, we will not have been the only people attempting to do so, but the conclusion for science studies and anthropology remains the same (and one demonstrated beautifully twenty years ago in *Leviathan and the Air-pump* [Shapin 1985]): that at its heart, scientific practice is also about social stability and legitimacy and that where such arguments erupt, one can clearly see both the state of the art and the art of the state.

EPNANO

The EPNANO project is still under way, and so the substantive issues remain open. There are however, some clear lines of interest. The most significant of these is the role of research into the potential health and environmental impacts of nanotechnology, an area that Rice, through CBEN, has seized on and turned into a robust field of inquiry. Mark Wiesner, one of the original Principal Investigators at CBEN, has been a core interlocutor in describing the process by which a certain kind of bargain was struck with respect to research on environmental and biological effects. Rather than simply funding research into toxicology or hazards, CBEN has promoted instead research that focuses on health and environmental uses of nanoparticles and on the challenges of engineering safe nanoparticles from the get-go (Kelty 2008a).

Several "problems" are being refined by this aspect of the research: the question of reflexivity in science and the creation of structures of "anticipatory governance" (Guston and Sarewitz 2002); the tension between risk calculation and other forms of foresight, prediction, and preparedness; the increasing separation of Environmental and Health Safety (EHS) issues from other areas of "social" implications (including legal, ethical, and cultural issues); the question of nano-technology as a "weakly contextualized science" (Nowotny, Scott, and Gibbons 2001) or as a "strategic" science (van Lente and Rip 1998) that defines a world-view and a general strategic focus, rather than being focused on solving specific problems of interest to the state.

Several researchers in the project have also found an interest in looking at "new objects" such as nanoshells, nanotubes, nanorods, nanocars, membranes, or nanotube fibers. When such objects can only be imaged through complex technologies and devices, how does one orient one's epistemological questions? Two research areas in particular have draw our attention: membrane engineering in Wiesner's case and vacuum technology in the case of Kevin Kelly. Building on work by Cyrus Mody (Mody 2001) on purity in the lab, this research direction has clear aesthetic appeal for EPNANO researchers—ranging from the material culture of science to the more metaphorical and allegorical uses of filters, mem-branes, and vacuums in understanding researchers' self-understandings as part of an emerging science. Naficy, for instance, posed the question of the "social-as-membrane" apropos of Wiesner's description of the interplay of science, eco-nomics, and environment, and Dib has explored the idea of nanoparticles as liminal objects that reflect prudence and ambivalence among researchers. Powell pursued a project more historical in nature, focused on the institutional creation of the National Nanotechnology Initiative and other agencies and institutes that promote nanoscience and nanotechnology.

While the projects described above are substantively specific (anthropology of science and technology) and focused on the use of new media and Internet-based tools, the conclusions I draw about composition, coordination, and collabora-tion are meant to apply across all domains of qualitative ethnographic work. Our informants-cum-collaborators are just as likely today (probably more so) to be producing and distributing their own media about the cultural and social issues that plague them—and they may do so either directly, with the increasing spread of new technologies, or indirectly, through the kinds of cultural changes that this increasing production and circulation of media can have on social groups of all kinds. Strategies of making and controlling media are as diverse and as culturally complex as the content of the media themselves.

But a more troubling issue for anthropology is how anthropologists and their informants might learn new strategies for making stable and robust conceptual connections across radically different projects (not just across area expertise or discipline, but outside of the academy and into unfamiliar forms of scholarly and critical practice). As I mentioned at the outset, the discipline has historically served as the mainstay of coordination of the making of conceptual connections. Whether it is the endless debates about the culture concept, the rich literatures in kinship, exchange, or political institutions—it is through disciplinary channels that an anthropologist working on heritage claims in Mexico (Breglia, this volume) might connect with a scholar working on expatriate Iranians in Washington, D.C. (Naficy, this volume), or South Korean venture capitalists (Chung, this volume). However, in a world populated by new objects (especially technical objects), new events, and new forms of organization, anthropologists are far more likely to find the kind of conceptual simpatico in surprising places—especially with other disciplines, often with informants themselves. In addition, the demand for inter- and trans-disciplinary research is high enough (i.e., our funding is increasingly contingent on it) that a new body of scholarship is in fact emerging, for better or worse, that is not structured through disciplinary channels. Are the classic channels of anthropology sufficient in these cases? Is there something more?

My example of the Linux kernel and of the stratagem of "adaptability" over against structured design is one kind of answer to this question: there are possibilities that have emerged which cannot fit into the disciplinary framework, and we do not know how to take advantage of them. Certainly there is nothing radical about the two experiments I have conducted—they remain projects that respond, in part, to certain kinds of disciplinary constraints, both at a substantive level (i.e., the "culture" of scientists and engineers) and at the level of practice (i.e., interviews and participant observation). But they are propositions about the possibility of a new form of shared and adaptable research method. A shared conceptual vocabulary, distinct from that entrenched in the journals and texts of anthropology, is certainly easier than ever to work on in common with others, even in public; likewise, the sharing of "data" (the material gathered at the inquiry stage) no longer need remain obscure, but can also be made public (or semi-public among a group of scholars) and worked on in common. Such practices might in turn become the discipline of anthropology (again), but to date they remain experimental. We don't yet know how these changes should be formulated and adopted, and thus modesty in proposing transformation is to be admired.

Perhaps the most important implication of these changes concerns the question of exclusivity. Anthropologists are by professional disposition interested in remaining anthropologists rather than joining in and becoming part of their field. Other social scientists show less compunction: political scientists work for campaigns and for foreign policy institutes; economists become civil servants and chairmen of the board. Anthropologists, especially those of the "critical" stripe, are far less comfortable joining in—or if they are it is, as Marcus points out, because they increasingly come to graduate school from an experience with NGOs, activist organizations, or other groups. The perceived virtue of this resistance is "critical distance"—but such a claim all too easily papers over the realities of contemporary fieldwork. In fact, it is an important reason to critically distinguish coordination from collaboration.

Collaboration is too weak a word to describe the entanglements that are by now thoroughly commonplace in cultural anthropology: entanglements of complicity, responsibility, mutual orientation, suspicion and paranoia, commitment and intimate involvement, credit and authority, and the production of reliable knowledge for partially articulated goals set by organizations, institutions, universities, corporations, and governments. Collaboration is perhaps too feel-good, too friendly a notion for the commitments, fights, and compromises that anthropologists frequently make in order to pursue some kind of conceptual innovation. And this is to say nothing of the problematic insertion of "ethics" and "institutional review boards" into the game.

So, for instance, in the ethics and politics experiments described here, scientists and engineers occupy a historically more powerful position in institutions, public life, and policy than anthropologists do. A common reaction to this situation (especially pronounced in some strands of STS) is to adopt the position of the critical analyst who unmasks the hidden structure of belief or interest operative in the activities of science and scientists. But such an approach is also inherently adversarial and blocks access to scientific and technical practices that might already be critical vis-à-vis some other more or less powerful constellation of interests. In our projects, therefore, we have explicitly sought out a different form of engagement: a search for what we refer to as "immanent critique" in the language and practices of scientists. Practically this means developing a process of dialogue, reinterpretation, and commentary that would render explicit the critical practices of scientists and engineers, in areas that might also interest social scientists (the stealth transformation of democratic practice by electronic voting machines; the politics of research on quasi-legal peer-to-peer technologies; and the production of critical research on the environmental and health effects of nanotechnology). While it may well be possible to perform critical, deconstructive, or oppositional readings of the informants we deal with, our attention has instead focused on finding those voices where they appear in the field first and trying to amplify them, transcode them, or simply explain them in our own work.

Naturally, there exist divergent audiences for such an endeavor: at least one is that of anthropology and science studies, which would seek to learn how such critiques are relevant to conceptual and theoretical problems "at home"; but at least one other is the scientists and their constituencies themselves, for whom our ("social science") research is increasingly a highly sought-after commodity—filling a much lauded, but ill-understood need for "social, ethical, and cultural" aspects/impacts of science and technology (indeed—just to emphasize the buttered side of our bread—were it not for this need, none of the research presented here would ever have been funded). Composition, therefore, confronts new challenges that extend (if not alter) the familiar notions of style, audience, idiom, jargon, and readability. Our primary audience will not always be anthropologists or social theorists, but it is social theorists or anthropologists who will always determine the value of, need for, fundability of, and quality of our work. Experimenting with commentary and composition is therefore a way to rethink the kinds of texts and new objects we produce so that they might fill both needs and respond to the reality of trying to do so (e.g., articles and books, documents and files, databases, software, content and version management, vocabularies and taxonomies, archives and search engines, and so on). It is a challenge to create new kinds of objects (not digital vs. analog, but new compositions of both) that are intelligible and that assist in conceptual innovation within anthropology, science studies, and the interpretive social sciences generally, and may even respond to the multiple, partial, incompatible demands we find in the field.

Bibliography

Agar, Michael H. 1995. *The Professional Stranger: An Informal Introduction to Ethnography.* 2nd ed. New York: Academic Press.

Amit, Vered, ed. 2000. *Constructing the Field: Ethnographic Fieldwork in the Contemporary World.* London: Routledge.

Ardren, Traci. 2002. "Conversations about the Production of Archaeological Knowledge and Community Museums at Chunchucmil and Kochol, Yucatán." *World Archaeology* 34(2):379–400.

Arnold, Wayne. 2006. "Thai Stocks Reflect an Ebb in Confidence." December 22. http://nytimes.com.

Ashforth, Adam. 2000. *Mudumo: A Man Bewitched.* Chicago: University of Chicago Press.

Austen, Jane. 2006 (1813). *Pride and Prejudice.* Ed. Pat Rogers. Cambridge: Cambridge University Press.

Bakhtin, Mikhail. 1982. *The Dialectical Imagination: Four Essays.* Trans. Caryl Emerson and Michael Holquist. Austin: University of Texas Press.

Bank of Korea. 1999. "Current Economic and Financial Movements." *Quarterly Economic Review,* April 27. http://www.bok.or.kr/template/eng/default/press/view.jsp?tbl=tbl_FM0000000066_CA0000000964andid=IN0000027273.

Barth, Theodor, and Maziar Raein. 2007. "Walking with Wolves: Displaying the Holding Pattern." *Journal of Writing in Creative Practice* 1(1):33–46.

Bataille, Georges. 1989 (1948). *Theory of Religion.* Trans. Robert Hurley. New York: Zone Books.

Bateson, Gregory, Don Jackson, Jay Haley, and John Weakland. 1956. "Toward a Theory of Schizophrenia." *Behavioral Science* 1:251–64.

Baygan, Günseli. 2003."Venture Capital Policies in Korea." OECD Science, Technology and Industry Working Papers 2003/2, OECD Directorate for Science, Technology and Industry. http://ideas.repec.org/p/oec/stiaaa/2003–2-en.html.

Beck, Peter. 1998. "Revitalizing Korea's Chaebol." *Asia Survey* 38(11):1018–35.

Beck, Ulrich. 1992. *Risk Society: Towards a New Modernity.* Trans. Mark Ritter. Newbury Park, Calif.: Sage.

——. 2001. "Redefining Power in the Global Age: Eight Theses." *Dissent* 48(4):83–90.

——, Anthony Giddens, and Scott Lash. 1994. *Reflexive Modernization: Politics, Aesthetics, and Tradition in the Modern Social Order.* Stanford: Stanford University Press.

Becker, Howard S. 1998. *Tricks of the Trade: How to Think about Your Research While You're Doing It.* Chicago: University of Chicago Press.

Behar, Ruth. 1996. *The Vulnerable Observer: Anthropology That Breaks Your Heart.* Boston: Beacon.

——, and Deborah A. Gordon, eds. 1995. *Women Writing Culture.* Berkeley: University of California Press.

Benkler, Yochai. 2006. *The Wealth of Networks: How Social Production Transforms Markets and Freedom.* New Haven: Yale University Press.

Berlin, Mitchell. 1997. "That Thing Venture Capitalists Do." *Economic Research,* January/February. Philadelphia: Federal Reserve Bank of Philadelphia. http://www.phil.frb.org/econ/br/br98.html.

Berliner, Paul. 1994. *Thinking in Jazz: The Infinite Art of Improvisation.* Chicago: University of Chicago Press.

Biehl, João, Byron Good, and Arthur Kleinman. 2007. *Subjectivity: Ethnographic Investigations.* Berkeley: University of California Press.

Black, Mary. 1963. "On Formal Ethnographic Procedures." *American Anthropologist* 65(6):1347–51.

Blanchette, Jean François. 2002. "'Dematerializing' Written Proof: French Evidence Law, Cryptography, and the Global Politics of Authenticity." Diss., Science and Technology Studies Department, Rensselaer Polytechnic Institute.

Bourdieu, Pierre. 1990. "The Scholastic Point of View." *Cultural Anthropology* 5(4):380–91.

———, and Loïc Wacquant. 1992. *An Invitation to Reflexive Sociology.* Chicago: University of Chicago Press.

Bowker, Geoffrey C. 2001. "Biodiversity, Datadiversity." *Social Studies of Science* 30(5):643–84.

———, ed. 1997. *Social Science, Technical Systems, and Cooperative Work: Beyond the Great Divide.* Mahwah, N.J.: Lawrence Erlbaum Associates.

Boyer, Dominic. In press. "Thinking Through the Anthropology of Experts." *Anthropology in Action.* Special Issue, ed. Michael Powell and Tara Schwegler.

Breglia, Lisa. 2006a. "Complicit Agendas: Ethnography of Archaeology as Ethical Research Practice." In *Ethnographies of Archaeological Practice: Cultural Encounters, Material Reflections,* ed. Matt Edgeworth, 173–83. Lanham, Md.: AltaMira Press.

———. 2006b. *Monumental Ambivalence: The Politics of Heritage.* Austin: University of Texas Press.

Brettell, Caroline B. 1996. *When They Read What We Write: The Politics of Ethnography.* New York: Bergin and Garvey.

Brodwin, Paul. 2005. "'Bioethics in Action' and Human Population Genetics Research." *Culture, Medicine, and Psychiatry* 29:145–78.

Bunzl, Matti. 2003. "Boas, Foucault, and the 'Native Anthropologist': Notes toward a Neo-Boasian Anthropology." *American Anthropologist* 106(3):435–42.

Burawoy, Michael, Joseph A. Blum, Sheba George, and Zsuzsa Gille. 2000. *Global Ethnography: Forces, Connections, and Imaginations in a Postmodern World.* Berkeley: University of California Press.

Callon, Michel, ed. 1998. *The Laws of the Markets.* Oxford: Blackwell.

Carruthers, Mary. 2000. *The Craft of Thought: Meditation, Rhetoric and the Making of Images, 400–1200.* Cambridge: Cambridge University Press.

———. 2008. *The Book of Memory: A Study of Memory in Medieval Culture.* Cambridge: Cambridge University Press.

Cefkin, Melissa, ed. 2009. *Ethnography@work.com.* New York: Berghahn Books.

Cerwonka, Allaine, and Liisa H. Malkki. 2007. *Improvising Theory: Process and Temporality in Ethnographic Fieldwork.* Chicago: University of Chicago Press.

Chun, Soonok. 2003. *They Are Not Machines: Korean Women Workers and Their Fight for Democratic Trade Unionism in the 1970s.* Burlington, Vt.: Ashgate.

Clarke, Adele E., and Joan H. Fujimura, eds. 1992. *The Right Tools for the Job: At Work in Twentieth-Century Life Sciences.* Princeton: Princeton University Press.

Clifford, James, and George E. Marcus, eds. 1986. *Writing Culture: The Poetics and Politics of Ethnography.* Berkeley: University of California Press.

Coleman, Gabriella. 2004. "The Political Agnosticism of Free and Open Source Software and the Inadvertent Politics of Contrast." *Anthropological Quarterly* 77(3):507–19.

Collier, Stephen, and Andrew Lakoff. 2006. "What Is a Laboratory of the Human Sciences?" Anthropology of the Contemporary Working Paper Series. http://anthropos-lab.net/documents/what-is-a-laboratory-in-the-human-sciences/.

Comaroff, Jean. 2005. "The End of History, Again? Pursuing the Past in the Postcolony." In *Postcolonial Studies and Beyond,* ed. Ania Loomba, Suvir Kaul, Matti Bunzl, Antoinette Burton, and Jed Esty, 125–44. Durham: Duke University Press.

——, and John Comaroff. 1993. "Introduction." In *Modernity and Its Malcontents: Ritual and Power in Postcolonial Africa,* ed. Jean Comaroff and John Comaroff, xi–xxxvii. Chicago: University of Chicago Press.

Coy, Peter et al. 1998. "Failed Wizards of Wall Street." July 1. http://businessweek.com/38/b3596001.html.

Crane, Gregory. 1991. "Composing Culture: The Authority of an Electronic Text." *Current Anthropology* 32:293–311.

Crane, Julia, and Michael Angrosino. 1984. *Field Projects in Anthropology: A Student Handbook.* Patterson, N.J.: Waveland Press.

Dabashi, Hamid. 2006. "Native Informers and the Making of American Anthropology." *Al-Ahram Weekly Online* No. 797. http://weekly.ahram.org.eg/2006/797/special.htm.

Deleuze, Giles, and Félix Guattari. 1987. *A Thousand Plateaus: Capitalism and Schizophrenia.* Trans. Brian Massumi. Minneapolis: University of Minnesota Press.

Denzin, Norman K. 1997. *Interpretive Ethnography: Ethnographic Practices for the 21st Century.* Thousand Oaks, Calif.: Sage.

——, and Yvonna S. Lincoln, eds. 2005. *The Sage Handbook of Qualitative Research.* 3rd ed. Thousand Oaks, Calif.: Sage.

Derrida, Jacques. 1976 (1967). *Of Grammatology.* Trans. Gayatri Chakravorty Spivak. Baltimore: Johns Hopkins University Press.

——. 1978. *Writing and Difference.* Trans. Alan Bass. Chicago: University of Chicago Press.

Devon, Ely, and Max Gluckman. 1964. "Conclusion: Modes and Consequences of Limiting a Field of Study." In *Closed Systems and Open Minds: Limits of Naivety in Social Anthropology,* ed. Max Gluckman, 158–262. Chicago: Aldine.

Douglas, Mary. 1970. *Natural Symbols: Explorations in Cosmology.* New York: Pantheon.

Downey, Gary Lee, and Joseph Dumit, eds. 1997. *Cyborgs and Citadels: Anthropological Interventions in Emerging Sciences and Technologies.* Santa Fe: School of American Research Press.

Dumont, Jean-Paul. 1978. *The Headman and I: Ambiguity and Ambivalence in the Fieldworking Experience.* Austin: University of Texas Press.

Durkheim, Emile. 1995 (1912). *The Elementary Forms of the Religious Life.* Trans. Karen Fields. New York: The Free Press.

——. 2006. *On Suicide.* Trans. Robin Buss. London: Penguin.

The Economist. 2007. "The Fall of Thailand?" May 22.

Edgeworth, Matt, ed. 2006. *Ethnographies of Archaeological Practice: Cultural Encounters, Material Reflections.* Lanham, Md.: AltaMira Press.

Eliot, T. S. 1971 (1917). "The Love Song of J. Alfred Prufrock." In *T. S. Eliot, The Complete Poems and Plays,* 3–7. New York: Harcourt, Brace, and World.

Emeagwali, Philip. 2001. *The Flight of Financial Capital from Africa.* http://emeagwali.com/interviews/capital-flight/africa.html.

Emerson, Robert M., Rachel I. Fretz, and Linda L. Shaw. 1995. *Writing Ethnographic Fieldnotes.* Chicago: University of Chicago Press.

Erber, Georg, and Harald Hagemann. 2005. "The New Economy in a Growth Crisis." In *The Regional Divide, Promises and Realities of the New Economy,* ed. Kurt Hubner, 20–43. London: Routledge.

Evans-Pritchard, E. E. 1951. *Social Anthropology.* London: Cohen and West.

Fabian, Johannes. 1983. *Time and the Other: How Anthropology Makes Its Object.* New York: Columbia University Press.

———. 2002. "Virtual Archives and Ethnographic Writing." *Current Anthropology* 43(5):775–86.

Faubion, James D. 1988. "Possible Modernities." *Cultural Anthropology* 3(4):365–78.

———. 1993. *Modern Greek Lessons: A Primer in Historical Constructivism.* Princeton: Princeton University Press.

———. 2001a. *The Shadows and Lights of Waco: Millennialism Today.* Princeton: Princeton University Press.

———. 2001b. "Toward an Anthropology of Ethics: Foucault and the Pedagogies of Autopoiesis." *Representations* 74(1):83–104.

———, and George E. Marcus. 2007. "Constructionism in Anthropology." In *Handbook of Social Constructionism,* ed. James L. Holstein and Jaber F. Gubrium, 67–84. New York: Guilford.

———, ed. 1998. *Essential Works of Foucault.* Vol. 2, Aesthetics, Method, and Epistemology. New York: The New Press.

———, ed. 2000. *Essential Works of Michel Foucault.* Vol. 3, Power. New York: The New Press.

Ferguson, James. 2006. *Global Shadows: Africa in the Neoliberal World Order.* Durham: Duke University Press.

Firth, Raymond, ed. 1957. *Man and Culture: An Evaluation of the work of Bronislaw Malinowski.* New York: Harper Brothers.

Fischer, Michael M. J. 1992. "Reading for the Ethnography." In *Burying SM: The Politics of Knowledge and the Sociology of Power in Africa,* ed. David W. Cohen and E. S. Atieno Odhiambo, 111–19. London: Heinemann.

———. 2000. "Before Going Digital / Double Digit / Y2000: The Nineties (A Retrospective of Late Editions)." In *Zeroing In on the Year 2000,* ed. George E. Marcus. Late Editions, Vol. 8, 13–34. Chicago: University of Chicago Press.

———. 2003. *Emergent Forms of Life and the Anthropological Voice.* Durham: Duke University Press.

———. 2007a. "Culture and Cultural Analysis as Experimental Systems." *Cultural Anthropology* 22(1):1–65.

———. 2007b. "Four Genealogies for a Recombinant Anthropology of Science and Technology." *Cultural Anthropology* 22(3):539–614.

———, and Medhi Abedi. 1990. *Debating Muslims: Cultural Dialogues in Postmodernity and Tradition.* Madison: University of Wisconsin Press.

Fisher, A. Melissa, and Greg Downey, eds. 2006. *Frontiers of Capital: Ethnographic Reflections on the New Economy.* Durham: Duke University Press.

Fitzgerald, F. Scott. 2004 (1925). *The Great Gatsby.* Ed. Harold Bloom. Philadelphia: Chelsea House.

Forster, E. M. 1921. *Howard's End.* New York: A. A. Knopf.

Forsythe, Diana. 1999. " 'It's Just a Matter of Common Sense': Ethnography as Invisible Work." *Journal of Computer Supported Cooperative Work* 8(1–2):127–45.

———. 2001. *Studying Those Who Study Us: An Anthropologist in the World of Artificial Intelligence.* Stanford: Stanford University Press.

Fortun, Kim. 2001. *Advocacy After Bhopal: Environmentalism, Disaster, and New Global Orders.* Chicago: University of Chicago Press.

———. 2003. "Ethnography in/of/as Open Systems." *Reviews in Anthropology* 32(2):171–90.

———. 2006. "Poststructuralism, Technoscience, and the Promise of Public Anthropology." *India Review* 5:2–3.

———, and Todd Cherkasky. 1998. "Counter-Expertise and the Politics of Collaboration." *Science as Culture* 7(2):145–72.

Fortun, Mike. 2005. "For an Ethics of Promising, or: A Few Kind Words about James Watson." *New Genetics and Society* 24(2):157–73.

Foucault, Michel. 1972 (1969). *The Archaeology of Knowledge and the Discourse on Language.* Trans. A. M. Sheridan Smith. New York: Random House.

———. 1973. *The Order of Things: An Archaeology of the Human Sciences.* A Translation of *Les Mots et les choses.* New York: Random House.

———. 1975. *The Birth of the Clinic: An Archaeology of Medical Perception.* Trans. A. M. Sheridan. New York: Random House.

———. 1980. *The History of Sexuality,* Volume I: *An Introduction.* Trans. Robert Hurley. New York: Random House.

———. 1985. *The Use of Pleasure.* The History of Sexuality, Vol. 2. Trans. Robert Hurley. New York: Pantheon.

———. 1986. *The Care of the Self.* The History of Sexuality, Vol. 3. Trans. Robert Hurley. New York: Random House.

———. 1988. "Practicing Criticism." In *Politics, Philosophy, Culture: Interviews and Other Writings, 1977–1984,* ed. L. D. Kritzman, 152–56. New York: Routledge.

———. 1997. "Polemics, Politics and Problematizations." In *Essential Works of Michel Foucault,* Vol. 2, *Ethics: Subjectivity, and Truth,* ed. Paul Rabinow, 111–19. New York: The New Press.

Franklin, Sarah, and Margaret Lock, eds. 2003. *Remaking Life and Death; Toward an Anthropology of the Biosciences.* Santa Fe: School of American Research.

Freilich, Morris. 1970. "Toward a Formalization of Fieldwork." In *Marginal Natives: Anthropologists at Work,* ed. Morris Freilich, 405–585. New York: Harper and Row.

Freud, Sigmund. 1963 (1905). *Jokes and Their Relation to the Unconscious.* Trans. James Strachey. New York: W. W. Norton.

Fujimura, Joan. 1987. "Constructing 'Do-Able' Problems in Cancer Research: Articulating Alignment." *Social Studies of Science* 17(2):257–93.

———. 1992. "Crafting Science: Standardized Packages, Boundary Objects, and 'Translation.'" In *Science as Practice and Culture,* ed. A. Pickering, 168–211. Chicago: University of Chicago Press.

———. 1997. *Crafting Science: A Sociohistory of the Quest for the Genetics of Cancer.* Cambridge, Mass.: Harvard University Press.

Geertz, Clifford. 1973a. *The Interpretation of Cultures.* New York: Basic Books.

———. 1973b. "Notes on the Balinese Cockfight." In Geertz, *The Interpretation of Cultures,* 412–53.

———. 1983. *Local Knowledge: Further Essays in Interpretive Anthropology.* New York: Basic Books.

Gerth, Jeff, and Richard W. Stevenson. December 22, 1997. "Inadequate Regulation Seen in Asia's Banking Crisis." http://nytimes.com.

Geschiere, Peter. 1997. *The Modernity of Witchcraft: Politics and the Occult in Postcolonial Africa.* Charlottesville: University Press of Virginia.

Ghosh, Rishab Ayer. 1998. "Cooking Pot Markets: An Economic Model for the Trade in Free Goods and Services on the Internet." *The Brazilian Electronic Journal of Economics* 1(1). Available at SSRN: http://ssrn.com/abstract=115288.

Giddens, Anthony. 1991. *Modernity and Self-Identity: Self and Society in the Late Modern Age.* Stanford: Stanford University Press.

———. 1999. "Comment: The 1999 Reith Lectures: New World without End." *Observer* April 11:031.

Glaeser, Andreas. 2000. *Divided in Unity: Identity, Germany, and the Berlin Police.* Chicago: University of Chicago Press.

Gluckman, Max. 1955. *Custom and Conflict in Africa.* Oxford: Basil Blackwell.

Gompers, Paul, and Josh Lerner. 2004. *The Venture Capital Cycle.* Cambridge, Mass.: MIT Press.

Goodman, Nelson. 1978. *Ways of Worldmaking.* Indianapolis: Hackett.

Graeber, David. 1996. "Manners, Deference, and Private Property in Early Modern Europe (in Shaping the Social Being)." *Comparative Studies in Society and History* 39(4):694–728.

Granovetter, Mark. 1973. "The Strength of Weak Ties." *American Journal of Sociology* 78(6):1360–80.

——. 1985. "Economic Action and Social Structure: The Problem of Embeddedness." *American Journal of Sociology* 91(3):481–510.

Granovetter, Mark. 2005. "The Impact of Social Structure on Economic Outcomes." *Journal of Economic Perspectives* 19(1):33–50.

——, and Richard Swedberg. 2001. *The Sociology of Economic Life.* Boulder, Colo.: Westview Press.

Grant, Bruce. *In the Soviet House of Culture: A Century of Perestroika.* Princeton: Princeton University Press.

Green, Stephen. 2000. "Negotiating with the Future: The Culture of Modern Risk in Global Financial Markets." *Environment and Planning D: Society and Space* 18(1):77–89.

Greenhalgh, Susan. 2008. *Just One Child: Science and Policy in Deng's China.* Berkeley: University of California Press.

Gudeman, Stephen. 1986. *Economics as Culture: Models and Metaphors of Livelihood.* London: Routledge and Kegan Paul.

Gupta, Ahkil. 1995. "Blurred Boundaries: The Discourse of Corruption, the Culture of Politics, and the Imagined State." *American Ethnologist* 22(2):375–402.

——, and James Ferguson, eds. 1997a. *Anthropological Locations: Boundaries and Grounds of a Field Science.* Berkeley: University of California Press.

——, and James Ferguson, eds. 1997b. *Culture, Power, Place: Explorations in Critical Anthropology.* Durham: Duke University Press.

Guston, David, and Daniel Sarewitz. 2002. "Real Time Technology Assessment." *Technology and Society* 23(4):xx.

Hacking, Ian. 1990. *The Taming of Chance.* Cambridge: Cambridge University Press.

——. 2006. *The Emergence of Probability: A Philosophical Study of Early Ideas about Probability, Induction, and Statistical Inference.* Cambridge: Cambridge University Press.

Hamilton, Jennifer A. 2008a. *Indigeneity in the Courtroom: Law, Culture, and the Production of Difference in North American Courts.* New York: Routledge.

——. 2008b. "Revitalizing Difference in the HapMap: Race, Biomedicine, and Contemporary Human Genetic Variation Research. *Journal of Law, Medicine, and Ethics* 36(3):471–77.

Hancock, Graham. 1994. *The Lords of Poverty: The Power, Prestige, and Corruption of the International Aid Business.* Boston: Atlantic Monthly Press.

Hardt, Michael, and Antonio Negri. 2004. *Multitude.* New York: Penguin.

Hazeltine, Barrett, and Christopher Bull. 1999. *Appropriate Technology: Tools, Choices, and Implications.* New York: Academic Press.

Hemon, Aleksander. 2002. *Nowhere Man.* New York: Nan A. Talese.

Herle, Anita, and Sandra Rouse, eds. 1998. *Cambridge and the Torres Strait: Centenary Essays on the 1898 Anthropological Expedition.* Cambridge: Cambridge University Press.

Herzfeld, Michael. 1997. *Cultural Intimacy: Social Poetics in the Nation-State.* New York: Routledge.

Holmes, Douglas R. 2000. *Integral Europe: Fast-Capitalism, Multiculturalism, Neofascism.* Princeton: Princeton University Press.

——, and George E. Marcus. 2005. "Cultures of Expertise and the Management of Globalization: Toward a Re-functioning of Ethnography." In *Global Assemblages: Technology, Politics, and Ethics as Anthropological Problems,* ed. Aihwa Ong and Stephen Collier, 235–52. Malden, Mass.: Blackwell.

——, and George E. Marcus. 2006. "Fast Capitalism: Paraethnography and the Rise of the Symbolic Analyst." In *Frontiers of Capital: Ethnographic Perspectives on the New Economy,* ed. Melissa Fisher and Gary Downey, 33–57. Durham: Duke University Press.

Hymes, Dell, ed. 1972. *Reinventing Anthropology.* New York: Pantheon.

Institute for the Study of Diplomacy, Georgetown University. 2006. *Discourse, Dissent, and Strategic Surprise: Formulating American Security in an Age of Uncertainty.* Working Group Report No V. February 27.

International HapMap Consortium. 2004. "Integrating Ethics and Science in the International HapMap Project." *Nature Reviews Genetics* 5:467–75.

International Monetary Fund. 2001. IMF Managing Director Congratulates Korea Repayment of 1997 Stand-By Credit. News release. August 22.

Jager, Sheila. 2003. *Narratives of Nation Building in Korea.* New York: M. E. Sharpe.

Jakobson, Roman. 1971 (1956). "Two Aspects of Language and Two Types of Aphasic Disturbances." In *Fundamentals of Language,* ed. R. Jakobson and M. Halle, 115–33. The Hague: Mouton.

James, Henry. 2007 (1878). *Daisy Miller.* Ed. David Lodge. London: Penguin.

Janelli, Roger, and Dawnhee Kim. 1993. *Making Capitalism: The Social and Cultural Construction of a South Korean Conglomerate.* Stanford: Stanford University Press.

Kaplan, Michael. 2003. "Iconomics: The Rhetoric of Speculation." *Public Culture* 15(3):477–93.

Keller, Evelyn Fox. 1985. "Dynamic Objectivity: Love, Power, and Knowledge." In Keller, *Reflections on Gender and Science,* 115–26. New Haven: Yale University Press.

Kelty, Christopher M. 2004. "Punt to Culture." *Anthropological Quarterly* 77(3):547–58.

——. 2005a. "Geeks, Internets, and Recursive Publics." *Cultural Anthropology* 20(2):27–36.

——. 2005b. "Trust among the Algorithms: Ownership, Identity, and the Collaborative Stewardship of Information." In *CODE: Collaborative Ownership in the Digital Economy,* ed. Rishab A. Gosh, 127–51. Cambridge, Mass.: MIT Press.

——. 2008a. "Allotropes of Fieldwork in Nanotechnology." In *Philosophy and Medicine* 101, ed. Fabrice Jotterand, 157–80. Dordrecht, The Netherlands: Springer Verlag.

——. 2008b. *Two Bits: The Cultural Significance of Free Software.* Durham: Duke University Press.

——, and Elise McCarthy. n.d. "Responsibility and Nanotechnology (I)." Unpublished manuscript.

Kim, Eun Mee. 1997. *Big Business, Strong State: Collusion and Conflict in South Korean Development, 1960–1990.* Albany: State University of New York Press.

——, and Jai Mah. 2006. "Patterns of South Korea's Foreign Direct Investment Flow into China." *Asian Survey* 46(4):156–74.

Kim, Hong Nack. 1989. "The 1988 Parliamentary Election in South Korea." *Asia Survey* 29(5):480–95.

Kleinman, Arthur. 1998. "Experience and Its Moral Modes: Culture, Human Conditions, and Disorder." *Tanner Lectures on Human Values.* http://www.tannerlectures.utah.edu/lectures/Kleinman99.pdf.

Kohno, Tadayoshi, Adam Stubblefield, Aviel D. Rubin, and Dan S. Wallach. 2004. "Analysis of an Electronic Voting System." Presented at IEEE Symposium on Security and Privacy, Oakland, Calif., May 2004. http://avirubin.com/vote/analysis/index.html.

Koo, Hagen. 2001. *Korean Workers: The Culture and Politics of Class Formation.* Ithaca: Cornell University Press.

KOSDAQ Stock Market, Inc. Database. 2001–07. http://kosdaq.com/market/market_
main.html/.

Krugman, Paul. 1998. *Curfews on Capital Flight: What Are the Options?* web.mit.edu/
krugman.

Kuhn, Thomas. 1962. *The Structure of Scientific Revolutions.* Chicago: University of
Chicago Press.

Lakoff, Andrew, and Stephen Collier. 2004. "Ethics and the Anthropology of Modern
Reason." *Anthropological Theory* 4(4):419–34.

Landecker, Hannah. 2002. "Commentary: 'Difficult Objects' in Anthropological
Research." Paper read at Rice Graduate Student Symposium, at Houston, Tex.

———. 2007. *Culturing Life: How Cells Became Technologies.* Cambridge, Mass.: Harvard
University Press.

Lassiter, Luke Eric. 2005a. *The Chicago Guide to Collaborative Ethnography.* Chicago:
University of Chicago Press.

———. 2005b. "Collaborative Ethnography and Public Anthropology." *Current Anthropology*
46(1):83–106.

Latour, Bruno. 1987. *Science in Action: How to Follow Scientists and Engineers through
Society.* Philadelphia: Open University Press.

———. 2005. "From Realpolitik to Dingpolitik, or How to Make Things Public." In *Making Things Public: Atmospheres of Democracy,* ed. Bruno Latour and Peter Weibel,
14–41. Cambridge, Mass.: MIT Press.

———. 2007. *Reassembling the Social: An Introduction to Actor-Network-Theory.* Oxford:
Oxford University Press.

———, and Steve Woolgar. 1979. *Laboratory Life: The Social Construction of Scientific
Facts.* Beverly Hills: Sage.

Law, John. 2002. *Aircraft Stories: Decentering the Object in Technoscience.* Durham: Duke
University Press.

———. 2004. *After Method: Mess in Social Science Research.* London: Routledge.

Lawson, Sean. 2007. "Info@war.mil: Non-Linear Science and the Emergence of Information Age Warfare in the United States Military." Diss., Science and Technology
Studies Department, Rensselaer Polytechnic Institute.

Lazzarato, Maurizio. 1996. "Immaterial Labour." Trans. Paul Colilli and Ed Emory. In
Radical Thought in Italy, ed. Paolo Virno and Michael Hardt, 133–47. Minneapolis:
University of Minnesota Press.

LeCompte, Margaret D., Stephen Schensul, and Jean J. Schensul. 1999. *Ethnographer's
Toolkit.* 7 Volumes. Walnut Creek, Calif.: AltaMira Press.

Lee, Byeong-Cheon. 2005. *Developmental Dictatorship and the Park Chung Hee Era: The
Shaping of Modernity in the Republic of Korea.* Trans. Eung-soo Kim and Jae-hyun
Cho. Paramus, N.J.: Homa and Sekey Books.

Lee, Kang-kook, and James Crotty. 2001. "Economic Performance in Post-Crisis Korea:
A Critical Perspective on Neoliberal Restructuring." *Seoul Journal of Economics*
46(6):881–97.

Lefebvre, Henri. 1991 (1974). *The Production of Space.* Trans. Donald Nicholson-Smith.
London: Blackwell.

Lester, Rebecca. 2005. *Jesus in Our Wombs: Embodying Modernity in a Mexican Convent.*
Berkeley: University of California Press.

Lévi-Strauss, Claude. 1966. *The Savage Mind.* A translation of *La Pensée sauvage.* Chicago:
University of Chicago Press.

———. 2001. *Myth and Meaning.* Foreword by Wendy Doniger. New York: Schocken Books.

Lévy-Bruhl, Lucien. 1926. *How Natives Think.* Trans. Lillian A. Clare. London: G. Allen
and Unwin.

Lie, John. 2000. *Han Unbound: The Political Economy of South Korea.* Stanford: Stanford University Press.

Lotfalian, Mazyar. 2004. *Islam, Technoscientific Identities, and the Culture of Curiosity.* New York: University Press of America.

Lucas, Gavin. 2000. *Critical Approaches to Fieldwork: Contemporary and Historical Fieldwork.* London: Routledge.

Luhmann, Niklas. 1995. *Social Systems.* Trans. John Bednarz and Dirk Baecker. Stanford: Stanford University Press.

Mahmood, Saba. 2005. *Politics of Piety: The Islamic Revival and the Feminist Subject.* Princeton: Princeton University Press.

Malinowski, Bronislaw. 1961 (1922). *Argonauts of the Western Pacific.* New York: Dutton.

———. 1967. *A Diary in the Strict Sense of the Term.* London: Routledge and Kegan Paul.

Maranhão, Tullio, ed. 1990. *The Interpretation of Dialogue.* Chicago: University of Chicago Press.

Marcus, George E. 1995. "Ethnography in/of the World System: The Emergence of Multi-sited Ethnography." *Annual Review of Anthropology* 24:95–117.

———. 1997. "The Uses of Complicity in the Changing Mise-en-scène of Fieldwork." *Representations* 59:85–108.

———. 1998. *Ethnography through Thick and Thin.* Princeton: Princeton University Press.

———. 2002a. "Intimate Strangers: The Dynamics of (Non) Relationship between the Natural and Human Sciences in the Contemporary U.S. University." *Anthropological Quarterly* 75(3):519–26.

———. 2002b. "Beyond Malinowski and after *Writing Culture:* On the Future of Cultural Anthropology and the Predicament of Ethnography." *Australian Journal of Anthropology* 13(2):191–99.

———. 2003. "On the Unbearable Slowness of Being an Anthropologist Now: Notes on a Contemporary Anxiety in the Making of Ethnography." *Xcp* 12:7–20.

———. 2005. "The Passion of Anthropology in the United States, circa 2005." *Anthropological Quarterly* 78(3):673–97.

———. 2006. "Where Have All the Tales of Fieldwork Gone?" *Ethnos* 71(1):113–22.

———. 2007. "Ethnography Two Decades after *Writing Culture:* From the Experimental to the Baroque." *Anthropological Quarterly* 80(40):1127–46.

———. 2008a. "The End(s) of Ethnography: Social/Cultural Anthropology's Signature Form of Producing Knowledge in Transition." *Cultural Anthropology* 23(1):1–14.

———. 2008b. "Contemporary Fieldwork Aesthetics in Art and Anthropology: Experiments in Collaboration and Intervention." In *Ethnographica Moralia,* ed. George E. Marcus and Neni Panourgia, 29–44. New York: Fordham University Press.

———. In press. "Collaborative Options and Pedagogical Experiment in Anthropological Research on Experts and Policy Processes." *Anthropology in Action.* Special issue ed. Michael Powell and Tara Schwegler.

———, and Michael M. J. Fischer. 1986. *Anthropology as Cultural Critique: An Experimental Moment in the Human Sciences.* Chicago: University of Chicago Press. 2nd ed. 1999.

———, and Judith Okley. 2008. "How Short Can Fieldwork Be?" (Debate Section). *Social Anthropology/Anthropologie Sociale* 15(30):1–15.

———, and Erkan Saka. 2006. "Assemblages." *Theory, Culture, and Society.* Special Issue: Problematizing Global Knowledge, ed. Michael Featherstone, 101–6. London: Sage.

———, ed. 1993. *Perilous States: Conversations on Culture, Politics, and Nation.* Late Editions, Vol. 1. Chicago: University of Chicago Press.

———, ed. 1995. *Technoscientific Imaginaries: Conversations, Profiles, and Memoirs.* Late Editions, Vol. 2. Chicago: University of Chicago Press.

Marcus, George E. ed. 1999a. *Critical Anthropology Now: Unexpected Contexts, Shifting Constituencies, Changing Agendas.* Santa Fe: School of American Research Press.

——, ed. 1999b. *Paranoia within Reason: A Casebook on Conspiracy as Explanation.* Late Editions, Vol. 6. Chicago: University of Chicago Press.

——, ed. 2000a. *Para-Sites: A Case Book against Cynical Reason.* Late Editions, Vol. 7. Chicago: University of Chicago Press.

——, ed. 2000b. *Zeroing in on the Year 2000: The Last Edition.* Late Editions, Vol. 8. Chicago: University of Chicago Press.

Maurer, Bill. 2002. "Anthropological and Accounting Knowledge in Islamic Banking and Finance: Rethinking Critical Accounts." *Journal of the Royal Anthropological Institute* 8(4):645–67.

——. 2004. "The Cultural Power of Law? Conjunctive Readings." *Law & Society Review* 38(4):843–50.

——. 2005a. "Introduction to 'Ethnographic Emergences.'" *American Anthropologist* 107(1):1–4.

——. 2005b. *Mutual Life, Limited: Islamic Banking, Alternative Currencies, Lateral Reason.* Princeton: Princeton University Press.

Mauss, Marcel. 1990 (1927). *The Gift: The Form and Reason for Exchange in Archaic Societies.* Trans. W. D. Hall. Foreword by Mary Douglas.

Miyazaki, Hirokazu. 2003. "The Temporalities of the Market." *American Anthropologist* 105(2):255–65.

——, and Annelise Riles. 2005. "Failure as an Endpoint." In *Global Assemblages: Technology, Politics, and Ethics as Anthropological Problems,* ed. Aihwa Ong and Stephen J. Collier, 320–31. Malden, Mass.: Blackwell.

Mody, Cyrus. 2001. "A Little Dirt Never Hurt Anyone: Knowledge-Making and Contamination in Materials Science." *Social Studies of Science* 31(1):7–36.

Mortensen, Lena, and Julie Hollowell. In Press. *Ethnographies and Archaeologies: Iterations of the Past.* Gainesville: University Press of Florida.

Nabokov, Vladimir. 1955. *Lolita.* New York: Random House.

——. 1969. *Ada.* New York: McGraw-Hill.

Nafisi, Azar. 2003. *Reading Lolita in Tehran: A Memoir in Books.* New York: Random House.

——. 2004. "The Republic of the Imagination." *Washington Post Book Review,* December 5.

Nordstrom, Carolyn. 2004. *Shadows of War: Violence, Power, and International Profiteering in the Twenty-First Century.* Berkeley: University of California Press.

Nowotny, Helga, Peter Scott, and Michael Gibbons. 2001. *Re-Thinking Science: Knowledge and the Public in an Age of Uncertainty.* London: Polity Press.

O'Donnell, Casey. 2007. "The Work/Play of the Interactive New Economy: Video Game Development in the United States and India." Diss., Science and Technology Studies Department, Rensselaer Polytechnic Institute.

Ong, Aihwa, and Stephen Collier, eds. 2005 *Global Assemblages: Technology, Politics, and Ethics as Anthropological Problems.* Malden, Mass.: Blackwell.

Orth, Maureen. 2004. "Losing His Grip." *Vanity Fair.* http://www.chaos2004.com/vanity3.php.

Parsons, Talcott. 1991 (1951). *The Social System.* London: Routledge.

Perrow, Charles. 1984. *Normal Accidents: Living with High-Risk Technologies.* New York: Basic Books.

Petryna, Adriana. 2002. *Life Exposed: Biological Citizens after Chernobyl.* Princeton: Princeton University Press.

Pollack, Andrew. 1997. "Crisis in South Korea: The Bailout." *New York Times.* December 4. http://nytimes.com.

Poovey, Mary. 1998. *A History of Modern Fact: Problems of Knowledge in the Sciences of Wealth and Society.* Chicago: University of Chicago Press.

——. 2002. "The Liberal Civil Subject and the Social in Eighteenth-Century British Moral Philosophy." *Public Culture* 14:125–45.

——. 2003. "For What It's Worth…" *Critical Inquiry* 30(1). http://www.uchicago.edu/research/jnl-crit-inq/issues/v30/30n2.Poovey.html.

Povinelli, Elizabeth A. 2002. *The Cunning of Recognition: Indigenous Alterities and the Making of Australian Multiculturalism.* Durham: Duke University Press.

Rabinow, Paul. 1977. *Reflections on Fieldwork in Morocco.* Berkeley: University of California Press.

——. 1999. *French DNA: Trouble in Purgatory.* Chicago: University of Chicago Press.

——. 2003. *Anthropos Today: Reflections on Modern Equipment.* Princeton: Princeton University Press.

——. 2005. "Midst Anthropology's Problems." In *Global Assemblages: Technology, Politics, and Ethics as Anthropological Problems,* ed. Aihwa Ong and Stephen J. Collier, 40–53. Malden, Mass: Blackwell.

——. 2007. *Marking Time: On the Anthropology of the Contemporary.* Princeton: Princeton University Press.

——, with Talia Dan-Cohen. 2005. *A Machine to Make a Future: Biotech Chronicles.* Princeton: Princeton University Press.

——, George E. Marcus, James D. Faubion, and Tobias Rees. 2008. *Designs for an Anthropology of the Contemporary.* Durham: Duke University Press.

Radcliffe-Brown, A. R. 1952. *Structure and Function in Primitive Society.* London: Cohen and West.

Raymond, Eric S. 2001. *The Cathedral and the Bazaar: Musings on Linux and Open Source by an Accidental Revolutionary.* Cambridge, Mass.: O'Reilly.

Reardon, Jenny. 2004. *Race to the Finish: Identity and Governance in an Age of Genomics.* Princeton: Princeton University Press.

Reddy, Deepa S. 2005. "The Ethnicity of Caste." *Anthropological Quarterly* 78(3):543–84.

——. 2006. *Religious Identity and Political Destiny: Hindutva in the Culture of Ethnicism.* Lanham, Md.: Rowman & Littlefield.

——. 2007. "Good Gifts for the Common Good: A Story of Blood in the Market of Genetic Research." *Cultural Anthropology* 22(3):429–72.

——. n.d. "Citizens in the Commons: Blood and Genetics in the Making of the Civic." Unpublished manuscript.

Reno, William. 1999. *Warlord Politics and African States.* Boulder, Colo.: Lynne Rienner.

Rheingold, Howard. 1993. *The Virtual Community: Finding Connection in a Computerized World.* Boston, Mass.: Addison-Wesley Longman.

Riles, Annelise. 2000. *The Network Inside-Out.* Ann Arbor: University of Michigan Press.

——. 2004. "Real Time: Unwinding Technocratic and Anthropological Knowledge." *American Ethnologist* 31(3):392–405.

——. 2006. "Anthropology, Human Rights, and Legal Knowledge: Culture in the Iron Cage." *American Anthropologist* 108(1):52–65.

Robben, Antonius C. G., and Jeffrey A. Sluka, eds. 2006. *Ethnographic Fieldwork: An Anthropological Reader.* Oxford: Blackwell.

Saka, Erkan. 2008. "Blogging as a Research Tool." E-seminar of the EASA Media Anthropology Network. May 19–June 1, 2008. http://www.media-anthropology.net/workingpapers.htm.

Sanders, Todd. 1999. "Modernity, Wealth, and Witchcraft in Tanzania." *Research in Economic Anthropology* 20:117–31.

Sanjek, Roger. 1990. *Fieldnotes: The Makings of Anthropology.* Ithaca: Cornell University Press.

Saussure, Ferdinand de. 1983. *Course in General Linguistics.* Trans. Roy Harris, ed. Charles Bally and Albert Sechehaye. London: Duckworth.

Scheper-Hughes, Nancy. 1997. "Demography without Numbers." In *Anthropological Demography: Toward a New Synthesis,* ed. David I. Kertzer and Thomas Earl Fricke, 201–22. Chicago: University of Chicago Press.

Shapin, Steven. 1985. *Leviathan and the Air-pump: Hobbes, Boyle, and the Experimental Life.* Princeton: Princeton University Press.

Shapiro, David. 1965. *Neurotic Styles.* New York: Basic Books.

——. 1981. *Autonomy and Rigid Character.* New York: Basic Books.

Sluzki, Carlos, and Donald Ransom, eds. 1976. *Double-Bind: The Foundation of the Communicational Approach to the Family.* New York: Grune and Stratton.

Smith, Daniel Jordan. 2001. "Ritual Killing, 419, and Fast Wealth: Inequality and the Popular Imagination in Southeastern Nigeria." *American Ethnologist* 28(4):803–26.

——. 2006. *A Culture of Corruption: Everyday Deception and Popular Discontent in Nigeria.* Princeton: Princeton University Press.

Spivak, Gayatri Chakravorty. 1987. *In Other Worlds: Essays in Cultural Politics.* New York: Methuen.

——. 1988. "Can the Subaltern Speak?" In *Marxism and the Interpretation of Culture,* ed. Cary Nelson and Lawrence Grossberg, 271–313. Urbana: University of Illinois Press.

Spradley, James P. 1979. *The Ethnographic Interview.* New York: Holt, Rinehart, and Winston.

——. 1980. *Participant Observation.* New York: Holt, Rinehart, and Winston.

Star, Susan Leigh, ed. 1995. *Ecologies of Knowledge: Work and Politics in Science and Technology.* Albany: State University of New York Press.

Stocking, George. 2001. *Delimiting Anthropology: Occasional Essays and Reflections.* Madison: University of Wisconsin Press.

Strathern, Marilyn. 1990. "Environments Within: An Ethnographic Commentary on Scale." In *Culture, Landscape, and the Environments: The Linacre Lectures 1997,* ed. Kate Flint and Howard Morphy, 44–72. Oxford: Oxford University Press.

——. 1991. *Partial Connections.* Sabage, Md.: Rowman & Littlefield.

——. 1992. *After Nature: English Kinship in the Late Twentieth Century.* Cambridge: Cambridge University Press.

——. 1999. "Refusing Information." In *Property, Substance, and Effect: Anthropological Essays on Persons and Things,* 64–86. New Brunswick, N.J.: Athlone Press.

——. 2004. *Commons and Borderlands: Working Papers on Interdisciplinarity, Accountability, and the Flow of Knowledge.* Oxford: Sean Kingston.

Strauss, Sarah. 2000. "Locating Yoga: Ethnography and Transnational Practice." In *Constructing the Field: Ethnographic Fieldwork in the Contemporary World,* ed. Vered Amit, 162–94. New York: Routledge.

Syring, David. 2000. *Places in the World a Person Could Walk.* Austin: University of Texas Press.

Taussig, Michael. 1987. *Shamanism, Colonialism, and the Wild Man: A Study in Terror and Healing.* Chicago: University of Chicago Press.

Taylor, Julie M. 1998. *Paper Tangos.* Durham: Duke University Press.

Thaler, Richard. 1994. *The Winner's Curse: Paradoxes and Anomalies of Economic Life.* Princeton: Princeton University Press.

Thomas, Nicholas. 1991. "Against Ethnography." *Cultural Anthropology* 6(3):306–32.

Thrift, Nigel. 1999. "The Place of Complexity." *Theory, Culture and Society* 16(3):31–69.

——. 2000. "Performing Cultures in the New Economy." *Annals of the Association of American Geographers* 90(4):674–92.

Toporowski, Jan. 2000. *The End of Finance: Pension Funds, Derivatives, and Capital Market Inflation.* London: Routledge.

Traweek, Sharon. 1988. *Beamtimes and Lifetimes: The World of High Energy Physicists.* Cambridge, Mass.: Harvard University Press.

——. 1995. "Bachigai [Out of Place] in Ibaraki: Tsukuba Science City, Japan." In *Technoscientific Imaginaries: Conversations, Profiles, and Memoirs.* Late Editions, Vol. 2, ed. George E. Marcus, 355–77. Chicago: University of Chicago Press.

——. 1996. "Kokusaika (international relations), Gaiatsu (outside pressure), and Bachigai (being out of place)." In *Naked Science: Anthropological Inquiry into Boundaries, Power, and Knowledge,* ed. Laura Nader, 174–97. New York: Routledge.

——. 2000. "Faultlines." In *Doing Science + Culture,* ed. Roddey Reid and Sharon Traweek, 21–48. New York: Routledge.

Tsing, Anna L. 1993. *In the Realm of the Diamond Queen.* Princeton: Princeton University Press.

——. 2005. *Friction: An Ethnography of Global Connection.* Princeton: Princeton University Press.

Tyler, Stephen A. 1987. *The Unspeakable: Discourse, Dialogue, and Rhetoric in the Postmodern World.* Madison: University of Wisconsin Press.

Tylor, Edward Burnett. 1994 (1871). *The Collected Works of Edmund Burnett Tylor.* Volume 4. London: Routledge/Thoemmes.

van Lente, Harro, and Arie Rip. 1998. "The Rise of Membrane Technology: From Rhetorics to Social Reality." *Social Studies of Science* 28(2):221–54.

Vidal, Gore. 1960. *The Best Man: A Play about Politics.* New York: Little, Brown.

Wallerstein, Immanuel. 1979. *The Capitalist World-Economy.* New York: Cambridge University Press.

Waquant, Loïc. 2003. *Body and Soul: Notebooks of an Apprentice Boxer.* New York: Oxford University Press.

Watson, C. W., ed. 1999. *Being There: Fieldwork in Anthropology.* London: Pluto Press.

Weber, Max. 2002 (1904–1905). *The Protestant Ethic and the Spirit of Capitalism.* Trans. Stephen Kalberg. Los Angeles: Roxbury.

Weinstein, Matthew. 2006. "TAMS Analyzer: Anthropology as Cultural Critique in a Digital Age." *Social Science Computer Review* 24(1):68–77.

West, Harry G. 1997. "Creative Destruction and Sorcery of Construction: Power, Hope, and Suspicion in Post-War Mozambique." *Cahiers d'études africaines* 37(3): 675–98.

Westbrook, David A. 2004. *City of Gold: An Apology for Capitalism in a Time of Discontent.* New York: Routledge.

White, Hayden. 1973. *Metahistory: The Historical Imagination in Nineteenth-Century Europe.* Baltimore: Johns Hopkins University Press.

White, Luise. 2000. *Speaking with Vampires: Rumor and History in Colonial Africa.* Berkeley: University of California Press.

Willis, Paul. 1981. *Learning to Labour: How Working Class Kids Get Working Class Jobs.* New York: Columbia University Press.

Winnicott, D. W. 1968. "Playing: Its Theoretical Status in the Clinical Situation." *International Journal of Psychoanalysis* 49:591–99.

——. 1971a. *Playing and Reality.* London: Tavistock.

——. 1971b. *Therapeutic Consultation in Child Psychiatry.* New York: Basic Books.

Wolf, Eric. 1982. *Europe and the People without History.* Berkley: University of California Press.

Woo, Jung-en. 1991. *Race to the Swift: State and Finance in Korean Industrialization.* New York: Columbia University Press.

Xiang Biao. 2007. *Global "Body Shopping": An Indian Labor System in the Information Technology Industry.* Princeton: Princeton University Press.

Zaloom, Caitlin. 2006. *Out of the Pits: Traders and Technology from Chicago to London.* Chicago: University of Chicago Press.

Contributors

Lisa Breglia is an Assistant Professor and Assistant Director of the Global Affairs program at George Mason University. She is the author of *Monumental Ambivalence: The Politics of Heritage* (University of Texas Press, 2006), a study of the local uses and meanings of archaeological sites in Yucatan. Her current research examines another of Mexico's most valuable and contentious resources: oil.

Jae A. Chung is a Professor at Aalen University, Germany.

James D. Faubion is a Professor in the Department of Anthropology at Rice University, author of *Modern Greek Lessons* (Princeton University Press, 1993) and *The Shadows and Lights of Waco* (Princeton University Press, 2001) and editor of several collections, including *The Ethics of Kinship* (Rowman & Littlefield, 2001) and two volumes of *Essential Works of Michel Foucault* (The New Press, 1998, 2000). He is currently completing a monograph on the anthropology of ethics.

Michael M. J. Fischer served as Professor of Anthropology and Director of the Center of Cultural Studies at Rice University before assuming his present post as Professor of Anthropology and Science and Technology Studies at MIT. While at Rice, he co-authored *Anthropology as Cultural Critique* with George Marcus. His recent publications include *Emergent Forms of Life and the Anthropological Voice* (Duke, 2003) and *Mute Dreams, Blind Owls, and Dispersed Knowledges: Persian Poesis in the Transnational Circuitry* (Duke, 2004).

Kim Fortun is an Associate Professor in the Department of Science and Technology Studies at Rensselaer Polytechnic Institute, and co-editor of *Cultural Anthropology*. Fortun received her Ph.D. in cultural anthropology from Rice University in 1993.

Jennifer A. Hamilton is Assistant Professor of Legal Studies and Director of the Law Program at Hampshire College in Amherst, Massachusetts. She has published several articles about race, law, and ethics, and is the author of *Indigeneity in the Courtroom: Law, Culture, and the Production of Difference in North American Courts* (Routledge, 2008).

Christopher M. Kelty is the author of *Two Bits: The Cultural Significance of Free Software* (Duke University Press, 2008), "Free Science/Free Software" (*First Monday,* December 2001), and several other publications on topics ranging from intellectual property, free software and open access, nanotechnology and society, and infrastructure and the media of knowledge production/circulation. After teaching for seven years at Rice University, he is now Associate Professor at the University of California, Los Angeles, in the Center for Society and Genetics and the Information Studies Department.

George E. Marcus is Chancellor's Professor, Department of Anthropology at the University of California, Irvine, and founding director of the Center for Ethnography there.

From 1975 to 2005 he taught at Rice University, and for twenty-five of those years was department chair.

Nahal Naficy is currently a research associate at Rice. Her Ph.D. dissertation focused on human rights activism and the coding of affect among NGOs in Washington. She is currently preparing a second ethnographic project on the ethics of kinship in contemporary Iran.

Kristin Peterson is an Assistant Professor in the Anthropology Department at the University of California, Irvine. Her research interests focus on international political economy, policymaking, intellectual property law, and science, health, and medicine. These topical and theoretical concerns are grounded in ethnographic fieldwork conducted in Nigeria and West Africa.

Deepa S. Reddy is Associate Professor of Anthropology and Cross-Cultural Studies at the University of Houston–Clear Lake. Her book on the contestations of identitarian politics in India, *Religious Identity and Political Destiny*, was published in 2006. She has written also on the globalization of caste via the discourses of race and human rights and on bioethics. Her current research interests range from (bio)ethics in human and animal research to medical tourism and drug development in India.

Index

and, 97–99; "cultural" and, 15n11; interdisciplinary study of, 16, 106; thick description and, 109
The Cunning of Recognition (Povinelli), 81
Current Anthropology (Journal), 184, 186n3

Dabashi, Hamid, 114–15
Daisy Miller (James), 118
Dali, Salvador, 171
Debating Muslims: Cultural Dialogues in Postmodernity and Tradition (Fisher and Abedi), x, xiv
deconstruction, ix, 157
Deleuze, Gilles, 17n12, 111. *See also* rhizome (concept)
Delimiting Anthropology (Stocking), 62n18
democracy, in Nigeria, 40, 47–48; elections and, 201–2, 204; in Iran, 127; in South Korea, 53, 53n3
Derrida, Jacques, 17n12, 181, 182n10. *See also entries for individual works*
design studio: as model for anthropological research practice, xii, xiv, 21–23, 25–31, 32n15
Designs for an Anthropology of the Contemporary (Rabinow, Marcus, et al.), 8n8
development aid. *See* humanitarianism
development anthropology, 135–36
Devon, Ely, 60
Diebold, 200–201. *See also* electronic voting machines (EVM)
Dikko, Alhaji Umaru, 41–42
Dill, David, 200
Druschel, Peter, 199
Dumont, Jean-Paul, 152
Durkheim, Emile, 54, 61, 147–48, 151

Ecuador, 47
Electronic Frontier Foundation, 201. *See also* Diebold; electronic voting machines (EVM)
electronic voting machines (EVM), 200–202, 204
elites: anthropological subjects and, 8n8; inequality, 40–41; politics and, 49. *See also* experts
ELSI-HapMap project: "Indian and Hindu perspectives on genetic variation research [in Houston]," 83, 87, 90–91, 93, 93n2, 94–96, 98–108, 110–11
emergence: anthropological concept of, 63, 72, 79, 154, 190; of assemblages, 176; emergent phenomena, 188, 204; nanomaterials and, 191, 203
emic (concept), 106, 110. *See also* etic
emotion, anthropological study of, x

empiricism, 38, 41, 51, 69, 71, 134, 140, 159; structure and, 171. *See also* positivism
"epistemic objects," xiv
"epistemic partners." *See* collaboration
epistemology: constructionism and, 155; dialogical approach and, x; of ethnographic research, x, xiv, 38–39, 41, 43, 45, 49–50, 64, 86, 119, 131–34, 138, 150, 154–60, 162, 184, 189, 196, 203; of finance, 57; "native point of view" and, 141, 150. *See also* authority; emergence; "the field"; ontology; positivism; representation; "self"/"other" distinction
Ethical, Legal, and Social Issues (ELSI) in genetics program, viii, 90, 92–95, 97–98, 100–103, 105, 111; relation to HapMap international genomics project, 92
Ethics and Politics of Information Technology (EPIT) project, 189–202, 204
Ethics and Politics of Nanotechnology (EPNANO) project, 189, 191–98, 202–4
The Ethnographer's Toolkit (LeCompte, Schensul, and Schensul), 33
Ethnographic Praxis in Industry Conference (EPIC), xiii
Ethnography@work.com (Cefkin), xiii
etic (concept), 110, 133. *See also* emic
Europe, 50, 54, 118, 154
European Association of Social Anthropologists (EASA) Media Anthropology Network, 32n15
European Union, 32n15
Evans-Pritchard, E. E., 146, 150, 157
"experimental moment." *See* critique
experimentation: ethnographic practice and, x, 6n5, 7–8, 12–13, 20, 26n13, 27, 31n14, 64, 131–32, 142, 170; pedagogy and, 9–10, 17, 30n14. *See also* Ethics and Politics of Information Technology (EPIT) project; Ethics and Politics of Nanotechnology (EPNANO) project
experts, 61, 114; anthropological research and, 8n8, 30, 59–60, 96–97; of bioethics, 84–85; of the Middle East, 115; of the U.S. economy, 40–41. *See also* collaboration; elites

Fabian, Johannes, 184, 184n1, 185–86
failure: ethnographic research and, 11, 45–46, 78, 133, 157, 159
feminism, xii; activism and, 75–78, 90, 96–97
Ferguson, James, 31, 38
"the field": anthropological conception of, 12, 73, 77, 89, 91, 95–96, 138; as assemblage, 90; pedagogy and, 180; structure and play within, 171